Messed Up

. . . . .

*Looking back on my life
by*

R. E. Miller

. . . . .

*Stories, reflections and thoughts about my life
written and collected in this
volume in 2014.*

In memory of my son,
Tyrone Lee Miller

Preface

In order to qualify myself, let me present my credentials: I am not a doctor of anything, nor am I traditionally educated by the normal standards that come from books.

This is my personal confession to the world and my desire to make a positive difference by telling my story. It has been said that disasters sometimes lead to good things and that some of our worst experiences become our best teachers. You be the judge.

My education comes from the lessons I learned from many wrong turns, mistakes and hardships in real life. I attended the School of Hard Knocks between the years of 1944 and 1973 where I earned a degree, majoring in Ignorance with a minor in Stupidity. Upon graduation in 1973, I began to use the lessons I had learned in practical and sometimes unusual ways to better myself and my circumstances. Most importantly, I discovered that I had freedom of choice. And I learned to have faith and believe without reservation in something that is yet to be, even though there may be nothing visible to support its possibility.

The story I am about to tell is one you may have heard many times before in many different ways, about someone's messed up life that somehow gets turned around. I have read many of such stories that have always left me envious, thinking, "Nice story, wish it was mine." It always seemed that no matter what caused all these "lucky" people to achieve their level of greatness against the odds, all had something special. There was always something that seemed to give them an edge that I didn't have. There was always something about them that I envied even before their remarkable stories began.

They always seemed to have so much going for them that it was inevitable that they would eventually succeed. It was only a matter of when.

Even the people who escaped the ghettos had someone pushing them, or pulling them, encouraging them, or maybe they had a special talent just waiting to be exposed. There was always something about all of them that I couldn't relate to because I had none of those things going for me. No one encouraging me, telling me about all my wonderful potential.

Instead, I was compared to people that were thought to be worthless. I was convinced that I was illiterate. The message was verbally and physically beat into me. I had nothing to draw from but the hard cold facts of the life I was living, with nothing but loss, rejection, sadness and confusion to guide me. I was a lost soul, wandering aimlessly through life without direction, or a reason, surviving from one day to the next, insecure and dependent, looking for a place to belong. It's incredible what insecurities will cause you to do to defend yourself from what you fear most of all. I believe my greatest fear was being alone and being different than others.

In 1973 something happened at around age 30 that awakened something in me that gave me hope. Hope that maybe there is something in all of us that we should know and understand about ourselves. Maybe we all have special talents just waiting to be exposed. Can there be something independent of outside influences that is more powerful than the misguided lives many of us are living? With that thought I set out in search of facts and reasons for my poor choices in life. This was not to be a search for blame to justify my poor choices. It was to be a search for the understanding of how my choices have come about and what I could actually do now to change the destructive path that I was on.

It was clear that no one was going to come to my rescue. If I was going to climb out of the hole I was in, I was going to have to first of all convince myself that I was worth saving. I thought, "Where did I start to go wrong?" Was I just born messed up and destined to destroy my life and everyone else's along the way? Or is there a logical explanation that will make everything clear to me?

I began to think back in time, as far back as I could remember about my life and where it all began.

When I did, I could see my childhood circumstances for what they really were. I could see how I misunderstood so many of those things that influence me. I saw things that were responsible for shaping my life into what it had become. It was as if I was looking at the life of a stranger in a movie, all that went wrong in his life. There were misunderstandings and bad habits developed in the imagination of a child that were brought forward into my adult life.

It became clear that insecurities often come from our childhood ways of dealing with what we imagined to be traumatic as children. This may be old news to you, but understand that I am not talking about something that was told to me, something that I can't connect with.

As adults we can see how our childhood imaginations often came with us into adulthood.

It's a safe bet that I am not going to tell you anything that hasn't been said by countless others in countless different ways.

Nothing I am saying is new, but it is unique because each of us experience life in our own way. I was unable to relate to the success stories of so many others until I myself became successful. All you will find that appears different here is that I had my own way of dealing with events.

Some of our characteristics are genetic and some are the result of the influences of people and circumstances along our way to adulthood.

Even though we all know these things we often fail to connect the dots between our childish actions toward situations as children and the way we respond to similar situations today as adults. Most of us misguided souls still habitually deal with the trauma the same way as we did as children. It has become a habit we never think to break. We never thought to tell ourselves that we are adults now and no longer need to fear those things we didn't understand as children. As adults we don't need to withdraw into ourselves, shutting everyone and everything out to protect ourselves from those dreadful things that lurk in the shadows that once devastated us as children.

My story and the way I tell it will definitely cause you to think and to compare your own life to mine. I have experienced a lot on many levels. Maybe you can relate. Violence, poverty, addiction, sexual, mental and physical abuse. I also understand criminal insanity and what it's like to lose your freedom and why so many return to prison over and over doing life on the installment plan. I know what it feels like to be illiterate. I know the insecure feeling of being different, out of place, lonely and rejected, and the frustration of not knowing how to express my emotions in a positive way. I know how it feels to destroy a marriage, then another and to abandon innocent children.

I also know the feeling of inner peace, what it's like to have wealth and freedom from addictions. And I know how it feels to have sympathy and understanding for those who abused and misled me. I know what it's like to be intelligent and what it's like to be happy and secure. I know what it's like to be different yet be content. I know what a wonderful, meaningful marriage is like having been married to the same woman for almost thirty years. And I know how it feels to have to make amends with my own children. It is my hope that my honesty in these writings will make a positive difference in their lives.

I hope that my story will cause you to believe that anything is possible, that even miracles do happen. You will find nothing in my life between 1944 and 1973 that would indicate that I had any chance or even a desire to change. The odds were stacked against me. My chances were slim, yet I was able to change.

The only way I can tell this story is to be honest, but honesty comes with much regret and shame for the things I have done. Reliving some of my past is very hard to do, and the realization of what my past has done to my children and grandchildren is the hardest and most regrettable of all my mistakes. I firmly believe that there is a reason for everything, but I am still in the dark as to what qualifies as a good reason opposed to a bad reason. Some of my children would have never been born if I had not been married five times and many of my more than thirty grandchildren would also not have been born. All I know is that there is a feeling of pride and love when I look at my great grandchildren and think to myself, "How can this be wrong and is this the good reason so many have suffered?" I don't know.

I was originally inspired to write this book after my 40-year school reunion several years ago.

I had not seen any of my classmates since 7th grade, but I still recognized most of them after almost forty years. All of them seemed to be pretty much in the same state of mind doing pretty much what their personalities as youngsters called for them to do as adults.

It was then that I realized just how far I had come from those days, back when I wanted more than anything to be intelligent like these class mates that I once envied. Back then I just wanted to fit in. I wanted the things we were being taught to come as easy to me as they did to all of them.

But the truth I faced at the time was that I didn't fit in and I didn't catch on like the other kids. I felt stupid and embarrassed and straight, red "F" report cards confirmed my stupidity.

By the time I reached third grade all this started to become evident to me. Up until then I had not given much thought to the differences between myself and my classmates.

To hide my embarrassment I acted up by being disruptive, giving the impression that I just didn't care when actually I cared very much. But pretending becomes who you really are, if you do it consistently and for a long time. You will probably see how well-concentrated thoughts of any kind work in a person's life as I tell my story.

On the last day of school, in the sixth grade, my teacher told the entire class that I would never amount to anything good and so it was that I was voted the most likely to never succeed. Yet on the day of our 40-year reunion I pulled up in a Cadillac, healthy, wealthy and wise, totally different then the disruptive brat they once knew.

I finally quit school in the eighth grade thinking that I would never be able to catch on anyway. What did it really matter? I thought that I would never amount to anything anyway.

I was reminded of two truths that day with my old classmates. One was the fact of where I had once been. And the other was the place where I had come and the direction I was headed. These two truths present themselves often in our life and it has been for the greater good that I have paid attention to them.

The thoughts I had that day caused me to think that maybe I had a story worth telling. But how can I best do that? I had never written a book. But if I could find a way, there was a possibility that my children and grandchildren, who hardly knew me, could possibly benefit by the telling of such a story, the story of my complete failure and destruction and the discovery that began a change in me that enabled the stress-free, confident life I came to enjoy.

And so I began to wonder, "What happened in my life that caused me to have such a low self-image?" If I wrote a book, maybe all I had learned from my mistakes could help others who are struggling against the same effects of low self-worth. What happened that changed everything for me most likely wouldn't be the same for others, but I had no doubt that my story might point others in the right direction as they relate many of my experiences to their own.

That's how this book began.

It won't be a story about how different I am then you. It's a story about how similar we all are. My life may have been more intense than yours or maybe less intense. Intensity isn't caused by the events of our life, but rather by how we personally process the events.

As for personal intelligence, Einstein said, "Everyone is a genius, but if you expect a fish to climb a tree it will live its whole life believing it is stupid."

As I contemplated writing this book, I realized that my grammar was poor and my spelling even worse. I thought, "How can I possibly do this?"

I also began to recall all the trials and tribulations of my youth and the struggles they caused me as an adult. I recalled the destruction and misery I had caused for myself and others for so many years.

It was almost more than I could bare. My heart was heavy with the pain that I caused the ones I loved.

But then the realization struck me that all the things good and bad that happened in my past had taught me all that I know today. In order for you to know how I have gotten to where I am, I needed to tell you the story of where I have been, where I am today and how it all started. So I reached out and got help from neighbors and friends to organize, edit and publish the huge assortment of stories I had collected in notebooks and in computer files.

The story that I am about to tell you is the story of *my* life. It is an account of events based mostly on memory with some events told to me by others. Many names have been changed for protection, often for my own protection.

As you read please understand that this is *my* truth and the way I discovered it. The way you understand and process my story and how my discoveries relate to you is your own personal guide to your own story. My story is only intended to help you think and to help you discover the meaning of your own, important story.

The Early Years

What We Were Taught

I came into this world in the summer of 1944. A much simpler time than now, moving at a much slower pace. We didn't have many forms of communication although we had at least advanced beyond smoke signals and even telegraph in most areas.

We hammered out our messages to the world on manual typewriters, or in long hand using fountain pens. Ball point pens had not been invented yet, let alone any kind of electronic device. Even tube devices were limited to radio and radio wasn't even an option in many parts of the country, as electricity had not found its way to the country yet and neither had indoor plumbing.

We mostly communicated through the newspapers and word of mouth neither of which were completely reliable. I guess things were really not so different than they are now in some respects.

The good part about limited forms of communication of this type is that we weren't constantly reminded of all the horrific things that are going on all over the world. These things seemed to fill our daily thoughts with negativity and hopeless despair when we tune into the morning news and listen to the same stuff in the evening just before bedtime. It's the last event we remember before falling asleep.

What are the chances that we might enjoy a stress free day when we are constantly allowing ourselves to be programmed with all these limiting energy sucking thoughts? But then we need to be informed about what's going on in the world right?

It's not so much the things we are exposed to in the news and in so many other ways throughout the day that creates so much negative energy that we often display on our way to work by way of road rage and many other ways. It's how we process what we see and hear that often causes us to think consistently about those things that eventually become what we believe.

It's not like there weren't horrific things going on somewhere in the world in 1944. We just didn't hear about those negative things constantly and most often not at all as children. So we were not affected by those things that control our thoughts and complicate our lives today.

I am not suggesting that progress should not be accomplished and I am not suggesting that we should bury our heads in the sand and live in denial. I am saying that we don't have to accept things that are not beneficial to us and concentrate our energy on positive possibilities.

As simple as life was in 1944 there was conflict in the world. The Second World War was near its end. Over 6 million innocent Jews were killed by Hitler and his army for no good reason in that war. Can't get too much more horrific than that, can you?

I suppose in a way that war had something to do with me coming into this world and the events that shaped my life in those early years between adolescent and adult.

We were in my day, all inspired by things like the pledge of allegiance to the flag in our schools when I was growing up. It helped us as children to develop a sense of pride in our country. There were only 48 stars on the American flag back then as Alaska and Hawaii had not become united with the other states. In those days prayer was even allowed in our schools, teaching us good moral values and standards to live by. In those days even though we were being taught that actions have consequences and that no one owed us anything we weren't willing to work for. We either worked hard to get what we wanted, or we worked smart and any other way was dishonest.

Most of us were required to attend Sunday school and church by our parents for the same reason. It helped us to be organized and to develop morals that gave us a sense of security in that we belonged. And something to believe in when things went horribly wrong.

We were never in danger of being sent to hell for eating red meat on Friday. It was just a rule to adhere to that taught us self-discipline.

Our teachers were not fearful of children bringing weapons to school. They were more concerned with the dress code. Girls were expected to wear dresses and if they showed up in slacks they were sent home. Boys were expected to wear a belt to hold their pants up. If we showed up without a belt we were given a length of rope to tie around us in place of a belt. Ridiculous and unfair to our rights to express ourselves as it was, it taught us good values and a sense of respect for ourselves and others.

I don't think there was a boy in the country who didn't carry a pocket knife to school and everywhere else. We even took our knives out and showed them off for show and tell when we got a new one. We never thought about stabbing our classmates with our knives, we thought of our knives as versatile, useful, creative tools, not weapons.

When we had differences that we needed to settle, we settled them with words or fists on the playground.

We wondered about life and death and were curious about it, but not at the expense of killing our class mates, just to see how it works, or how it would feel to end someone's life, because we had morals and the fear of consequences.

Many of us were misfits and felt out of place, different and insecure. I was one of the many, but I never thought of killing my classmates as a solution, because I had morals and the fear of consequences.

But in spite of simpler times and all the teachings and discipline I received there were circumstances and situations that were no different than they are now for our young people who are lost and unable to process what is happening in their life.

Even though I had been taught good values, I was confused about their application. I felt so out of place and misunderstood with so many things going wrong in my life that I had no way of explaining these feelings to anyone. I was sure that no one understood me and what I was going through and that I was all alone on my own with no visible way to go.

So I forgot all I was taught and opened myself to any possibility where I could feel like I belonged. I became a soul without direction or reason. Looking back I can tell you without a doubt, that these insecurities were the base for all my poor decisions and the cause of all my troubles.

This is my true story of how I became lost in the swamp of despair and how I found my way out. This is not about a religious belief or a suggestion that you become anyone other than who you were truly meant to be, that is something only you can determine. My only reason for the words I write is to open your mind to yourself and the limitless possibilities of the things you desire in this life.

My Father and Mother
I was raised by a mix of poor, wealthy, and middle-class family members for the first 7 years of my life. I didn't know the security of having a father.

Still, I had a family that tried to care for me. Nevertheless, I come from a broken family like so many others have for whatever reason.

My mother is still living today. My biological father passed away back in the mid 1980's.

My parents divorced when my father, who was in the Army at that time, got another girl pregnant while on leave. If you were from Texas in 1944, and if you got a girl in "trouble," you were expected to do the honorable thing and marry the girl. To make sure that young men did the right thing, many marriages in Texas were performed at gunpoint. I am fairly certain this is where the phrase "shotgun wedding" came from. The father of the girl my dad had gotten pregnant let it be known that he would shoot my father dead if dad did not do the honorable thing and marry his daughter.

This presented a bit of a problem. Not only was my dad already married, his wife was pregnant too! So my father went to my mother and begged her for a divorce. Mom agreed to the divorce. Then, to show his appreciation, he lied to everyone and blamed my mother for his mistakes.

He claimed that I was not his child. He said it was my mother who had cheated on him while he was overseas and that she caused the divorce. That was how he justified cheating on my mother.

My mother left Waco, Texas shortly after the divorce was final. She moved to Victoria, Texas where I was born.

My first name came from the actor Randolph Scott who was popular with the girls back then. Mom liked him and his name, but shortened it to Randy. For years I was often asked if my name was really Randolph or Randall. My middle name Earl came from an uncle on my father's side who was quite wealthy. My mother was told that I would be rewarded when I was older if she would name me after my uncle Earl. I have not yet received anything and don't expect that I ever will since they are both dead.

I think my aunt's intentions were good, but circumstances caused by my mother and I leaving Waco played a big part in that intention and it was thought for many years that my mother and I had died in a car crash.

There had been a car accident, but we obviously survived. I don't know who started that story or why it got started. When I showed up 18 years later everyone was surprised. Grandpa, being the kind, soft-hearted soul he was, cried, when he discovered that I was alive.

We returned to Waco shortly after I was born to visit Grandpa and Grandma Miller.

My grandma Miller picked cotton for a living like a lot of women and children did back then, including myself. Grandma Miller was about 12 years of age when she became blind as a result of coming in contact with a pesticide poison that the cotton had been dusted with. The pesticide was transferred from her hands to her eyes as she wiped the sweat out of her eyes with her bare hands one hot sweltering afternoon in one of the many cotton fields around Waco, Texas.

The loss of her sight only increased her sense of touch.

Her touch was more accurate than most people's eyes. Before my mom and I left Waco, Texas again, Grandma Miller ran her hands over my face, and said to my dad, "This is your son." Eighteen years later, everyone was surprised that I was alive, but it came as no surprise to Grandma when I showed up looking like my dad's twin. Fortunately for me, he was a good looking man.

The only one that wasn't surprised that I was alive was my dad. Hmmm. It makes you wonder.

I didn't see my father again until 18 years had passed. At that meeting, it was as if I were looking at an older version of myself. If anyone ever had any doubts about who my father actually was, they didn't need a DNA test to finally know the truth. But I'm getting ahead of myself. I'll get back to that meeting with my dad a little later.

I could have easily grown up hating my father for disowning me and disgracing my mother the way he did. My mother had plenty of reasons to have ill feelings toward my father.

She could have instilled those thoughts about him in my mind. But she didn't. All she ever said was, "When you're old enough, go see him and find out what he's like for yourself." And that's exactly what I did. My aunts, on the other hand, made sure that I knew what a rat my father was. Every time I did something wrong, one of them would remind me that I was just like "my no good father." I suppose it was their way of standing up for my mom and warning me. But it just made me feel more worthless.

I actually found him to be a very good person. He worked hard at a job he loved to support eight children and "Betty," the girl he left my mother for. I don't think Betty was a bad person either. She was a bit spoiled, lazy and very insecure. And, oh! She was blind in one eye.

I didn't judge my dad then, and I'm not judging him now for the broken relationship between him and my mother. Did all that happened between my mother and father have a personal effect on me? Indirectly, yes, it did. However, I'm sure that they didn't decide to bring me into this world as a plan to hold me personally responsible for their failed marriage or to punish me for it. I believe it was nothing more than a set of circumstances that stemmed from a young man thinking with the wrong head when he was tempted to cheat with a young, shapely girl, or remain faithful to a bulging, pregnant wife. After all, he wasn't planning for more than a fling, so who would ever know if he decided to cheat. Right?

Charles, My First Stepfather

Mom and I were alone against the world. Looking back to 1944, I feel respect for my mom and how brave she was.

After leaving Waco, my mother and I went back to Victoria, Texas where she met and fell in love with my first stepfather, Charles.

He was a really nice guy, who was also a divorcee. He had a 12-year-old daughter by the name of Charlene. Charles worked for the railroad. I was two years old when they married. Charles, his daughter Charlene, and his parents loved me dearly, as mom tells me. Personally, I don't remember that, but I'll take mom's word for it.

After they were married, all was good for a few months. Then, Charles was killed on the railroad. That was in 1946, and odd as it may seem, I can still remember two days from back then. I remember in detail, as if it were yesterday, what the kitchen looked like. I remember where I sat. I was on one of those steel folding step stools and it was pulled up to the kitchen counter. I ate a bowl of chicken noodle soup with lots of crackers. My bowl sat on a cutting board that pulled out of the cabinet. I remember a doorway to the right of where I was sitting in the kitchen, and someone putting their leg across the doorway so that I could not enter the next room. I believe that leg belonged to Charles, because the feeling I remember was a good one. I believe this was one of his endearing ways of playing with me. I can see it all now as if it were yesterday. I can still feel that feeling of goodness, but I can't remember his face. My guess is that I remember this one particular day because it was the last day of his life. There just isn't any other reason why I would remember all those details. I also remember the funeral. I remember a very small church. I can see the coffin up front. The church was packed with people. Many more people were standing outside the church because there wasn't enough room inside.

Here are some events that led to the death of Charles.

He and my mom were out late at night with friends having dinner and cocktails, when, at 2 am Charles was called into work to replace his brother, who also worked for the railroad. He had gotten sick and sent home.

I suppose no one even heard his brother come in at 2 am in the morning while everyone was asleep.

When Charles showed up for work he was tired and a bit inebriated, but not noticeably so. He was leaning out from the caboose waving a lantern to indicate to the engineer where the end of the train was, when they passed some culverts stacked up by the side of the tracks. He didn't see them. He was struck in the head, knocked under the train and killed.

When word first came of his death, everyone thought it was his brother that was killed, because he was supposed to be working that shift.

I'm with you on this one. I'm wondering why his wife didn't know that he had come home. I'm missing something here, but this is the way my mom told it to me. Maybe he didn't go home. I don't know.

This was the very first experience that I can remember of my life.

If you're with me so far, you may realize that at the age of two, my experience and my memories are of loss. There were good things that happened in my life around that time. I have consciously remembered happier details after all these years, but the things that dominated my subconscious mind for so many years, were loss. And so, insecurity was born in me. Little did I know then that things were about to get worse. A lot worse. And insecurity would lead me to make many poor decisions in an attempt to capture that feeling of belonging.

Mom took Charles death very hard and had a breakdown. I was sent away to live with relatives. The year was 1946.

Grandpa and Grandma Winters,

The first relatives I lived with were Grandpa and Grandma Winters, my mother's parents. I lived with them for about three years. Upon reflection, some of the things that we are influenced by in our lives are nothing more than misunderstandings that caused resentment, anxieties, fears and insecurities.

The events during the time I spent with grandpa and grandma, back in the mid 40's, are pretty sketchy.

The things I remember with most clarity are those things that have had an emotional impact on my life; good and bad alike. There was a chain of emotional events that happened early on in my life that I misunderstood when I was a child.

Now, as an adult, I am armed with knowledge and wisdom. I can go back and look at those emotional turning points in my life and understand them for what they really were and I am free to make a rational decision to let go of those things that have harmed me and are responsible for holding me back for so long.

They may seem silly, odd or innocent to the person passing by. But those days with Grandpa and Grandma would define who I was to myself and how I would express myself to others.

Grandpa was as mean as a junkyard dog. He stood about five foot six, and weighed about 140 pounds soaking wet. He feared no man. Grandpa was a hard-working man that would drink nothing but hot scalding water. Grandpa seldom, if ever, touched liquor. He never drank coffee. Every morning he washed his eyes out with rubbing alcohol. Yes. You heard me right. He ate handfuls of Arm and Hammer baking soda for multiple reasons. As strange as all this may seem, grandpa lived to be 101.

Grandma was a kind, gentle soul, who produced 16 children before she passed away in her early 60's. I remember her with great fondness.

My Mom, as well as some of my aunts, told me stories about their upbringing and what they and their brothers had endured at the hands of my grandpa while growing up.

The two oldest boys, Otis and Bill, at one time were hung by their toes and grandpa whipped them until their backs bled. Another time, they were ordered to stand barefoot on the edges of steel drums in the hot Texas sun for punishment. As the stories go, the two oldest boys were the most rebellious and suffered the most punishment.

Grandpa once went to the country school where all of his children attended, and then timed himself as he ran home as fast as he could. The time it took him to reach home from school was the amount of time everyone had to get home after school.

They had to run home so that they could work in the fields until sundown. Then they were allowed to clean up for supper, eat, complete their school work, and go to bed.

They were all required to maintain good grades, or bear the consequences of a whipping with grandpa's razor strap. They were never allowed to bring guests home after school, or any other time, without permission from grandpa. Permission was rarely ever granted. If they were ever late for any reason getting home from school, they were given a knife and told to go and cut a good, keen switch that grandpa used to whip them with.

Mom once told me a story about a little dog she had. When the weather was bad, the dog would come inside and lay just inside the door. Grandpa didn't approve of animals in the house. One day, grandpa had been in town getting supplies, because the weather wouldn't permit work in the fields. When he entered the front door, he saw the dog lying asleep just inside. He walked over to the dog, put his foot on the dog's neck and applied pressure until the dog quit struggling and died. .

The first recollection of a relationship with grandpa was when he bought me a toy that cost him somewhere in the neighborhood of eight dollars. (Eight dollars in the 40's might be like $80, or more, today. For some people, 8 dollars represented a day's work back then.) Being the mechanically inclined kid that I was, I took my new toy into the backyard and proceeded immediately to part it out with a hammer. Grandpa was not very impressed with my mechanical skills.

He rewarded my efforts by whipping me like a redheaded stepchild. I had not intended to be bad; I was just being a curious little boy. At age three, I had never encountered anything like that whipping before. And so, fear was born.

The next event that I can remember, is having a goat for a pet. All of the animals on the farm, with the exception of the dog and the horse, were there for one purpose and one purpose only. Food. At my age, I didn't know that it was a bad idea to get attached to the animals. They were only part of the food chain on the farm. We didn't get a lot of company that I can remember, except for my cousin, Sandy now and then. So the animals were my playmates. I spent a lot of time with the goat, because it followed me around the farm and was a good companion. Until Grandpa slaughtered it. I cried when he cut its throat, so grandpa cut the goats' penis off and gave it to me for a keepsake to remember my playmate by. That's not weird, is it?

My next memory is Sandy and me riding bareback on the back of this big horse while grandpa led the horse up a hill. The hill was quite steep and rocky. As gravity would have it, both Sandy and I started to slide off the back end of the horse. I landed flat on my back, cracking the back of my head on a big flat rock. My cousin, Sandy, landed on top of me, knocking the wind out of me. I was told not to cry or I would really get something to cry for. (Don't think for one minute that I didn't remember what that something was.) So, I sucked it up and quit crying. But geez, Grandpa! I was only three years old and smacking my head on that rock hurt a lot!

I can remember being physically hurt a lot while growing up, but I don't remember crying much after this age. I remember pretending to cry when receiving a whipping so that whoever was whipping me at the time would stop. Even though it didn't hurt enough to cry. It was an embarrassment. I'd do anything to make a whipping stop.

The Toy Truck and a Snake

The next emotional impact involved a little yellow plastic truck. As I recall, I was playing out in the front yard. It was a hilly yard as it descended down maybe 100 yards to the lumber shed, barn and other outbuildings. I was playing on the side of one of the hills, digging a hole in the rock hard earth so that I could cover the opening with sticks and then park my truck in the makeshift garage. At one point, I put the truck in the hole that I was digging. I began to chop around the truck with the head of a garden hoe that was missing the handle when I accidentally struck the back of the truck breaking off a piece of the tailgate.

Fear gripped me, as I recalled what had happened the last time that I broke a toy. I ran to the lumber shed and hid that truck within a niche between long and short boards in the shed.

So, at three years old, I learned to hide things I didn't want people to know about. Fear for the condition of my butt was my motivation for hiding the truck in that stack of lumber. And deception was born out of fear.

I had pretty much forgotten about the truck by the time grandpa went to the shed and began to pull out lumber for a project he was working on. I followed grandpa everywhere he went around the farm. I was standing just outside the lumber shed door next to the table saw he had set up, when grandpa discovered a diamondback rattlesnake in the stack of lumber coiled around my little yellow truck. The snake was getting ready to strike.

To the best of my knowledge, grandpa had no fear of anything, least of all snakes. He had what we referred to in Texas, as a "what not shelf," That shelf was usually cluttered with all kinds of things; hence the term "what not." (Texas folks like to keep it simple so their descriptions of things are most often simple.)

Grandpa's shelf was located in the living room of the house. The shelves were loaded with snake rattlers that he kept as souvenirs of the rattlesnakes he had killed around the farm. On this day, grandpa pulled his hatchet out of the hammer loop of his overalls, and began to turn the snake into snake sushi. As grandpa chopped the snake into pieces, he threw them out the door of the shed. One piece, the one that contained the head and about a foot of snake, hit me right above the shoulders and wrapped around my neck. I don't remember my exact reaction but it was one of hysteria I can assure you. My first thought, once I calmed down, was that I deserved this as my punishment for breaking that truck. This was my first confirmation of fear and my introduction to anxieties born of an over active imagination. As I recall, grandpa handed the truck back to me, and never said a word about the broken tailgate. Looking at the incident now, I believe he most likely thought that he had broken the truck himself during his battle with the snake. What I am sure of, is that I did not like that snake wrapping around my neck along with all the snake blood and guts that got all over me. From that moment on, I was petrified of snakes.

The Plum

My mind now takes me to a situation that started at the well. In the 40's most people didn't have running water. That was a luxury of the rich, as was electricity in those days, because the power lines had not made it to the country yet. We got our water from a well just a short distance away from the house. The well consisted of a deep hole in the ground with rocks and mortar set around it. This rock wall was to keep rodents from falling into the well, decaying, and then contaminating the water. It's most likely why Grandpa boiled his water before drinking it. In order to get the water out of the well, a bucket with a rope tied to it was lowered into the well until it was submerged in the water, then it was pulled up. Occasionally the bucket of water would come up with a water moccasin snake hitching a ride in it.

All around grandpa's farm yard there were apple and plum trees. The ground was often littered with fruit that had fallen from the trees. On this particular day, grandpa pulled up a bucket of water that contained a water moccasin. He poured the water out and the snake began to slither away. Grandpa pinned it to the ground with a rake just an inch or so away from one of the plums on the ground. As the snake thrashed about struggling to free itself, its mouth was wide open exposing its fangs. I remember feeling terrified. Then, grandpa ordered me to pick up the plum that was an inch or so away from the snakes reach. The snake seemed to be striking at the plum. I don't remember if I did, or if I didn't pick up the plum that day, but logic tells me that I did. I don't remember any consequences for disobeying. What I do remember is thinking that the plum episode was more punishment for breaking the stupid tailgate on that doggone truck.

I didn't really resent my grandpa for the next fifty years because of all of these events and the way I remembered them. But I wondered why he did all those things that seemed so mean to me and

I certainly didn't think all those events had anything to do with my adult life.

I would never have reprocessed those days on grandpa's farm, until one day many years later my wife said something that sparked my mind and caused me to take a closer look.

Now that I am old enough to understand and those days are so far away, I can feel safe and secure looking back at them. I can see now what really happened. I am able to look at all sides of those days without emotional attachment.

It seems like all my life was just a confirmation of those first things I learned in life and the way I understood them at the time. As you will begin to see as I tell you the rest of my story, those early years had a huge impact on me. I only felt loss, fear and rejection. I took these experiences into my heart. I actually believed that I was bad. Worse yet, I believed that I deserved to have bad things happen to me. I lived in fear. I had no security and bumbled through these years getting intense discipline when I only needed correction. I don't remember much affection except from grandma and there wasn't anyone reaching into my broken life and reassuring me. But, times were different in those days.

Looking Back At Grandpa

Here is an account of what I think really happened back then.

In spite of the things I just told you, grandpa was good to me. Whatever he did to his own children, he did not do to me. I'm not excusing grandpa for what he did. What he did was inexcusable. Just like my parents and the circumstances that ended their marriage, the relationship between grandpa and his children had nothing to do with me either.

Yes, he was a strict man with very little or no time for nonsense, ignorance or crybabies. This is who grandpa was. I've come to realize that he didn't really mean to hurt me. He actually thought he was helping me.

The whipping I received for breaking that expensive toy may have been deserved. There may have been better ways of dealing with me, but back then the lessons we learned and the way that we learned them, were lessons that would not soon be forgotten. And, obviously, I didn't.

The snake wrapping around my neck from the lumber shed was an accident. I just happened to be standing in the wrong place at the wrong time.

My hysteria over that snake incident was grandpa's motive for his actions at the well. It was his way of teaching me to overcome my fear of snakes. To this day I'm not overly afraid of snakes. I still don't like them. And I especially don't like being surprised by them! Hysteria over snakes did not continue to be a problem due to the fact that grandpa forced me to overcome my unreasonable fear of them.

The episode with the goat, while somewhat odd, was actually my grandpa's way of comforting me for my loss. The penis of the goat was the only part of the goat small enough for me to carry in my pocket and it was not considered edible. Thank God for that, because I would just hate to have to tell you that I ate goat penis when I was young.

The situation when I fell off the horse was like I said; grandpa had no time for crybabies. Does anyone, really? To this day I can endure a lot of physical pain without any need of medication.

Now that all of this is behind me and I understand it, I clearly remember the good things about grandpa too.

I have made a conscious decision to balance the bad things with the good that I know. I was too young to understand many things so many years ago. I am not blinded by my own pain anymore. And miraculously, I can trace some very positive traits back to those early days on grandpa's farm. I owe him some gratitude.

Grandpa's Toolbox

Grandpa was a carpenter. He taught me about the tricks of the trade, the names of the tools, and what their uses were. Grandpa would often tell me to bring him a certain tool from his toolbox and I would always know what that tool was, because he had taught me. He enjoyed working with wood and I guess I got that from him. Today, I have a garage full of woodworking equipment. I'm not a very good carpenter because I'm a perfectionist, although I do get by. I am pretty good at building cabinets, restoring furniture, and building one-of-a-kind things, thanks to Grandpa. His skills with wood left a lifelong legacy between us. Fortunately that first whipping didn't cause me to lose my interest in taking things apart. I am also very mechanically inclined and understand complicated mechanical things with ease.

Mixed Up Food

Looking back, I've realized that grandpa sometimes had great patience with me. I clearly remember one night at the supper table. I had this habit of mixing all my food up with my milk. Grandma scolded me, but grandpa just calmly said, "That's all right, he's going to eat it." And I did. Grandpa gave me the green light to mix to my hearts delight! As an adult, I have been known to mix up some real strange things that many people tell me tastes pretty good. I smile when I try mixing some new concoction, and I think of grandpa. But I have stopped mixing my food up in my milk glass. (Thought I'd mention that just in case you drop in for supper sometime.)

A Mouth Full of Hair

I can also remember going into town with grandpa to get my hair cut. During the haircut, I was talking and talking. Grandpa told me that I should be quiet before I got a mouthful of hair. He no more than said it and guess what? You guessed it! A big gob of hair fell into my mouth. I shut my mouth and never said another word. We walked all over town and he kept talking to me but I wasn't answering him. Finally he stopped and said, "What's wrong with you, boy?" Feeling ashamed and a little embarrassed, I opened my mouth and showed grandpa the hair. All he said was, "Good Lord, boy! Spit it out!" He didn't even say, "See, I told you so."

Cracklins

And then there's my great fondness of eating "cracklins". This was a delicacy that came when Grandpa slaughtered the hogs. I can picture him as he heated a 55 gallon drum of water. He started by building a fire under the drum and bringing the water to a rolling boil. Then, using a hoist, he would lower the hog while still alive, head first, into the boiling water. Now this may sound cruel, and it probably was, but then Grandpa was not very considerate of animals or people for that matter. But there were a number of reasons why grandpa did it this way. One reason I do know is that the hair comes off of the hog easily when scalded, so then grandma could make cracklins out of the hog skin. She would keep them in a big tin canister under the counter in the kitchen.

Cracklins are made from the pork skin with the fat intact after skinning the hog. The pork skin is then cut into one-inch squares and then deep fried until they float to the top of the oil, then they are removed from the oil with a slotted spoon and put on a draining rack and seasoned with salt and pepper. Grandma always dusted them with a bit of flour before storing them to keep them from sticking together. I can't begin to tell you how good they were. They just melted in your mouth. Sometimes when grandma and grandpa were outside, I would sneak inside and get a handful because I loved them! If you know what cracklins are, you know what I'm talking about. Every time I would get into the container, I would leave a trail of flour across the floor and they would always know that I had been into the cracklins.

Ranger

I also smile as I fondly recall our dog Ranger. He was a big Doberman that was confined by a real long heavy chain. Ranger killed everything that came within the radius of that chain. In the morning we would find dead porcupines, armadillos, possums, skunks, snakes and virtually anything that came within Rangers reach. No one could get near that dog except Grandpa, Grandma and myself. Peddlers and strangers didn't come near the house because Ranger could reach the house on his chain, and when Ranger came out of his doghouse, people ran like heck to get out of his reach! Grandpa, being the carpenter that he was, built Rangers house with a hinged roof that could be opened to expose the inside of the doghouse. Every now and then, when I would come up missing, Grandpa always knew right where to look for me. He would walk over to the doghouse, open up the roof, and there I would be, curled up next to Ranger, both of us fast asleep.

Sandy

I couldn't always predict Grandpa. One time I was certain I'd get a whipping was when I got caught playing "you show me yours and I'll show you mine" with my cousin Sandy under the porch in front of the house. My grandpa and uncle AJ (Sandy's dad) thought it was funny. We didn't get in trouble at all. The strange thing is that I knew something wasn't right about it even at age five but my curiosity about the difference between boys and girls got the better of me now and then.

Electricity

My most peaceful memory is a beautiful evening outside with Grandpa and Grandma. We were sitting out in front of the house watching the Northern Lights, as Nat King Cole could be heard on the radio coming from the house. He was singing "Mona Lisa." As dreamy as this all was, it kind of puzzles me that I can remember the radio playing but can't remember electric lights in the house. I only remember eating by lamplight. There must have been lights, if there was a radio. While I don't know how electricity got to the farm, I distinctly remember that radio playing and Nat King Cole singing. A truck must have shown up one day and put in wires. But, this is my first recollection of electricity on the farm and a dream-like peace still comes to me as I think back to that evening on the porch.

Church

The most memorable experience with churches that I can remember is my step-father Charles' funeral. I do also recall Grandma teaching Sunday school and I never missed a Sunday of church and Sunday school, because Grandma wouldn't allow it. They were Baptists. The church they attended had something that looked to me like a small swimming pool up in front. People, as they came of age, were submerged at baptism. I thought that was really scary for some reason.

I recall all of the pews had little slots in the back of them to hold hymn books and shot glasses filled with wine. Once, I went crawling around in the back pews drinking all of the wine. That is the last thing

I remember about my life with Grandma and Grandpa on the farm just outside Dallas, Texas.

I cared deeply for my Grandma. I never felt any confusion about her and the way she treated me. On the other hand, for the majority of my life, I was confused by my memories tied to my Grandpa. He was stubborn. He was mean. He was strict. He was a lot of things. But most of all, as I look back, he was good to me.

While it took me a long time to understand those events and the major part they played in my life, now I understand. I would have never come to this conclusion about Grandpa if I had not felt for so many years that I was missing something about all those events that just didn't make sense. He was good to me so why did he do all those things that seemed so mean? Now I know.

In recent years, I have looked back to try to understand the roots of my negative attitudes, behaviors and insecurities. The years when a youngster is deciding who he is cannot be handled too carefully. I was five when I first drank that wine in the back of the church pews. Little did anyone know that alcohol, drugs, sex and violence would consume the majority of my years to come.

At this point, my life was repeating a predictable pattern. Maybe you feel trapped in this vicious cycle right now. Maybe my story can help you understand what is happening in your life. I bet you haven't done anything worse than I have. I was on a crash course of self-destruction, rejection and fear.

I didn't get a happy, secure childhood. I wasn't able to handle all that was bottled up inside of me, even at such an early age. I was five years old and life was already pretty messed up. We have a ways to go and there's a lot of crap along the way, but I promise you, there's a happy ending.

Aunt Kate and Uncle Louis
I don't remember what the reason was, but when I was five, I was sent to live with my aunt Kate. She and Uncle Louis had four kids. They lived in Mart, Texas a little town outside of Waco.

Aunt Kate was a lot like Grandpa and a little bit like Grandma. She could be sweet one minute and meaner than heck the next. She was a seamstress and worked in the cotton fields during picking season. Uncle Lewis worked as a mechanic for a Ford dealership in Waco, so during cotton season, all of us kids would head to the fields with Aunt Kate. My cousin Patsy and I were both five and we were required to pick cotton too, mostly because it provided a way to keep an eye on us and work at the same time. Aunt Kate would sew these long canvas sacks with a strap on them that went around our shoulders. We were so little that the sacks would drag along behind us down the rows as we picked cotton and stuffed it into the long sack. Once the sacks were full, they were brought to a cart at the edge of the field. The cotton was then weighed, recorded and dumped into the cart. The cotton pickers were paid by the pound of cotton that they picked. I don't remember what that amount was, but I do remember picking such a small amount that it didn't even register on the scale. I was scolded by Aunt Kate and told that I had better quit playing and pick some cotton or else. The next day, I picked a nickel's worth of cotton according to the scale. I had put a big dirt clod in my sack to add more weight. At the end of the day, all of the pickers would ride back to the farmhouse sitting on top of the cotton in the cart. I remember searching everywhere for that dirt clod as we rode back to the farm. I was just sure that someone was going to find that clod of dirt and discover what I had done. This was my first experience with being purposely dishonest.

It seems like a lot of negative things happened the year or so that I lived with my Aunt Kate and Uncle Louis. Maybe it is just the fact that I can trace some deep problems back to those days.

It is said that at age six we begin to develop habits that eventually define us. I think that age is more like five for the majority of us. This seems to be the age that most people can clearly remember back to. Of course, we all have random memories, but I am setting age five as a good age for each of us to go back and take a deeper look.

Looking at our childhood is something we don't usually do consciously or think to connect it to any of our current behavior. However, this is the age where we start storing our experiences in our subconscious minds. By repetition, we develop habits. Once recorded in the subconscious mind, habits become very difficult to overcome. Most people don't understand habits and how they develop and never think to change them and instead do all they can to justify them usually by blaming someone or something for their shortcomings. We become complacent as we allow circumstances to shape our lives never knowing that bad habits can be overcome several different ways.

By definition, a habit is something you do without thinking. The point here is that all of our habits, either good or bad, often start to develop at this age. While I had done some far less than desirable things, I had also convinced myself of some things that weren't even true and I will bet that you have too.

One of the biggest lies that I defined myself by, was that I was stupid.

First Year of School

Patsy and I were the same age and we both attended our first year of school together in Mart. I spent most of my first school year sick. I was told that I had pneumonia four times that year. Common sense tells me that I most likely had pneumonia once and relapsed three times. I was seldom in school and when I was there, I didn't learn much because I was so far behind. Patsy was rather slow scholastically and brought home poor report cards, so did I.

Naturally, I didn't think of myself as being just behind. I figured that I must be slow too. I thought that I wasn't as intelligent as the rest of the class. I felt different and out of place. I never developed a love of learning the school stuff and began to believe the lie that I was stupid. I was five. I didn't understand that an entire year of being sick would knock anyone off course in school. I just decided that I was never going to be like the other kids in the smarts department.

Here is another example of how we can convince ourselves at an early age of things that are not necessarily true. But these things tend to affect and define the rest of our lives. Sometimes, we do not leave those childhood misunderstandings behind. We believe them and eventually begin to live them out until, suddenly, it isn't just a misunderstanding, but now our reality. The important fact is that we need to go back and define it. All too often, we end up being defined by the misunderstanding! How backwards is that?

Back to my time with Aunt Kate. She had a lot of my grandpa in her and she reacted to life accordingly. As a child, you will remember that besides running home from school every day so that she could work in the fields, she was also required to keep good grades. Knowing her, my guess is that she didn't have very good grades which meant she had to take a walk with grandpa where she got the razor strap at the end of the walk. That leather strap that Grandpa sharpened his razor on really hurt. So, to teach us to become brighter students, the razor strap became her method. Patsy and I were often required to take a walk that ended in the bathroom. Once there, we were told to lean over the bathtub so Aunt Kate could whip us with Uncle Lewis' razor strap.

This didn't help either of us become better students. In fact, it did just the opposite by convincing us that we were, indeed, stupid and illiterate. Sometimes while trying to beat good sense into a kid, we beat in the wrong message. Each whipping beat the message into us. I really got the strap when I failed the first grade because of being sick all year. So, it appears that some of Grandpa's meanness got to me after all. He sure taught Aunt Kate a lesson she never forgot, and she then passed it along. What a legacy.

One evening at the supper table I was doing something that Aunt Kate didn't approve of and the situation got out of control. Exactly what I was doing I don't recall. What I do recall, is stabbing her in the hand with a fork when she tried to slap the crap out of me. She got in a few whacks before I nailed her with the fork trying to protect myself. I was pleased that she had to stop to nurse her hand. That was the last time she ever attacked me at the table. Did I purposely hurt her? No. The fork was already in my hand when she began to slap me. She actually stabbed herself when I put my hands up to protect myself from her attack. What an environment around the dinner table. And to think I was only five!

Memories of fear and violence are foremost in my recollection of those days.

While I wasn't afraid of Aunt Kate, these days confirmed my worthlessness to my subconscious mind. She had a lot of good qualities. She had taken me into her home. She didn't treat me any worse than her own kids. She was doing what she thought was in our best interest. I don't blame her for those days. She was not an out and out mean person. She did have a bad temper at times and like grandpa, she didn't put up with any nonsense. She had been a student in the painful history lesson of how she had been raised. She didn't know how to do anything else. She handled us kids just like she was handled. Generational habits are powerful.

Watch for them to pop up over and over in my own life's story.

In those early years I was the one who was hurt. But, as you'll soon learn, I became the one to pass on all the pain, fear and insecurity to the next generation. You may wonder how I can see the best in Grandpa, Aunt Kate and all of the people who were supposed to be keeping me safe as a little kid. Actually, I didn't see the best in them for years. Slowly, I had to process all of this crap that was done to me. Then, I had to look into all of the pain that I then imposed on the people I have loved the most.

While there is no excuse for hurting someone, there is an understanding that comes when you realize that your intention was never to hurt them. You have either believed lies, or acted on bad habits so completely that you no longer consider the impact on those around you. I understand that all of these people loved me and truly cared about me. They just couldn't figure their own lives out enough to reach into mine. When you realize that people have not purposely hurt you, it is easier to forgive them. Do you understand the concept here? It is a powerful and freeing idea. Forgiveness. Forgiveness towards all of the people who wronged you, also gives you the freedom to receive forgiveness for all that you have done wrong. Most often, you must start by forgiving those people who mislead and hurt you. You must not stop there. You then need to walk through this pain and receive this same forgiveness for yourself. You will not complete the transformation of forgiveness until you offer it towards your biggest failure. It doesn't matter how the pain started and who continued it. It matters that it stops. Not just on the conscious level, but deep into your soul, spirit, and heart.

Forgiveness allows me to share my story with you. Never assume that I think it's alright to hurt another human being in any way. However, we have all been hurt, and we have also caused pain. Let's accept that we are human, get through the pain of the past and become better people in the future. It is said that you cannot change the past. I encourage you to look at the past long enough to let it change you today. This is not easy, but if you change your Today and you continue to change Tomorrow, suddenly your Yesterdays are something you can be proud of.

There is never a time when we are not programming something into our minds. I was definitely learning throughout those early days. And I was not learning good life skills. For the most part, I was programming my mind and life for a coming disaster.

There are a bunch of little things that I remember from back then. While they may appear meaningless, these situations were defining me.

Like being so small that I could actually sit down in a five-gallon bucket. I remember not being able to get out by myself and getting stuck. I think that was my first introduction to claustrophobia.

My First Bike

One experience that started happy, was getting my first two-wheel bike from Mom on one of her visits. I remember trying to ride it and falling many times. I finally figured out that it's not such a long fall if I sat on the back fender. So, that was how I learned to ride a two wheel bike; sitting on the back fender with my feet on the pedals stretching forward over the seat to reach the handlebars. I loved my bike and I was proud that it came from my mom.

I remember getting caught (again) playing "you show me yours and I'll show you mine" with my cousin Nancy in the outhouse. I think we were playing doctor and I was sewing her up. I was pretty sure that I had invoked the spirit of some doctor and that I was performing major surgery when we got busted by Aunt Kate. I got the proverbial "shame on you," but Nancy, being four years older than me, got the "shame on you, you should know better." That embarrassed her so much that she ran away from home. She didn't get far before she came back though. If memory serves me, maybe a few houses away. As a curious little boy I played that game until I was eight. But, I perfected it so that I didn't get caught. Actually I discovered from that incident that it was in some way wrong and that I should be more secretive about my curiosity concerning the difference between girls and boys. I knew that hiding things wasn't a good idea because of the episode with the snake. But then it seemed that I should hide certain other things. Can you see how this could be confusing to a five year old? I see it now as a natural part of growing up. Neither right nor wrong, but rather curious.

In order to get a better understanding of this I did some research and discovered that it was actually considered to be a healthy natural thing for curious children to explore these areas. It is just one of the phases that children go through. Playing doctor was mentioned as one of the games children play. It was also suggested that this phase be treated with understanding and that children should not be punished or made to feel ashamed but rather made to understand the difference between girls and boys and the importance of being respectful of each other's privacy.

A Great Loss

The next significant event in my life is when Grandma Winters came to visit us one day. She, Uncle Louis and I went into town so Grandma could go to the beauty parlor to get her hair fixed. I went along with Uncle Louis to pick up supplies from the general store. When we came back to pick up Grandma, she was sitting on the curb with a bottle of grape soda that she had hardly touched. She said she wasn't feeling very well and got into the front seat of the car. I sat in the back, and Grandma gave me the grape soda. She instructed me to drink it quickly before I got back to the house where Patsy would feel left out. When we got home, Grandma laid down on the bed to rest. She called me over to the side of the bed. She took my hand and with a little squeeze said, "Be a good boy and take good care of your mom." Then she died.

Wow. What strong words to leave with a five-year old! I know Grandma meant well, but those words have been a hardship for me, because I was unable to care for myself, much less my mom.

I remember Aunt Kate quickly giving Grandma a shot of insulin and then slapping her face as she called to her. I became angry with Aunt Kate and yelled at her, "Leave my grandma alone!" Someone ushered me out of the house and over to the next door neighbor's. I don't think I was gone more than a few short hours, but when I came back, there was a coffin in the parlor. Grandma's body was in that coffin and all my aunts and uncles were there. I know mom must have been there too, but that's not even in my memory bank. My grandma's death was very hard on me. I loved my Grandma Winters. She was my security blanket and so far, I had lived with her and Grandpa longer than anyone else. My world was continually changing. I had very little happiness and security in those days.

Shortly after Grandma's funeral I was moved again. My mom came to get me and my stuff. I remember when she went to load up my bicycle Aunt Kate wouldn't allow her to take it. Aunt Kate said it was payment for taking care of me. So, what I thought was mine, was taken away. I never saw my bike again.

Bloody Bones
From Aunt Kate's, I went to live with Uncle Otis and Aunt Eunice and their three children, Robert, Gracie and Bonnie, in San Antonio, Texas. I can't remember what Uncle Otis did for a living at the time but Aunt Eunice was a hairdresser. She worked out of the house. The year must have been around 1949. My cousin Robert, who was several years older than me, was going down a really steep hill on his bicycle. We were headed for home and it was raining hard. I sat on the back fender with my bare feet supported by the braces on the bike. About half way down the hill and going at breakneck speed, my left foot slipped from the fender brace into the spokes. My foot was severely damaged as we slid to a sudden stop. It was as though the rear brake had been slammed on. My bare foot stopped the forward progress of two boys barreling down hill. This set up a miserable ordeal of bandages and dressings. I protested the treatment

and often couldn't even be found. It hurt to remove the bandages that stuck to the mangled flesh. It hurt even more to bathe the wounds. My foot resembled raw hamburger. In order to make me cooperate, Robert would put on this mask and pretend to be a ghoul by the name of "Bloody Bones." My choices were simple. Either cooperate or be eaten by Bloody Bones.

I always cooperated in the end because who wants to be eaten by a ghoul named, Bloody Bones?

Long after my foot had healed, Robert still came to my bedroom window at night wearing the mask to frighten me. Apparently, he got a kick out of it, but I was seriously frightened.

One time when we were playing "hide and seek" I went to hide behind an open door. Bloody Bones was standing there waiting for me. It was in the middle of the day and I thought I was safe. Bloody Bones had previously only come out at night. Being attacked by day was too much for me. I ran out of the house and hid by a retaining wall and refused to come inside for a long time.

Of course, the ghoul I'd seen behind the door was only the mask hanging behind the door. But at six years old, I was convinced that it was Bloody Bones himself waiting to get me. In addition to living in fear of Robert's scary mask episodes, Uncle Otis would often come home drunk and fight for what seemed like hours with Aunt Eunice. She would be yelling and screaming as he slapped her around. I was too young to understand what was happening, but I remember all of us sleeping in the next room. My cousins, Gracie and Bonnie, would cry and that bothered me too.

My First Puppy

Sometime in this period, my mom came back into my life. She rented a small two-room bungalow down the street from Uncle Otis and Aunt Eunice. I no longer had to fear Bloody Bones at night because I stayed in my new house with my mom. I did have to stay with Uncle Otis and Aunt Eunice during the day while Mom was at work. As long as I didn't have to stay there at night, I was OK with it. I don't remember it being so bad, partly because I got to bring my new puppy with me! I loved that puppy!

Mom had been dating a guy that worked heavy construction. I really liked him and he was good to me. He used to drop five dollar bills in the back seat of his car for me to find. Mom never let me keep them.

One day he took me to the pet store and let me pick out a puppy and bought it for me. I was thrilled that mom let me keep it. She was very upset, however, when my puppy chewed up everything in our little house. So, now during the daytime when I stayed with Aunt Eunice, she cared for the puppy as well as me.

When we lived in that little house, I was diagnosed with Anemia and was prescribed Mogen David wine in small doses as a cure. Wow!

I recall the lady next door with a mean kid that peed on my back and his mom worked at a drive-in and was bit several times by a copper head snake. It had hitched a ride on the running board of her car. She thought it was a stick and kicked at it and got bit several times. I remember her leg. It sure looked ugly.

These days were good until the day Mom and I packed up to move to Dallas. We went to get the dog and Aunt Eunice wouldn't let us have it. She said she had spent money on feeding it and it should rightfully be hers. I remember mom pulling on one leg, and Aunt Eunice pulling the other. They continued to fight until I said, "Let her have the dog." I could see we either had to leave my dog or they were about to injure it. We left San Antonio without my little friend and I never saw it again.

Now I had lost a puppy and a bike. Both had meant a lot to me. I didn't have much and what I did have was being taken away from me. I was hearing the people who were caring for me say that they deserved to keep something of mine because they had helped care for me. I don't know about you, but I would never take a kid's bike from him or his puppy, for that matter. The under-current to these situations, is that I had been a burden. I don't remember feeling that anything important was mine to keep forever.

Another thing I misunderstood was the drunken fighting between Uncle Otis and Aunt Eunice. It wasn't him that was drunk. It was her who was drunk and did the slapping. She finally shot and killed him many years ago. My guess was that she was drunk at the time.

Mom and I lived for a short while with my cousin Billy Jean. At twenty three, she was actually my mother's age and the daughter of Mom's older brother, Bill. There was another girl about Mom's age and the three of them didn't get along very well. Eventually we moved again.

I'm not exactly sure where we moved to. All these moves were getting confusing. But I do remember spending a lot of time at my mom's new boyfriend's house. His name was Jack. Jack lived with his parents in a huge house. We spent one Christmas there and I got lots of really neat Christmas presents.

The next Christmas, we were in a little one room apartment. It was just Mom and me. We had a little, foot-tall, plastic, transparent tree with little colored bulbs on it. There were a couple of little Christmas presents under it. I believe one of them was a Roy Rogers watch. We were poor. This was quite a contrast from the previous Christmas. I remember Mom sitting there reading a letter from Jack who was now overseas somewhere.

The Big Hole
During that time, Mom worked in a liquor store to make ends meet. I was supposed to go straight home after school, but one day instead of doing what was expected of me, I went to check out this hole that was being dug at a friend's house. I don't know what the hole in the ground was for, but a big dirt hole to a seven year old can be very exciting! After messing around for an hour or so, I headed home. My route home had me pass right by the liquor store where my mom worked. When she saw me cruising by she called for me to stop and then came across the street and grabbed me by the arm. She took me into the back room of the store and beat the living daylights out of me. Another one of my beloved Grandpa's blessings.

Uncle Bud and Aunt Marie

I believe our next move was to somewhere near San Antonio. We spent some time with Uncle Bud and Aunt Marie. They eventually became multimillionaires and were already quite wealthy back then in the early fifties. As the story goes, when they were first married, Uncle Bud and Aunt Marie started out with ten dollars between them. Aunt Marie worked for several years, while Uncle Bud attended college and got his degree in chemistry. Uncle Bud went to work for a local testing laboratory in San Antonio and after a short while was able to purchase the laboratory from his employer. The laboratory was located on the third floor of a large building where they also lived. I remember sitting in one of the windows in that building watching the battle of flowers as the parade passed by below. That was a good day.

Being a single mom couldn't have been easy. Mom put in a lot of hours at the liquor store to meet our financial needs. This meant I was staying with other people after school and on weekends. Some of these places and people were pretty bizarre.

One lady I stayed with would take my toys away and give them to her children as soon as my mom left. I didn't like this place. She didn't want any of the kids she babysat to wet their clothing or the bedding during naps, so she didn't allow us to drink water. Remember we were in Texas in the middle of the summer heat. I can still picture one little kid sitting in his highchair. He couldn't have been more than one or two years old and our babysitter came by with a damp rag to wipe his face. In an attempt to quench his thirst, he grabbed the rag and began to suck on it frantically.

I was all too familiar with thirst. I was just as desperate as that little guy in the highchair. The only difference was, I could walk around and search for something to drink and my search led me to the back yard which served as a livestock yard. There wasn't any grass left, but there were a few holes full of muddy water. With the temperatures reaching into the hundreds almost every day in the summer, the family's ducks would sit in the water in the holes and cool themselves. One of the other boys and I were so thirsty one day, we went outside and drank muddy water from one of those dirty pools.

I have vague memories of living with quite a few other people for short periods of time during those years between two and eight years of age. The last place I remember living before leaving Texas, was a Mexican village outside of San Antonio. I made friends there with kids and met their older siblings and parents. I saw and heard things that scared me. One friend's older brother told me how his dad burned him with a spoon when he lied. And, looking back, I think his dad abused him, because he tried to mess with me in that way.

I still don't think I can fully comprehend the back-lash from that time. I was getting all scarred up, mostly on the inside. In fact, today, I have a visible scar on my arm where Jackie burned me with the tip of a red hot knife. Can you imagine what we all would look like if our emotional and mental scars were as visible as the physical? In a way they are visible, as we act out the pain that we have felt. My life was severely damaged by other damaged people. Jackie was abused by a man he couldn't stop. And then he came after me. And I couldn't stop him. Again, we see a looping cycle.

A Box of Crackers

I would like to challenge you to try a little experiment. Go get yourself a nice new box of crackers. Take all of the crackers out and stomp on the box. Crush it in every way you can think of. Burn a few edges with a lighter. Rip it in two. Now go get the contents of that box and try to get them to fit back in nicely. Go ahead. Yell at the box if you want to. Curse at it and tell it that it is a stupid, worthless box. Let it know that as a cracker box, it has the sole purpose of holding crackers. If it can't hold crackers and if it doesn't look like a nice cracker box, what is it good for? Who would want it?

I can guarantee you a few things. That box will never be like it was before you attacked it. If it stands a chance of functioning as it was intended, someone is going have to heal it up. There will need to be some tape, some gentleness, patience and someone with the vision of what that box can still be. The point I am trying to make is quite simple really. We have people who have been as damaged as that box you just mangled. They feel like junk and look like garbage. They are embarrassed and ashamed of themselves. They look around to all the other perfect boxes and get really angry. Why did they have to experience such thoughtless, severe treatment? There aren't any easy answers to the "why" questions. And each person in this situation feels hopeless.

My life was just like that box.

I felt so many negative emotions as I experienced those random acts of abuse and violence.

Can you relate to my story? If you can, then I want to encourage you to begin a healing process right this very moment. Acknowledge the fact that you have been through some horrific events. Be honest with yourself. Look back and grieve the parts of your life that weren't your fault. However, this process will not be a positive one if you are only feeling sorry for yourself. Another common pitfall is to become obsessed with anger towards the people and situations that harmed you. I urge you to just simply be honest. Right now, you need to understand your "why?" question. You need to understand that just like that cracker box, you have been unable to keep up with all of the people around you who have never been damaged. Unlike the box, you have a heart, spirit, soul, and mind. You don't have to live out your days angry or moping around. We all have the potential to change our attitudes. Once our attitudes change, we can, with self-discipline and purpose, change the course of our life. That is the beauty of free will. We must take responsibility for our lives right now! We can become anything we set out to be. This process must begin with one simple step. We must honestly look for truth.

The older I become and the longer I search for truth, the more I realize that the truth is constant. I just become more aware of it as I search for it. Truth has been there the entire time. I just never seriously looked for it. Now, I never grow tired of the search. I was numb for so many years. Then I became destructive to both myself and anyone around me. When I realized that I had done unimaginable damage to others, I reached for drugs and booze to wipe out my conscience. I couldn't face myself.

But there I go again, getting ahead of myself. Let's get back to my childhood.

Wally

I was really happy to be with my mom, as she was the only one I really felt loved by since Grandma Winters was gone. I was seven years old when my mom met a guy named Wally Leines. Wally was in the Air Force at the time and stationed at Kelly Field near San Antonio. Wally used to take me to the base sometimes. I would swim in the swimming pool or we would go to a movie that was being shown. I liked Wally, and between him and my friend, Sonny, I had some great days.

One evening, Sonny and I were at his place sitting on the end of the bed watching Roy Rogers on television. Wally knocked on the door and ask if I wanted to go to the movies. I don't remember who invited him in the house, or if anybody did, for that matter. But he was standing in the house when Sonny's dad came in the back door and spotted him. Sonny's dad reached into his back pocket and pulled out an automatic pistol. Recalling it now, I believe it was a 45 automatic. Wally was trying his best to explain that he was only there to ask me if I wanted to go to the movies.

Sonny's dad wanted to know if either Sonny or I had invited Wally in. We were both scared so we said "No." I believe Wally was called a few choice names and then ordered out of the house. I never did go to the movies with him that day, and I felt terribly guilty for not standing up for him in front of Sonny's dad.

Wally became my mom's third husband and I felt guilty the entire forty-four years I was around him. Eventually, he died of cancer in 1996. For some reason, I never mentioned that situation at Sonny's home to him. How easy would it have been to ask him about it? Instead, I thought he disliked me because of that day when I failed to stand up for him.

As I think back now to that day so long ago and all that happened shortly thereafter, I believe Wally forgot about that incident years ago. It was my overactive imagination that caused the guilt I felt about that day. Wally was always good to me. Like, I can remember being very sick and Wally wrapping some sheets around me. The sheets were filled with something awful smelling, but he was sitting up with me all night until my fever broke in the morning. That doesn't sound like a man with a lot of animosities. Also, I can remember having an asthma attack and Wally stood there beside me. I felt assurance as he placed his hand on my shoulder and told me that everything was going to be all right.

I have a few random memories from those days. I was always barefoot and after stepping on a rusty nail, I got blood poisoning. That was a big deal back then. I also remember all of us sitting outside at the Sinclair's when out of nowhere, this maniac driving a car that had no tires on the wheels, came down the road and wiped out all of the mailboxes across the road. He continued on without stopping. It was as weird as it sounds.

I also recall attending school for a short time while we lived there in that village but I can't for the life of me remember the school or any of the kids in my class.

I recall Sonny's dad gunning for this creature that was getting in the hen house and eating his eggs. He finally found it slithering across his drive way behind his car. A ten-foot chicken snake looks a lot like a rattler but is not poisonous. Sonny's dad took the opportunity to jump in his car and run back and forth over it until he was satisfied that it was dead. Having accomplished the supreme over-kill he got out of the car and took the snake by the tail, swung it over his head and let it go into the tall bushes across the road where it hung draped in the trees looking kind of eerie.

Being the curious little boys that Sonny and I were and the fact that I was no longer afraid of snakes, thanks to Grandpa, we decided to pull the snake out of the trees and drag it back across the road. The snake was very heavy and that dead snake began to move and coil somewhat. We instantly let go. I don't remember what we did next, but I have never liked being surprised by snakes.

Are you beginning to understand where all our fears that we carry through our lives comes from and how they affect us in the present? We can look back at those times when we, as creative children, let our active imaginations create a marker in the pages of our life that we turn back to whenever a similar situation appears in our life. Now I know why I don't like being surprised by snakes and why it is that I am not afraid of them. But I will still have the same feelings concerning snakes and many other things until I face my fears and stop relying on those memories. Those memories got control of my emotions. I am grateful to my Grandpa, for that lesson years ago which forced me to face my worst fears today. I am no longer afraid to open myself up to everyone, after being so afraid for so long to open myself up to anyone.

Then we moved yet again. This time we left Texas. Wally was now permanently in our lives. We lived for a short while in Oklahoma where I attended school briefly, before we continued on to Des Plaines, Illinois.

Once there, we lived for a short time with Aunt Dorothy and Uncle Stanley and their four children. They lived right by the rail road tracks and we spent considerable time smashing pennies and rocks under the passing trains. I used to place a penny on the track and run like heck because I thought the penny would derail the train. I got along great with my cousins, Jimmy and David. They were like the two big brothers that I never had. I attended second-grade while living with them. I remember it was the year Dwight D. Eisenhower was elected President of the United States.

Broken Bottles
Once summer came, Wally was discharged from the Air Force and he, Mom, and I moved down the street to live with an elderly couple. We lived with them when my oldest sister Joyce was born. I think Wally went to work for the sanitation department and Mom worked at a supermarket in town. I was happy to be there with my cousins partly because the people we lived with had a cute little dog. "Pepper" used to howl along with Wally when he played the guitar and sang. We all got a big kick out of that!

It was fun while it lasted, but our living arrangement came to an end one day after just a few months. It was all because I was accused of breaking some bottles in back of the house. I told everyone that I didn't do it. But the older couple was dead certain that I had broken those bottles. Even my mom sided with them.

Good old Wally calmly asked me, "Did you break those bottles?" I said, "No, I didn't." He stood up for me when they insisted that I incriminate myself. He told them, "Randy didn't do it."

Now, Wally had a deep authoritative voice that warned you not to dispute his spoken word. After all, he did stand six foot four and weighed about 220 pounds. He was pretty quiet, but when he spoke, it would be in your best interest to listen. (Unless, of course, you were a crazy Mexican with a 45 in your back pocket.)

Regardless of Wally's confidence in me, we were asked to move out after that. Mom still didn't believe me and asked me one last time to tell the truth. I stuck to my story, which was true. Still, Mom warned me, "If you're forty years old and I find out that you broke those bottles, Randy, I'm going to whip you."

Well, mom it's been over half a century now and I have to tell you, I did NOT break those bottles and I never knew who did. I don't know what reason I ever gave mom to doubt me that day. But I have to admit that in time, I gave her plenty of other reasons to doubt me!

Hulahan

Just before we moved, we finally got to get a dog of our own. The people that owned the supermarket where mom worked had a pair of Great Dane's. They had just been blessed with a litter of puppies when a city ordinance came out saying that it was unlawful to have more than one dog without a kennel license. So, they began giving purebred puppies away and mom, to my joy, brought one home.

As we were told, the parents to our puppy were show dogs. The mother was given to some people who lived in Michigan over 500 miles away, but two weeks later the dog showed up back at the front door!

Wally took possession of our Great Dane puppy and named him "Hulahan." I think the name came from the way Hula swayed when he walked unsteady because of his big feet that his body was yet to match and dad picked up the name from when he was overseas while in the Air force. I can still see that dog with his bobbed ears sticking straight up. We had them held up with wires wrapped in gauze to keep them straight. What a crazy sight!

After we were kicked out, Mom, Wally, my new sister Joyce, Hula and I were off to Minnesota in a black 1950 Ford. We were pulling a trailer containing Hula and our belongings.

If we pause and reflect right now, you may begin to realize how many times I was moved within the first eight years of my life and the various people I was exposed to. How could anyone not be confused having been raised in so many places with different sets of values? There is also the fact that I barely had a chance to get used to one situation before I was placed into another. I had absolutely no sense of security and was always searching for a way to belong.

Minnesota

Upon reaching Minnesota, I was sent to live with Wally's parents. I can't recall where Mom, Wally, and Joyce were, but I loved living out in the country! Wally's folks still had five kids at home and we lived out in the middle of nowhere. The eight of us lived in a tall skinny house with only four rooms. One room downstairs served as a kitchen, dining room, living room and family room. The other room was a bedroom and there were two bedrooms upstairs. The house was so small that the stairway to the upper level was almost straight up and down like a ladder. We had electricity but television had not yet come to the country. For entertainment we listened to shows like "The Shadow," "Boston Blackie," and "Amos and Andy" on the radio. I believe that year was one of the most peaceful times of my life. It was the best time that I can remember of my childhood. We played anti over, caught fireflies after dark and spent hours rolling in the grass. We would come in tired at night and count wood ticks that we collected while rolling in the grass to see who had the most. We milked cows and not only did we separate the cream from the fresh milk, we also churned the cream into butter. Besides the milking cows, there were pigs, chickens and a horse named "Star." All summer long we'd swim in the deep ditches alongside the driveway. Life was good.

We all attended school in Gary, a small town about twenty miles away that we got to by bus.

I was in the second grade and didn't really have any friends. This was most likely a result of moving to Minnesota in the middle of the school year. I didn't struggle with school as much there and that helped me.

Everything began to change, however, when I moved back with my mom and Wally. We lived just a little ways out of a little town by the name of Rindal. It was a tiny town that consisted of a creamery, general store, one church, a gas station and a few homes. Wally was now my official dad and for the first time, we were living as a family in our own home. Where we had moved to was not far from my new grandma and grandpa's home, but it put us in a different county. I couldn't go to school in Gary, but was now required to attend school in a town by the name of Fertile. The school was under construction as they were adding on to it. At first it looked like I would be attending a one room country school. As summer ended, the school board decided at the last moment that the new school was far enough along to begin classes.

At this point everything started to go wrong. My new dad didn't seem to pay any attention to me anymore. The security and good feeling of belonging that I had while living with Grandma and Grandpa Leines for that short time was gone like so many other good things that, for one reason or another, just seemed to disappear from my life. I wasn't catching on to things in the new school like the other kids were. To hide my embarrassment I gave up trying. I became disruptive as I clowned around for attention. When I wasn't being disruptive, I day-dreamed. I was a crummy student who was soon on bad terms with my teacher. For punishment, I was most often sent to the principal's office. I usually got spanked, adding to my misery, I was little for my age so some of the kids picked on me. I was such a hassle to my teacher, that she was no doubt very happy when we moved away before the end of the school year.

We left Rindal on a Friday. Our driveway was a little over a mile long, so I had a long walk after the bus dropped me off. When I got home that day, I opened the front door to find the house was completely empty. I turned around and started back down the driveway wondering what I was going to do without a family. Maybe I should have been surprised or frightened but I actually felt nothing and thought that it was just another loss in my life. I was about three quarters of the way down the driveway again when Mom and Dad showed up in our black 1950 Ford. I'm still not sure why I wasn't aware of the fact that we were moving. My guess, is that there just wasn't much communication to kids in those days.

Some of the things I remember best about living there was that we had brought a television set from Des Plaines. But television signals had not come to the country yet. Even though our old Emerson TV displayed no picture at all, people came from all over the country-side to see what a TV looked like. I remember how excited we all were when the first station made it to where we lived. It was Channel 6.

We watched shows like Charlie Chan, Boston Blackie and Flash Gordon. Usually it was two hours or more of test pattern, which is a bunch of lines and circles on the screen, because of transmission problems and an hour or so of TV. We had company a lot and no one complained or got impatient waiting for a picture to replace the usual test pattern.

Hula was getting really big. To show just how big there is a picture somewhere of Dad standing in front of Hula holding him up by his front feet stretched out. He was as tall as Dad.

Dad did a little farming on the little bit of land that belonged to the place where we lived. The machine that is used to plant the seeds is called a drill which is a wide contraption that is pulled behind the tractor with metal compartments in sections that contain the seed to be planted. Beneath the compartments containing the seed are disks that part the soil as seed is deposited, closing the soil over each seed. The seed is deposited by small gears that turn the little grains into a tube, called a drill, that projects between the disks that part and cover the soil. There's a platform in back of the drill that I rode on as dad planted the seed.

One day, I watched the seed being turned into the tube and decided to see what would happen if I stopped the seed. Not a good idea. I didn't see the gear coming around and my finger was almost cut off and I got one more of the many scars that remind me of some of the dumb things I did as a kid. And as an adult. That day I was able to run home and have my Mom fix me up.

Dad planted flax and I remember playing in the flax bin until I was told that a kid somewhere in the country had jumped into a flax bin and smothered to death. Flax in a bin is like quick sand. Only it sucks you under faster.

The Wrong Foot

We moved to Bejou, a little town of about 200 people. ("Bejou" is the Sioux Indian word for "hello.") I was still in the third grade, starting over in a new school yet again. The school was small with only four class rooms with a small room that was the principal's office, a small lunch room, two bathrooms and a basement for the boiler room and janitor's quarters. The grades only went up to the eighth grade. Each of the four teachers in the school taught two grades at a time in one room. First through fourth grade was taught on the first floor and fifth through eighth grades were upstairs.

I immediately got off on the wrong foot. My teacher was asking each of us what our nationality was and came and stood over me. "Full-blooded Texan," I declared, which got a good laugh from everyone. I was honestly embarrassed because I thought that really was my nationality since that was where I came from.

The next thing I recall was getting caught making a spitball out of my spelling words paper. "This boy ate his spelling words!" the principal was told. Out came a rubber hose and I got a taste of it. That principal and I, and his rubber hose, got to know each other very well!

While I most often precipitated my own dilemmas at school, there were a few times that I just got unlucky. Like the time I found a half-dollar coin in an envelope. You know, the kind you drop into the offering plate in church on Sundays. It was just lying there on the bathroom floor so I decided to keep it. I hid it under the rubber mat in front of the drinking fountain just outside the boys' bathroom. I would not have done that if I thought it was right for me to keep the money. I would have just stuck it in my pocket. I have no idea how they figured it out, but somehow I was singled out and forced to tell where it was hidden. I was punished and labeled a thief, although I didn't really steal anything.

And not every part of this school year was bad. The best part about my new class was that there were eleven girls and only three boys, including myself. I was the most popular and always the first one chosen for any sport. I was the best athlete in all sports which was very positive for me. I was proud of my athletic abilities and it was a source of confidence.

Not so in the classroom. I felt out of place there. No one dared to tease me about my learning difficulties. All of the girls liked me and I could and would beat up both of the other boys if they said anything about it. But there wasn't enough flirting or fighting to cover up that I couldn't read as well as the other kids. I couldn't spell worth a darn either, no matter how hard I studied. Mom would help me study my list of twenty spelling words, reading them off to me, pronouncing and spelling each one for me over and over until I remembered the correct spelling. I tried my best to memorize those words. By the time mom got to the bottom of the list and then returned to the top, I had already forgotten the words at the top. She would become angry and accuse me of not even trying. I heard that phrase a lot. Not only from my mom, but from teachers as well. Being accused of not trying was a lot better than being accused of being stupid I supposed. So I pretended not to try. The sense of being a disappointment to all of the adults around me was more than I could face.

I am sure that my learning disability was nothing more than my poor self-image and the result of the message that Aunt Kate beat into me along with the confusion of moving from one school system to another where studies were always a little different. The truth is, I never had a learning disability. I was just a victim of circumstances that no one can be held responsible for. Not even Aunt Kate. She was a victim herself teaching me what she had leaned the same way she learned it. The lie was already in full bloom in my heart and others didn't need to remind me that I was a stupid boy. I felt that I was the dumbest kid in my grade and acted accordingly.

A Confusing Scenario
Let's look at things again and try to gain some insight as we go. We could go back to the very beginning and blame my dad, David, for cheating on my mom and causing their marriage to end. I could blame Aunt Kate for her negative responses when I first started my school days. I could blame my mom for putting me in all of those situations. I could blame it on bad luck or a million different reasons, but it wouldn't change anything, especially the circumstances that are now in the past.

Sure, a lot of things could have been done differently. Had some issues been better handled, my life would have gone in a different direction. But the reality of the situation is that things were the way they were. I still don't believe anyone hated me so much that they intentionally misdirected my life. Everyone that had anything to do with my upbringing did what they were taught to do. To hold a grudge or to blame someone else for my shortcomings now, is to release control of my life and become a slave to past injustices.

I am telling you that I no longer live like that frightened, abused, stupid boy. I have realized that I no longer need to! I have the ability to be successful at anything I set my mind to. Had I known this at eight years old, I would have done very well in school. But I didn't know, or at least I didn't understand and my parents and teachers never gave a thought as to why I wasn't catching on. I had been convincing them that I just didn't care enough to try.

Now, here's a confusing scenario for you. I was pretending not to try, yet I honestly believed that I was illiterate. Wow! Talk about living a lie.

Bejou
Bejou had a population of 212. At least, that's what it said on the sign as you entered town. And I pretty much had a fist fight with every boy around my age. Even if I was little for my age, I was scrappy. I had a lot of internal issues, so I was all too happy to beat the crap out of any boy who dared to bother me.

There was a liquor store and two saloons in Bejou. The people who owned the saloon at the end of town wanted to retire due to poor health, so Mom negotiated a rental agreement with them and took over the saloon. We moved down the street into a bigger house. Our new property had a lot of crab apple trees and other big trees to climb. My buddies and I would climb up into the branches and throw crab apples at passing cars.

We did a lot of crazy things. We used to have occasional BB gun battles (it's a wonder we still have our eyes). We had crab apple fights, good old fashioned mud ball fights after a hard rain and "match fights" with farmers matches rigged up with clothes pin guns. We'd walk the ditches for miles and search for bottles to turn in for two cents each. We'd spend all of our money as soon as we got it so I often didn't have enough for toys and candy. So, I'd buy one and steal the other. It never even bothered me. At one of the stores in town, the owner took care of his elderly sister who was in a wheelchair. I stole the most from them. I think they maybe knew about it, but the store keeper, Papa Halstrom, would pretend to sleep, so I got away with a lot. One thing about them I'll never forget. Folks said that when his sister died, there was forty thousand dollars cash stuffed in the little pillow that she sat on!

Remember our dog, Hulahan, the Great Dane? Hula now stood about three feet tall and weighed around 190 pounds. Dad had to chain him to our house as Hula often got into fights with a boxer from the other end of town. I don't know how either of them lived through some of the fights they had.

One of the outstanding characteristics of Great Danes is that they tend to be very protective. One day right out in front of my house, the neighborhood bully stopped by on his bicycle. I don't remember why, but he slapped me across the face. I probably don't remember the reason because he most likely didn't have one. He just enjoyed doing mean things. Hula was watching. He broke his chain and had that kid pinned to the ground in an instant. The bully was squirming on the ground and begging me to call my dog off. I did, but not before I had the final say. "You're not so tough now are you?" I never had another problem with that kid. Whenever I would see him he would sneer at me but never picked on me again thanks to Hulahan.

I made it all the way up to the sixth grade in Bejou before we moved again. This time we moved back into the country to a tiny town called Bear Park. This could hardly be called a town, as it consisted of a general store, a town hall, a Lutheran Church a few hundred yards down a gravel road, a graveyard alongside the Church and one old house across the main gravel road that ran in front of the store. Mom had once again negotiated a deal, this time with Papa Halstrom, and was hired to run the store. Our house was not far from Rendahl which put me in the Fertile school district again, where I would be attending the sixth grade. I must've left one heck of an impression on my third grade teacher, because when she heard I was coming back, she went and warned the sixth grade teacher about me, the little terror with horns.

Willie
By this time I was almost normal size for my age. I think it was one of my first days at school when I met what turned out to be my best friend back then, Willie. Although we were technically cousins, I don't think Willie or I ever thought of ourselves as relatives. We were like brothers. Most of all, we were best friends. Willie had a mess of sisters, six to be exact and not a single brother. The day we met, he was sitting on a mission style sofa in the hallway at school. Willie had broken his leg when a wall of unsecured lockers fell on top of him.

Willie couldn't get around very well, so at recess time he sat on the couch in the hallway, letting the kids coming by take rides up and down the hall on his crutches. Some kid was leaning on his crutches when I came by. Without a word, Willie snatched them away from the kid, and handed them to me to try. We were best of friends from that moment on. We rode the school bus and did everything together. Willie only lived a couple of miles from the store and he often rode his bicycle over. He was just a few months older than me but a grade higher because I was held back my first year of school. Being a grade apart didn't bother either of us. We still rode the bus together and sat in the same seat every day listening to the popular songs of that time on the bus radio. We'd belt out everything from Elvis to Jerry Lee Lewis as we sang along. We played "Name That Tune" to each song that came on the radio. The year was 1955.

Willie and I got together almost every weekend. If he wasn't staying at my place, I was staying at his. Willie's house kind of reminded me of the one I lived in when I first came to Minnesota. There were only four rooms, none very big. Their kitchen may have measured 5 x 10 feet with one of those old-fashioned wood-burning cook stoves taking up most of the space. They squeezed a couch and one end table with a radio on it around the dining set and there was a tiny master bedroom on ground floor. The stairway to the upstairs was again more like a ladder, leaning in the opening of the ceiling as it was almost straight up and down and very narrow. How nine people fit in that house was amazing in itself, but there was always room for me and I was made to feel welcome. I suppose it was much the same for Willie at my house except we had a lot more space.

Every Saturday was catechism at the Lutheran church in Rendahl. We had to study for a test about biblical subjects and occasionally read from the New Testament. The Reverend gave up on calling me to read because I couldn't pronounce any of the words. Mom would quiz me on all of the questions but I just couldn't seem to retain any of the answers. Mom would become very angry with me and accused me of not trying again. The problem was I just couldn't focus and I felt stupid. Believe it or not, I actually failed catechism. That's not easy to do! Don't you just know how much that did for my self-esteem?

If that weren't enough, on Fridays in school, we had what they called parochial school. One day I got the Reverend so angry with me, that he kicked me out of the class and told me not to return. I think it was because I got into an argument with the little girl that sat next to me over a broken color crayon.

We were as poor as church mice that year. Dad wasn't working and Mom was expecting my brother Lee. Mom and dad had crawled around in potato fields on their hands and knees gathering up little or damaged potatoes the digger left behind. That's what we lived on that year. Nothing else. It was so cold in the house that in the morning the glass of water beside my bed would be frozen. Mom always seemed to be mad at me and often threatened to send me to reform school. I didn't really know what a reform school was but it didn't sound good.

Anyway, the set of color crayons was a gift from my Aunt Marie in Texas. They were in a little leather pouch with fringes on it. The little girl asked me if she could see my crayons and when she handed them back, one was broken. I think it was already broken before she ever touched them, but I blamed her just the same. She had a fifty cent piece in her purse, so to get even with her for breaking my crayon, I stole her coin. That's what the argument was all about. The little girl was crying because I was accusing her of something she denied doing. I wouldn't let it go so I got kicked out of parochial school. Being kicked out for something I thought was someone else's fault didn't do much for me, or my opinion of ministers of the faith. I felt justified in stealing from that little girl.

As I remember that event today, I feel a lot of remorse for hurting that little girl's feelings and stealing from her. Her name was Sarah. She was a very sweet, thoughtful and polite little girl, who obviously liked me. I showed my appreciation for her friendship by hurting her feelings and stealing from her. I saw Sarah recently at a 40-year school reunion. This was the first time I had seen her in all those years. She grew up to be everything and more than she was as a little girl. Sarah is married to a very wealthy man who treats her with all the respect and consideration that she deserves. But more about that reunion later on.

So, I brought the fifty cents home and gave it to my mom to buy something to eat. She asked me where I got it and I said that I had found it.

Religious Teaching

For those of you who are not familiar with parochial schools it's a religious teaching of the Lutheran faith which was taught in school by a minister every Friday. Parochial school was really a good thing for children who needed guidelines and boundaries. I was already a rebellious boy, and by getting kicked out of this class, we can safely assume that I entirely deserved it. Unfortunately, religion in schools suffered the same fate as the Pledge of Allegiance to the flag.

To this day I believe in the need for religious orders that help keep people organized and respectful to one another. Even though they don't all agree with each other, they still believe in the same higher power however which way they see and understand it.

Churches give us a place to go and be reminded of the things that we tend to forget. Religion gives us something to believe in when we are not sure of ourselves and a positive way to go when we have lost our way.

I believe in all religious beliefs even though they are a business like any other business that provides a product or a service for a price. I don't attend church often because I don't need to, but when I do I pay for the entertainment and sermon when they pass the offering plate.

While I was in serious need of self-discipline in my life at this age, I have to chuckle at some of the adventures Willie and I masterminded. One of our favorite targets for our pranks was our cousin, Junior. He had four sisters and needed us to put some testosterone in his world. Besides, Junior was a couple years younger than we were and spoiled rotten. Willie and I took it as our personal responsibility to torment him any way and every way that we possibly could. We were very tough on him!

One of our meanest schemes probably warped Junior for life. Just outside of Rendahl there were two buildings. This was actually right across the gravel road at the end of the drive way where we lived when Mom and Dad moved without telling me. One of the buildings was a cinder block building where they kept dead bodies in the winter, as they waited for the ground to thaw for spring burials. The other building looked like a small house with a picture window in front. Curtains and all.

This building was never locked and contained a variety of caskets. One day, Willie, Junior, and I went inside and we talked Junior into getting into one of the coffins. As soon as he did, we slammed the lid shut and ran out the door screaming "Watch out!" Before we could get to the road, Junior came crashing through the window. Glass was flying everywhere and he hit the ground running. We actually had to run him down out in the field across the road! It took both Willie and I to tackle him and calm him down.

We just loved to plot mischief against this poor kid and we saw a perfect opportunity one day at our swimming hole. Really, it was just a gravel pit full of water, but we had rigged a homemade diving board out of a plank, bailing wire, scaffolding and a 30-gallon drum which was the anchor at the end of the board buried in the sand. We really did a pretty good job engineering with junk parts. It worked okay except for once in a while, the end of the plank would come out from under the wires that ran from side to side connected to the lip of the drum that we had buried in the sand, as the board worked its way forward it would come loose and dump us in the water without warning. It also lacked spring, because of the way it was secured under the bailing wire, so we were always tinkering with it.

Willie and I were down at the swimming hole when Junior came by that morning. He was fresh from Sunday school and wearing his Sunday best. I can't remember which of us talked Junior into going out on the end of the diving board, but we convinced him to check out the bounce by telling him that we had made some adjustments. The adjustment was one of us standing on the other end of the board. When Junior got to the end of the board over the water, we stepped off, and he was dumped right in!

Junior lives in Alaska now, and we talk on the phone every now and then. We laugh about the dumb things we did when we were young. He asked me one time why we were so mean to him and I told him, "Because you were a brat and we really needed somebody to pick on."

Candy and Cookies

Mom was still running the general store in Bear Park through this time. And when I say it was a general store, I mean that in every sense of the word. There was a gas pump on one side of the store and a vessel in front of the store where kerosene was stored. One crank on the kerosene spigot equaled 1 gallon of kerosene. We sold a variety of machinery parts and other hardware, besides a full line of groceries, clothing, packaged meats, bulk candies, nuts, cookies and farm fresh eggs that the farmers brought in to trade for groceries. We also sold some pharmaceutical drugs, ice-cream, knickknacks and much more. I could pretty much have anything I wanted anytime I wanted it. As you can imagine, with my lack of self-discipline, I developed some bad eating habits and ballooned up to about 175 pounds. I was about 5'2" and 12 years old. Being overweight was out of character for me, as I had always been pretty lean. Willie had fun teasing me, but that didn't bother me because we were friends.

When I got to school that fall, the extra weight helped me hold my own in my battles with the other boys. There were definitely kids that could beat me up, but most of them knew that I would never back down from a fight, so they left me alone. One of the kids I looked up on my first day back at school in Fertile was a boy who had picked on me in third grade. I think I ran him to the bus every day. There was one other kid that did continuously pick on me in the sixth grade. I warned him to leave me alone until I finally retaliated and threw him on the ground. I'll never forget the look on his face when he realized that I had over powered him. It was the look of surprise and fear. There was really no point in beating him up, because now he knew to leave me alone. He kind of became a friend after that.

While the boys and I seemed to be getting to an understanding, my scholastic achievements were a disaster. I was so disruptive in class that my teacher moved me to the front of the class. When that didn't work, she moved me about five feet in front of the first row. When that still didn't work, she moved me and my desk outside the door and into the hallway. She'd also sent me to the principal's office quite often but it never did any good. I managed to get pretty much straight F's. At the end of the year she passed me just to get rid of me.

I remember that last day in sixth grade. I happened to be sitting up in my special spot in front of the class when she gave me my report card. It said "passed." I was so excited I fell over in my desk! The teacher came over just as I was picking myself up and she turned towards the class and said, "Here is an example of what you never want to become; he will never amount to anything." I can't really say if that was the most demoralizing moment I ever experienced or not. Her statement just sealed what I suspected about myself all along. I had just heard it clearly spoken in front of all of my peers. I was already convinced that I was indeed illiterate. Now, I was worthless as well. Randy Miller was destined for failure and it was announced to everyone.

I think back about that teacher now and I feel remorse. I had driven her to the point of complete frustration where she felt she had to degrade me in front of the entire class. She wasn't in any way a mean person. In fact, she was a very nice lady and actually a kid herself, as she was about 24 years old. For years, every time I accomplished something I would remember her in a positive way and think, "I wish you could see me now."

It would be nice to tell you that I set out to defy her statement. But, it would take me years to complete anything positive. I do know this: had she thought for one moment that what she said would have had such an impact on me, I know she would have never made that statement. Back then, teachers weren't trained to recognize problem children like they are today, not that they always use what they know. Isn't it strange that, as well-informed as teachers and parents are today concerning the detection of troubled children, troubled kids bring guns to school and kill classmates and themselves? Are we really paying attention? I think it was beyond any of my teachers to even contemplate the thought that I might actually be smart enough to play the part of an illiterate kid, pretending not to care, all the time being quite intelligent. I had everybody fooled. That included myself. But it was really only circumstances and the way I reacted to those circumstances that caused me to live a lie for the first 29 years of my life. Sure, I can blame the roots of this lie on all those people that had an impact in my upbringing. I could blame them for not taking the time to understand me and what I was going through. But what difference could it possibly make now for me to add insult to injury by allowing myself to remain a victim of those circumstances? It simply no longer matters!

What matters is right now. Today. This very moment. Sure, those things that happened a long time ago made a difference in my life, and most definitely caused me to doubt myself. So what? Now that it's in the past, should I pick up that club and beat myself with it every now and then so that I might be reminded of what could have been, "if only?" Or, should I drop it once and for all and make the very most of right now? The fact is, we've all done a lot of negative things that have definitely affected others and the lives they are living today. It all comes back to one thing. Whatever happened was yesterday. Right now is all we really have. If I can understand and forgive all those people I have blamed for my shortcomings for so long and take control of my life once and for all, then I can be free to forgive myself for the wrong I've done to others and make this day, at this very moment, the beginning of a new and better life. It may seem like I am repeating myself. I am. This whole forgiveness issue is a very big deal. We need to remind ourselves of this concept continuously, and then again. It is the key to becoming all that you were created for all along. The pain and fears from the past need to be wiped away. There isn't room to bring in the positive and good things your life can have, if you are filled with the bad and negative.

Here's another experiment for you. Take a little white board, and write down all of the horrible things that have happened to you. Include every bad experience you can think of. As you write, you will find that one word runs into the next, and pretty soon there is just a blob of words all jumbled together. Don't erase a thing.

Now, begin to write down each and every good memory that you can think of. Bet you can't pick out the pleasant words as they blend into the crappy words beneath them. Can you see the problem? You have to find forgiveness and apply it. The bad memories have to go in order to fill your life with good ones.

Everyone has something to be thankful for. Start with a fresh perspective and apply some energy to this. It is very important if you truly want to start living a life that you are consciously choosing. If you do not set out to control your own life, someone will come along and control it for you. If not in the present, then you will be controlled by something that overpowered you in your past. Guaranteed. Do you have dreams? What is stopping you from reaching those dreams? Your will is more powerful than any circumstance, past or present. You may need to make slight adjustments or your life may need serious reconstruction. What do you want? Who do you want to become? No one's life is perfect, but there is happiness, peace, and contentment to be found. You need to regain your focus and seek wise counsel if you feel you have completely lost your way.

Just a word of caution: old habits are the next culprit on the road of transformation. Watch for them. They will creep up on you and when they do you will be confronted with two truths I will and I can't both are true but there is only one way to go and the choice is yours to decide. Be ready and prepare a strategy. Forgiveness first. Then wrestle with those habits! Imagine what you want out of life without limiting yourself to anything and imagine who you want to become. Don't be misled by anyone or anything that isn't in tune with your desires. Pay close attention to everyone and everything around you. You will discover people who think like you who are willing and able to help you realize your dreams. Resistance only serves to remind you that you are in the right place heading in the right direction. After all, forward movement into resistance is what lifts and keeps a ten-ton aircraft flying.

My life would have been a lot less painful had I known all of this back in my early years. With disbelief I started seventh grade, and that progressed from bad to worse. My sister Kathy and my youngest brother Dennis, were born by now, and my dad, Wally, had even less time for me. He never seemed to approve of anything that I did, and we didn't really do anything together. I got some attention from him when I did bad things, so that was what we shared the most. In retrospect, I never had an active male role model in my life. I was on the outer fringes of great relationships several times, but never had a strong connection with any lasting impact. By the time I was a father, it was very obvious that I didn't have a clue what a guy should do with his kids. Wally tried, and I did too. We just never tried at the same time.

Dad lived for sports when he was young. He played basketball in school and was fairly good. So, I became interested in basketball. He was 6'4". I was just over 5 feet and pretty pudgy. Okay, I was fat! When I first started, I couldn't dribble the ball worth a darn. I seemed to have two left feet. If I had the ball and someone was near me, I had to get rid of it, because I couldn't handle it, and they would take it away from me. With a little practice, I could have overcome my awkwardness but I didn't see it that way. I thought I was naturally uncoordinated, even though years later I was the first pick for sports.

Keep in mind, there's a difference between playing with gifted sports minded kids, and playing with eleven giggly girls and two sissy boys. Then there was the fact that I was not as agile as I once was now that I was carrying 70 pounds of extra fat. To compensate for my lack of ball handling skills and my chubby body, I learned to hit the basket from anywhere on the court. At one time, I could hit 3 out of 5 one-handed push off shots from half court. I became very proficient at hook shots, and I rarely ever missed a free throw. When I wasn't shooting baskets on the court, I was shooting paper wads at the garbage cans. I did become fairly good on the basketball court, which helped me regain my confidence in sports. But I was never good enough for Dad to notice.

    He sang and played the guitar and even sang on the radio a few times. He was the lead singer in local country western bands around the area. For all of his years of experience playing and singing, I didn't think he was very good at it. Looking back, if either of us had noticed the other and found some common ground, I think we could have been really good for each other. Maybe if I learned to sing I could get his attention. So, I practiced a lot and made sure that he heard me. Even so, if he ever did notice, it was never made apparent to me. You could always tell when dad liked someone; he either teased them or picked on them. He never did any of those things with me. He liked to hunt but he never took me hunting with him. I would have jumped at the chance to go and spend some time with him, just the two of us. Every once in a while, he would ask me to go someplace with him or do something, and that made me think, "Maybe he does care!" But that didn't happen very often. A couple of times he took me several miles away from home and left me there. I didn't understand why he did that and I never asked him. It's safe to assume I was being punished for something. That's enough to indicate that we didn't communicate well, and we were out of rhythm with each other. I don't know how to process relationships like ours. I wish I could give you some formula for success when two people just don't click, even when both are desperate for acceptance. Maybe there isn't an answer, but it is something I hope to understand some day.

I tried everything to have dad approve of me. Besides the basketball and singing endeavors, I tried becoming an artist. I had drawn some things that others said were quite good. I showed them to dad and his response was "What's that worth? How much money are you getting for that?" I pretty much lost interest in art after that comment.

I thought I'd get his approval for sure when I got a job at the sugar beet plant. This was during a time when there were no jobs available. For several weeks, I rode seventy-five miles to Grand Forks with two guys that worked in the plant. They worked the midnight shift. I'd sit in the lobby and ask for a job. One night, someone was missing and they asked me to work. I was really excited because it was a better paying job than dad had. When I told him the good news he just said, "How long do you think that's going to last?" I quit shortly after that. Why he reacted to me that way, we will never know. Probably, I was just more trouble than he knew how to handle.

I know all these things make him sound bad, but he really wasn't. He died of cancer in 1996 while I was holding his hand. There were a lot of things I wanted to clear the air about before he died, but the thing I mostly wanted him to know was how sorry I was for causing him so much embarrassment.

He just said "That's all right. Things happen and you turned out good."

I think I made a pretty good impression on him in the years before he died. But just so you know, I realized I needed to ask for Wally's forgiveness. As a kid, I made it awfully hard for a man as proud as he was, to hold his head up in the community where we lived. In rural Minnesota we are related and well-informed of each other's private business. I was in trouble more often than not, and everyone knew about it. Wally had every right to have a cold heart towards me.

At the end of his life we finally clicked. We accepted each other, and I get a lump in my throat now, as I think of Wally and honor him. He was a good man.

So, here we are back in seventh grade where I pretty much stayed in trouble at school all the time. I was placed in a class with eleven other "slow learners." We were taught by our English teacher who volunteered to whip us into shape in addition to his obligations to teach the rest of the seventh grade. Of the eleven of us in that class, nine of them had actual learning disabilities and were not trouble makers. The other kid in the class that I remember best of all was Mike. The two of us seemed to be on the same page and tried our best to make our teachers life a living hell. But, that English teacher could hold his own.

He had this piece of wooden wall trim that measured about 3 feet long, 2 inches wide and three quarters of an inch thick. When we would cut up in class, he would wait until we were not expecting it, calmly walk up behind us and smack us across the back with that piece of trim. Man, did that sting! But it really didn't do any good. We thought of it as playing a game. Mike wised up to the sneak attacks, and when the teacher got near him with that piece of trim, Mike began to scream like he was being murdered. It wasn't long before the trim was side-lined, and the new punishment was him digging his fingers into our collarbones. Personally, I preferred the trim because it didn't hurt nearly as much as his fingers digging! Mike started screaming every time the teacher got near him, so the teacher backed off. That turned all of the attention on me. I thought screaming like Mike was kind of like crying, and I wasn't a crybaby.

I just took my punishment and kept on being a brat in spite of the consequences of my bad behavior. I think that was the first year that I actually pulled B's out of English because I was in a class with slow learners and the work was really, really easy. Maybe I should have known then that I really wasn't slow, and that I was only fooling myself. But, it is really difficult to realize the truth when your whole life is built on a lie, a lie that you've convinced yourself is the truth, and will do everything you can to confirm it.

That was me. I hid it all behind my bad behavior. If anyone suspected I had a disability, I would do something extraordinary so that they would believe once again that there was nothing wrong with me. I wanted them to think that I just didn't care.

My math teacher was a tough guy too. He used to make me stand in the back of the room with an eraser in each hand held above my head. Or, he would pull the back of my hair or physically slapped the crap out of me. I didn't care. I knew I was disruptive, I thought I deserved it, and this was a part of my life at school. I failed his class... go figure.

Many times I was sent to the principal's office where I was told to bend over and grab my ankles. The paddle he used was a thick piece of wood that resembled an oversized Ping-Pong paddle with many holes drilled in it. After the principal was done spanking me, he would make me sign the paddle. My name was all over that paddle, until the day I decided it was getting too demeaning. The last time he told me to bend over and grab my ankles, I just said no, and walked out of his office.

Of course I got expelled, which made me think I should have taken the spanking because now I had to explain to Mom why I wasn't in school. You know how moms are; they don't hurt you physically but they really know how to get to you emotionally.

At this point, Dad didn't have much to say about anything I did or didn't do. I think that hurt most of all because I really wanted him to care. But, like I've said, all I ever got was the feeling that he didn't have any time for me. I often thought it was because of that incident back in Texas when that Mexican pulled a gun on him. Or maybe it was because he had four of his own kids now, and I was a problem he didn't need. And, to make matters worse, my problems weren't getting any better.

I was pretty hard on all of my teachers in order to maintain my rebellious image. We had this one teacher who was of considerable size and had a reputation for being very strict. One day, I was walking down the hall not paying attention to where I was going and I bumped into him. He pushed me up against the lockers, got in my face, and told me "When you see me coming down that hall, you step to the other side!" I quickly replied, "When I see you coming down the hall, there ain't no other side!" Instead of beating the living crap out of me, he started laughing and walked away.

Another time in health class, I kept talking to someone while the teacher was trying to conduct the class. When he had finally had enough of me he said, "Miller, if you open your mouth one more time you're going through that door. In fact, I don't think I'm going to open the door. I'm going to use your head for a doorknob." I looked over at the door that was standing wide open and couldn't resist saying, "The door's open!" The next moment was very embarrassing as he jerked me out of my desk by my shirt, almost ripping it off my back. I don't think my feet touched the floor between the time he jerked me out of my desk and the time I was in the hall, slammed up against the wall. I was scratched and bruised with my shirt hanging half off exposing my fat. As I recall, I really didn't say "The door's open!" as an invitation, or to be a smart mouth. It was more a question of how he was going to open an already open door with my head.

This teacher was also the physical education teacher. I actually got good grades from him because I was pretty good in sports by then. I think he thought that he could do something with me that none of the other teachers could do. He wanted to break me, which is interesting, because none of my teachers viewed me as being breakable. I came off arrogant and strong willed. I think his idea was to make me fear him. He definitely was rougher, and seemed more serious than the other teachers, but he was still a teacher, and I had no fear of any of them. His tactics didn't work, although I was careful not to give him too much trouble, because I really didn't enjoy physical pain.

My buddy Mike and I got to be pretty close friends, but we were in trouble a lot. At lunchtime, we could be found at the gas station in the back room smoking cigarettes. If we weren't there, we were uptown stealing cigarettes, food, and other small items such as lighters and pocket knives from the Coast to Coast hardware store. It never bothered either of us. It never occurred to me that I was doing something wrong. I was so selfish that I just took whatever I wanted.

Sometimes mom sent me back over to the store she managed to get something she needed at home. I took that opportunity to steal money from the cash register. At first, I stole only a few coins because coins were all that were left in the cash register overnight. I soon progressed to dollar bills, then fives. Mom kept the daily store money in the house after closing. It was kept at the top of a cabinet in the kitchen in a big roll secured by a rubber band. After everyone was asleep, I would sneak down stairs and steal some of the money. I was careful not to take so much that mom would notice. One day, I finally made a mistake that got me caught.

It was mom's birthday. I bought her a bottle of Ban deodorant because I thought that little round ball on the top of the bottle that spread the deodorant was cool. Although I was given to telling a lot of lies, I really wasn't very good at it. Especially with Mom. She always seemed to know the truth. I often asked her how she knew, but her answer was always the same; "A little bird told me." Once she found out that I had stolen from her to buy her a birthday gift, I got a severe beating with a belt. I pretty much gave up stealing from her after that.

The Skunk

My cousins from Des Plaines, Illinois came for a vacation, and their visit marked a new phase in my life. Up until that time, I smoked cigarettes on occasion because the kids I hung with were doing it, but I never inhaled, because I didn't know how. My older cousins taught me how to inhale and I was hooked for the next 40 years. I remember my first drag. I almost passed out as it took my breath away and made me cough. Kind of makes you wonder why you would ever want to try it again after such a horrible experience.

First off, I was looking for anything to help me feel better about myself. I had a very low internal self-image. I was looking for anything that would help me feel accepted, respected. I was the class clown, the teacher's nightmare, my parents' problem child, and I didn't like myself at all. I was ready to try anything that could possibly make me feel good. Soon, I was addicted to nicotine. The year was 1956. I was eleven years old.

I remember that year because my cousins came to visit us in a brand-new blue and white 1956 Chevy. We did a lot of driving around in that new car and we got a life lesson the hard way. There was an older guy who often came to the store for supplies. He told me once that if you pick a skunk up by its tail, it can't spray you. So we put that theory to the test when the boys and I discovered a small skunk in the ditch while out driving in the country. Someone, and I assure you that someone was not me, got out of the car and picked the skunk up by its tail. It was put in a paper sack and placed it in the back seat of the car. Do I need to tell you the rest?

They spent a lot of money on tomato soup attempting to rid that brand-new car of the skunk smell! Uncle Stanley has been dead and gone for many years now but my cousins still tell that story today. Only they make it sound like it was all my idea to pick up that skunk! The question is, why would anyone even contemplate the thought of putting a smelly skunk in their brand-new car? Who would even think of it? They were older than me. Why would they listen to an eleven-year old?

The Farm

Part way through the school year, Mom's store was sold, so we moved again. Mom and Dad bought the farm that once was the house Dad's mother and all of his uncles grew up In. It was a fairly good-sized house, although it started out to be a log cabin years ago. It had been updated with siding, there was a big barn with a loft and a tin car shed. There was no electricity, indoor plumbing, or telephone, and as it turned out, the well water was contaminated. We had to carry water in ten-gallon cream cans from other sources. Most often we trooped across a field to grandpa and grandma's place. This was the grandparents where I first lived when we first came to Minnesota.

This move put me right back into the Gary school district. I was a whole grade behind in math now, and the principal of the Gary school couldn't come up with a solution that would work in their system. So, they moved me up a year. Odd as it was, math turned out to be my strongest subject that year. This was also my last year in school.

Joyce and Lee were now attending school and we all rode the bus together. Every day when we came home from school, the first thing we'd do is flip the light switch just inside the door to see if we had electricity yet. Dad and grandpa worked for months installing electricity but it was a slow process because the house didn't have wall cavities having been at one time a log cabin. Once the electrical work was finished, we had to wait until the electric company brought power to us.

I don't remember living without electricity being a bad thing, but living without plumbing really sucked! The toilet was located a few hundred feet away from the house, making it especially nasty when it was 40 below in the winter. You couldn't see 12 inches in front of you through the blizzards that are common in that part of the country, way up in northwestern Minnesota. People actually got lost, and froze to death while trying to find their way to or from the outhouse or the barn in a bad blizzard. So, a lot of people installed life lines which were nothing more than a rope or wire stretched between buildings that you held onto so that you wouldn't get lost. We didn't have life lines on our farm, so when I needed to use the bathroom in the winter, I whizzed right off the porch. That worked well in the winter, but in the summertime, on a hot day, you realized why the toilet was located so far from the house. When I was growing up, outdoor toilets didn't smell like porta potties do today; they smelled exactly like what they were full of.

I don't remember having too many problems with teachers my last year of school. Of course, there was the time my history teacher explained that a human being could only live a certain number of days without sleeping before they would die of exhaustion. I don't remember what that number was, but I topped it by saying very convincingly that I stayed awake for a few days longer than her theory allowed. When she asked me, with much interest in her voice, how on earth had I ever survived staying up for so many days at one time, I told her that I'd slept nights. That got a big laugh from the class, but my teacher didn't find it so funny. I had one liners left and right, and came away from the eighth grade pretty much unscathed. I finished my last full year of school with all B's and C's, which was really good for me.

I remember one day I was sitting in class, when my little brother Lee knocked on the class room door and asked if I could come out and talk to him. He told me that two of the kids in my classroom had been teasing him at noon hour and had thrown his ball on top of the county shed. I went back into my room and grabbed the two boys. Our teacher never said a word as I marched them outside, and made them climb up on top of the county shed and get my brothers ball. It turned out to be a bonanza as they kept throwing balls off the roof asking, "Is this your ball?" Lee had lots of balls when they were finished. And the boys never teased my brother again.

I did come back to school for a couple of weeks in the ninth grade. No one even recognized me right away because I had grown five or 6 inches and stood 5'9". I was slim and trim at 136 pounds. I was very glad to be through with school. I had never felt comfortable there, and my opinion of myself was at an all-time low. The worse I felt about myself, the more I acted out. I was very angry in general, and couldn't find a voice for my feelings. I always envied my classmates because they seemed to have everything I wanted. That misconception alone was cause for mega insecurities. Maybe I wasn't so naïve that I believed Grape Nut Flakes was a venereal disease, or that Peter Pan was a bed pan for sick people, but what I did believe was just as ridiculous.

My Pretended Self

As a teenager, I always wanted to be someone other than who I was. Playing pretend and wanting to be someone else are quite different concepts. I spent years wishing I actually was someone else. Not just the typical super-hero, but some popular boy I picked out. I pretended I was him. That behavior was so unhealthy! My pretended self over-powered who I really was, leaving me empty, shallow, and insecure. One classmate in particular, was a kid who was always cool and very popular. I was notorious and feared, so I'd pretend I was him. Not in a way that made me change my behaviors, but in a negative all-consuming fantasy world. I didn't like myself. I couldn't handle my life, or understand what was going on inside of myself. I felt like junk, and my inner dialog was defeated and hopeless. I honestly believed that I was worse than everyone around me. I didn't feel that I belonged anywhere. I couldn't receive love or even look for it. I was only surviving. My life was out of control, and I had very few skills.

At my 40-year school reunion I met up with my old class mates. I had not seen any of them since middle school. I got there a little late, so everyone had eaten and were enjoying cocktails. It doesn't take a lot of liquor before people begin to show their insecurities. I discovered that most of my old class mates had only changed in appearance. They were the same old likeable people that I had at one time envied. I realized that I had changed and that there was no one there that I would change places with. A feeling of well-being came over me, giving me a sense of pride at that moment. That is saying a lot since I was the one voted most likely not to succeed so many years ago.

I also discovered that the cool kid I had always admired, had died in a car crash when he was in his early 30's. The talk was, that it may not have been an accident, because at the time of his death, his life was in turmoil and he was deeply depressed. I was very sad to hear of his death. I was humbled when I realized the many times I had wished I was dead and even plotted against my own life. Life is precious. Every life.

Young, Dumb and Bulletproof

With my school days over, I could concentrate on other things.

Willie and I turned 16 that year and Willie got his first car; a light green 1949 two-door Ford Coupe. I think it burned more oil than gas but it had a mean sounding Hollywood muffler, burned rubber and got us everywhere we wanted to go, as long as we kept it full of oil and gas. Half of which we stole from farmers around the area.

We had wheels now, so Willie and I began to experiment with liquor. We decided to celebrate the New Year in Bejou and this was the first time I ever experienced being drunk. I remember the feeling like it was yesterday. Back in the day, nobody really thought there was anything wrong with treating teenagers to alcohol. On special occasions, in fact, most of the bars in the area served liquor to minors. Yes, it was against the law, but it was also a way of life in the country where everyone worked hard all week and unwound in the bars on the weekends.

New Years was special; everyone got drunk. I was sitting in a booth with a buddy who was feeding me shots of whiskey, when all of a sudden it hit me. I just started to laugh uncontrollably. I really liked the feeling. It felt like all of the burdens that concerned me to the point of depression were lifted and nothing mattered anymore. Willie and I did a lot of drinking after that. We didn't need an occasion in order to justify it either. I got sloshed hundreds of times throughout the next few decades. But I never experienced that first good feeling ever again.

Willie and I worked for local farmers in the summer. We did custom baling, harvesting crops and other field work. During the potato harvest, we would load all of the potatoes that had been hand-picked by women and children. Potato season was to the northern states what the cotton fields were to the South. Once the loading season was finished, we would go to Grand Forks and work in the potato factories where they were sorted, stacked, sewed into bags and shipped to the processing plants.

Custom baling was a real treat for me. Willie never did any custom baling, as he usually drove a tractor and plowed fields at that time of the year. The custom bales were shipped by rail and the farmers were paid by weight, so it was necessary to get as much weight into a single bale as possible. At five o'clock in the morning, when there was still dew on the grass, it wasn't uncommon for a bail to weigh in at 220 pounds or so. I never could figure out why the process they used required handling one bale five times between the times you pulled it out of the baler to the time you put it in a box car. But, the guy I bailed for was a chiseler who got me drunk on weekends and paid me $5.00 a day for 12 to 14 hours of work and rarely ever gave me the money he owed me.

Custom baling is hard work. The crazy thing, is that I loved it. It made me feel good to work hard and I wasn't always so angry. To this day I prefer to work hard.

Willie and I had many adventures in his old '49 Ford. The first winter, I believe that car was in the ditch as often as it was on the road.

We were quite the duo; young, dumb and bulletproof.

One night, we had been in town drinking quite heavily. Willie was pretty much smashed but I was still sober enough to be the designated driver. He got into the passenger seat and more or less passed out. We weren't too far out of town, when he asked me to pull over so that he could throw up. He hung his head out of the car and did that very thing. When he was finished, he closed the door and I started to drive off. I was just picking up speed when he decided he also had to whiz. In spite of the fact that I was moving along at a pretty good speed, he opened the car door and stepped out. I stopped the car and ran back to where he was lying face down in a ditch. I was thinking that he was surely dead, but to my surprise when I got there, he groaned and said, "What the hell happened?"

Good thing he was drunk, because I don't think he would have survived it sober!

Another one of our episodes took place one evening just after dark. We were attempting to steal gas from one of his uncle's storage tanks used to fuel the tractors on the farm. We made too much noise and someone came out of the house. We took off across the field using the same path the tractors used. It was bumpy with many dips and ditches to negotiate. This might sound like a perfect getaway, but we had a slight problem. Willie's car had a pin missing from the carburetor linkage which caused the gas pedal to stop working at times. Normally this didn't cause much of a problem. We would just get out, raise the hood, and reconnect the linkage.

But, that's not so easy to do when you're trying to make a getaway. We were flying over the rutted field when we realized we were in trouble. Headlights were coming headed our way. I took the wheel while Willie got under the hood to work the throttle control on the carburetor by hand. Imagine, if you will, trying to drive a vehicle with the hood up so that you can't see with someone hanging on for dear life under the hood with nothing but their feet sticking out getting spanked by the hood every time we hit a bump.

It was a challenge for both of us, but I'm sure it was most painful for Willie. We got away that night. It wasn't until just recently that we found out who was driving the car that was chasing us. Of all people, it was his mother! It was a good thing that we didn't stop, because I would rather have dealt with all of Willie's uncles than to face Willie's mom.

The fall of 1960 Willie and I went to Grand Forks to work in the potato warehouses. There was a gas war going on, so at ten or eleven cents a gallon, we could fill the gas tank for around a dollar. We went through a lot of gas and even more alcohol.

One evening after work, Willie and I hooked up with this Indian dude because he could buy us liquor. He talked us into buying white port wine. You know, the good stuff with an expiration date on it. I think it cost $.98 a quart. Anyway, between the three of us we drank nine quarts. We ended up parked on Main Street. Willie was passed out behind the wheel when the police arrived. They tried to wake Willie up, but once Willie passed out it was almost impossible to revive him. The policeman started twisting Willie's arm. Willie finally did wake up, and when he did, he came up swinging. Had it not been for that, we may have avoided jail. But off we went to jail. The cellblock they threw us in was wall-to-wall drunks and only had two beds for maybe ten people. We dragged the people occupying the beds off and took over. The next day broke me of ever drinking wine again. That was absolutely the worst hangover I had experienced. The next day they let us go. We went back to where the car was, picked it up and headed back to the great Northern flophouse hotel where we were staying.

We headed back to Grand Forks for testing as Willie and I decided to join the Navy. I just barely squeaked by. There were a hundred or more guys testing, and I managed to score lowest of any one, with a score in the low 30's. It was a sure thing that I was going to be scraping paint off a ship and swinging a mop. Willie, on the other hand, had done quite well. He had scored in the high 90's. We were sworn in and it wasn't long before we were aboard a prop jet on our way to basic training in San Diego, California.

I was excited to go, and didn't realize that I was headed for more disappointments to add to my list of failures. I did just fine in basic training until they gave us the first test. I knew all the answers to the questions but I couldn't read fast enough to get through the multiple choices shown on the slide projector. I ended up guessing at questions I knew the answers to and failed the test. When you fail a test you are set back a week. Willie and I were separated and I joined a new company. I was successful in everything in the Navy except for those darned tests. I watched other guys trying really hard to learn their left from the right so that they could stay in the Navy but they were always sent home. I'd seen other recruits being sent home for failing tests. They all expressed a wish to stay in, but were sent home anyway. I noticed that the guys who wanted out, tried everything to get out, and couldn't get out no matter what they tried. I thought the best thing for me to do was to play games like I had been used to doing in school. So, I pretended to want out and they kept setting me back, without sending me home. I became insubordinate which meant hours of extra exercises to break my will.

One night, I even jumped the fence, pretending to escape. It was easy to fool them, because when the psychologist asked me to answer the questions on those tests I answered all of them correctly. I knew the answers when he read them to me verbally. After almost 5 months of basic training, which was originally supposed to be only nine weeks, they threw up their hands, gave up on me, and sent me home.

I look back now and wonder if I had told them the truth about being a slow reader, they might have sent me home like they did everyone else who really wanted to stay. Or would they have taken a chance on me?

I wonder how different my life would have been had I stayed in the Navy? I am positive that I wouldn't be writing these lines today. The reality of the situation, is that I was discharged and sent home in shame. They gave me an honorable discharge, but everyone in the country knew that I had somehow failed. The Vietnam conflict wasn't many years after that, when a lot of people around the country that I knew were drafted into the service and came back in a box. I often felt guilty as though I had schemed my way out of my patriotic duty and really wasn't any better than the draft dodgers. Who knows if things would have been different; perhaps I would've come home in a box.

If I've learned anything from my past, I have learned that there is a reason for everything. Sometimes we may not be aware of what that reason is right away, but eventually, we can usually see a bigger picture and understand. Sometimes we never know. But, this you can be sure of: if anything had been different this far into my life, it would have changed everything. And then I wouldn't be writing this. Which leads us to wonder at this book in your hands, and how my life will affect yours. It really is a mind blowing thought process, isn't it?

After being discharged, I headed for Minnesota. Coming home was very difficult. I no longer had my good buddy Willie to chum around with, and I really didn't know what I was going to do. Thankfully, Junior and I got close and added a few stories to our history.

No Taillights, No Brains

We had always used Willie's car, so with the money the Navy gave me at discharge, I bought, of all things, a green 1949 Ford. I had problems with the transmission the first day I brought it home. I couldn't get the overdrive to work so I took it apart and must have put it together wrong because it was worse than ever after that. Finally the transmission stuck in first gear.

Willie's old Ford was sitting in the weeds at his parent's place, so I went over to his house and asked his dad if I could have the transmission out of it. Although he was using it for parts on his own car, he said yes. I went about the business of taking it out. I couldn't get under the car so I cut a hole in the floor-board and took it out from the top. If you know anything about '49 Ford flatheads, you have got to be impressed. Once the transmission was in my possession, Junior and I went over to Rendahl, parked the car in the grass across the street from a service station, and commenced to change transmissions.

In each of the '49, '50, and '51 Fords all that holds the motor in the car is two motor mounts in front on either side of the engine. They are secured to the frame and separated by rubber that is secured by two pieces of metal fastened to the motor and frame. The only other thing that holds the engine in place, is the two bolts towards the back of the transmission mount. Junior and I succeeded in getting the old transmission out and replacing it with the one from Willie's old car. I connected the drive shaft, and Junior put the two bolts back in the transmission mount. We cleaned up our mess, packed up the tools and took the car for a test drive towards home. It worked just fine! We were quite impressed with ourselves, as our previous top speed had been 20MPH in first gear.

I was cruising about 50 or 60 miles an hour down a gravel road when the hood flew up and laid right across the windshield completely blocking my view. I panicked and slammed on the brakes. When I did, the whole engine launched forward and drove the fan through the radiator. Junior had forgotten to replace the transmission mount bolts. Somehow, we made it back to Willie's house without burning the engine up. I asked his dad for the radiator out of Willie's car, but he was in a crappy mood that day and told me no. Junior's dad had an old junked '48 Ford with a good radiator. It was totally different than the radiator in the '49, but I made it fit.

What a time I had with that old car! But it finally met its Waterloo. I was working for a farmer east of Bejou. Just as I was going for some second-gear scratch, I snapped the camshaft and kicked a rod through the block.

Once again I was without wheels. The next Friday, I went in to Fosston and bought a gray 1950 Ford from a dealer. I didn't know it at the time, but the car didn't have taillights. That proved to be my next problem. The very next day, Saturday, I headed to Bejou to find some fun. One of the guys around my age had his daddy's 1958 Ford for the evening. He thought his dad's six-cylinder engine was faster than my flat head V8. We decided to find out east of town at the end of the pavement where all races were held. I was leading the way and pulled off to the shoulder waiting for the '58 to pull alongside of me. I didn't know I didn't have taillights and was just sitting there waiting. It was dark out. A race isn't any good without a crowd, so I watched in my rearview mirror as some headlights came up. The '58 Ford swerved around me, just as another car was passing him. The '58's left rear quarter panel was smashed, and the other car went off in the ditch, but not before rolling over a couple times. Fortunately, no one was hurt.

Now, you have to remember that I wasn't the most popular person in the country. I had been in trouble for a decade, and everyone in both cars involved in the accident were close friends and part of a click that didn't include me. They all decided to blame the accident on me. I was out numbered eight to one, so to be assured that I would be able to leave in one piece, I had to agree that the accident was my fault. Sure, I didn't have taillights, but I was pulled off the road, and didn't have a dent or scratch on my new car. I actually thought that they would wake up in the morning and realize that there was no way they could hang this on me. But, lo and behold, the very next day, the father of the boy driving the '58 Ford, showed up with his damaged car demanding compensation. I explained what had really happened, and that it wasn't my fault, but no one believed me. It was my word against eight of them. I was amazed that the adults believed them, even though there wasn't a scratch on my car.

That is the crappy part of having a bad name. You take the hit for all that you do wrong, plus anything anyone else wants to try to pass on to you. It wasn't until many years later that the truth was finally discovered. While bartending at my parents bar, my dad, Wally, overheard the other guys laughing and joking as they sat in a booth drinking beer. They were laughing about how they had gotten away with lying about what really happened that night. It didn't really make my dad happy, since he was the one who paid the bill. It certainly didn't do me any good for dad to have another reason to be disappointed in me. I don't remember anyone ever apologizing to me for not believing me. But then, that wasn't the way things worked in our family. I guess it really didn't bother me that I didn't get a formal apology, because after all, if I had not been there to race, I wouldn't have been a part of that situation. And, I wasn't completely without fault, in the fact that I didn't have taillights.

This wasn't the last time I would be blamed for something I didn't do. Circumstantial evidence from past events caused people to blame me for all sorts of things that I was not guilty of. A lot of people in the community viewed me as an outlaw, yet I really don't know why. I don't think I did anything that other kids around the country didn't do while growing up. While I pretended to be a tough guy, everything I did, or was accused of doing, was devastating to me on the inside. I was always a lot more tender than anyone knew. I held my head up and did my level best to have an attitude of, "I don't give a crap." But that was such a lie! If people knew how sensitive I was, I think they would have been surprised.

I've spent some time honestly looking at those days, and the two things that really damaged my reputation, was my behavior in school, and my discharge from the Navy. While I was a good, hard worker, and hadn't done terrible things yet, I was treated very poorly. I think stories about me were part truth, and a lot of gossip. In the country where I lived, everyone knew everybody's business. If I passed gas in the presence of one person, someone miles away would be talking about what I had to eat that particular day. Only they would turn a bologna sandwich into a nine course meal. Things can get pretty boring in the country, and people's favorite pastime was to gossip about each other. Events were more often than not blown way out of proportion. I believe I was one of those colorful kids, and that caused everyone's attention to be focused on me. If I was in the area and things went wrong, then I somehow got the blame. I'm not really sure why I didn't stand up for myself, because I often knew who was really responsible.

I suppose that a few rounds of people not believing the truth, and my ability to truly get in trouble, made for a bad mixture. Besides, I didn't have many friends, and who likes a tattletale?

After that accident, I just kept on getting into trouble with my car. Finally, Dad took my keys.

Fixing Things
I loved to fix machinery.

While I'd get hired for plowing, raking, disking, and dragging, it was all just plain boring to me. I took the work for the breakdowns. I used to pray for breakdowns because I enjoyed fixing things. I could forget my problems and just get lost in an engine. I was good at tinkering and fixing, and there wasn't much else I was good at back in those days.

My favorite rig was the John Deere D. If you're not familiar with farm equipment, it's a tractor with steel wheels as big as a house! It moved at the speed of moss; in high gear and wide open, it topped out at about 3 mph. It started on gas and ran on something they called distillate. I did a lot of daydreaming on that tractor. I dreamed about all the cars that I wanted and all the nice things I would have some day. I reminisced about past events, and wondered about the future. I remembered Willie and me riding home on the school bus together, engaged in conversation about relationships with girls. His idea was to love them and leave them, but I always wanted just one special girl. Perhaps a girl that I could save from a life of poverty and misery. As it turned out, I lived Willie's dream for many years, while he lived mine. I will explain later.

Wrecking the Plow
Back to the moment. Dad was in town and I was sent out to do some plowing on the south 40. I was backing up to the plow with that old John Deere. The break and the clutch were one and the same.

When you released the clutch with a long lever, it automatically applied brake shoes to a small flywheel on the right-hand side of the tractor. The shoes were worn out, so the tractor didn't always stop when it was supposed to. The plow had these levers that stuck up so that you could actually reach out behind you from the tractor seat and raise and lower the plow with these handles. As I backed up to attach the plow, I released the clutch and applied the brake. The tractor kept on going backwards and the levers on the plow were about to pin me to the seat when I jumped off. I looked up as the tractor was going over the plow and for an instant, I thought the tractor was going to tip on top of me. Fortunately, it settled down and stopped with the plow completely mangled and broken beneath it.

I walked back home and waited for Dad to come. He showed up with Mom and he saw the wreck but didn't say a word about it. He just took off somewhere after dropping Mom off at the house. I explained to her what had happened thinking for sure that I was in big trouble. Even though I hadn't done anything wrong, something was wrecked and I was there. Dad walked back into the house smiling and seemed relieved that I wasn't hurt. That was kind of a special moment for me. But it was just a moment. It wasn't long before the relationship between us went back to crap.

I was 18, restless, and tired of my life. I decided to go and visit some of my aunts and uncles in Texas. I took a bus to San Antonio, where I looked up my Uncle Otis and Aunt Eunice. By this time, Aunt Eunice had a beauty shop with employees in part of her house, and Uncle Otis worked in a service station. I worked with him for a while at the service station and then went to stay with my Uncle Bud and Aunt Marie. You remember them, don't you? They were officially millionaires who now owned six testing laboratories. I earned a little money by doing some work for Uncle Bud, but was pretty much just mooching off my relatives.

Meeting My Father

And then one day, while Aunt Marie and I were in Waco, I asked her about my real father. She suggested that we stop at a service station and look him up in the phone book because she thought he was still in the area. There was only one David Miller in the book so I called the number. An elderly lady answered the phone. It was kind of an awkward moment for me when I asked if David had ever been married before and if he had a child. The lady obviously didn't know how to answer me, so she put me on hold for a while and then came back and said, "Yes." I then said, "I am probably that child. My name is Randy Miller."

"Oh, my God!" she said, "I will send somebody right over to get you."

Shortly, two of my long lost cousins, John and Herby Boyette, came to pick me up looking like, as Aunt Marie put it, like they had just come from Tobacco Road. They did look a bit rough, maybe really rough, but they were good old boys.

The first thing I discovered from them was that I had eight brothers and sisters. I knew I should have one half-brother because the girl my father married was pregnant just a little after Mom. Turns out, I had a half-brother 6 months younger than me who was 18 years old, the same as me at the time. My father and Betty had two sets of twins, twin boys and twin girls for a grand total of four boys and four girls.

Herby had things to do and left John to show me around. The first place John took me was where my father worked as a laundry pickup and delivery driver. He was out on a route when we went to find him. My cousin brought me around to all of his co-workers and asked them who I reminded them of. They all said without hesitation, "David Miller." When his truck finally pulled in and I stepped onto the truck and came face to face with him. John asked, "Do you know who this is?" My dad looked at me and calmly said, "Randy." His first question to me was rather odd; he asked me what my last name was. When I answered him he said, "Your mother told me she would never change your last name." Somehow I think that oversight had nothing to do with any promise my mother might have made to my father. But I figured, "Whatever fries your chicken", and let it go. He told me all about how he had never looked for me because he had heard that my mother and I were killed in a car crash years ago. Yeah right! I didn't believe him, but it didn't bother me either.

The next people I visited was Grandma and Grandpa Miller. I guess grandpa was always kind of emotional so he broke down and started crying when he saw me. Even though grandma was blind, she was visibly happy that I had come back to find my dad's side of the family.

By this time, I had heard a lot about my 18-year old brother who was considered the bad ass of the family who liked to fight with guns, knives, fists and feet. Ray was constantly in trouble with the law. I was really anxious to meet him, but no one seemed to know where he was. Finally, that evening he showed up. The first thing he had to do was punch me a couple of times. While it was in fun, as though he were trying to determine whether I was a real or not, there was also a fair amount of emotion to go with it. This kept up and it wasn't very long before I was pretty tired of him punching on me. Fun or not, I drove him in the chest with a good stiff right that caused him to gasp for air. Once he regained his composure, he said "Damn! You hit back." We had just established that I wasn't going to take any crap and those punches sort of caught us up in the brother department.

Later that night, we hooked up with a local guy my brother knew and scored some liquor. We got so blitzed that I honestly can't tell you exactly what happened. All I know is we both ended up in jail for drunk and disorderly conduct.

After five days in jail, they let us go and it was then that I got to meet the rest of my brothers and sisters. Betty, seemed to accept me into the family, but a short time later, I think she was behind it, when my dad told me that I had to leave. His exact words were Ray you can stay, but, "Randy you have to go." What a slap in the face that was. It was evident that I was not going to find a place I belonged here with my dad and all these new brothers and sisters. I headed over to grandma and grandpa's place, and dad later called me and apologized. The damage was already done. Ray and I decided to hitchhike back to Minnesota. Even though he had a place with dad he decided to stick with me. I'm not sure what I expected from my biological father, but I can tell you that I was hurt when he asked me to leave. I knew that he had abandoned me back when mom was pregnant. What my head knew went directly to my heart. I felt abandonment to my core when he told me to leave, yet still accepted my brother. We were both causing trouble, so I couldn't understand why I was the only one rejected. I guess I just made his life more complicated.

I was looking for a place to belong where I didn't have a hole in my heart, and where I felt accepted just as I was. But it looked like this wasn't the place.

Clearly, I didn't get much love from him. I didn't give him much either. Actually, all things considered I probably got more than I expected. I was pretty used to rejection and pretty much expected it, but for a couple of weeks I felt a part of something and then like always, it was gone.

We never did get to know each other well enough to do any bonding. I saw him only three times in all my life that I remember and the third time he was dead. I can't honestly tell you what I really felt at the time, seeing him there, dead. I think I was numb beyond any emotion, beyond anger. Looking back, I think there were maybe a couple of times when he actually tried to bond with me. Once he told me to call him Dad.

The pain from that experience in Texas, quickly turned into anger. I felt cheated out of a father-son relationship, and the honest truth, is, I was. Just being his son wasn't enough to give me a place in his home, let alone his heart. My brother had a place and I didn't. Same relationship, same dad. I just wasn't worth it. Do you hear the same old wounds surfacing again? I know that I could continue to be angry about a lot of things that could have been, but never were, because of my dad's actions years ago. But my anger won't change anything. It will only continue to suck the good life out of me and leave me cold-hearted, empty and mean.

Anger and Frustration

Do you have a deep burning rage over past circumstances in your life? Right here, we need to take the time to understand the circumstances and accept them for what they really were.

It doesn't do any good to ignore or deny anger and frustrations. No matter how deep you bury them, they will continue to control you. It is only when you finally review the issues and realize that it was never about you personally that caused others to make poor decisions in regards to your well-being. Once you reach this understanding, it is time to let it go.

It is never someone else that makes us angry or abusive; it is our own emotional experiences that cause us to act this way. There are some things that people do to us, or fail to do for us, that we may never understand, but our first responsibility is to understand our self, in this we may come to understand those reasons that have caused us so much emotional stress. Then we can find our own answers to our short comings within that understanding that will enable us to survive all of life's bumps and bruises.

The only understanding we may ever come to know of the actions of someone else, is that each of us are subject to our own set of circumstances in life, but we are accountable only for our own actions. All actions from others, towards us, are nothing more than the results of their own personal reactions to a specific set of circumstances that are controlling them. As long as we let the memory linger and obsess about something we have no control over, we are indeed being controlled, manipulated, and even corrupted, by the things we dislike most about our past. It is our responsibility to ourselves to let anger and resentments go and become free to move on. If we continue to hold on to all of the pain in our past, our entire lives are soon consumed. Once we are consumed with our pain, we are then completely out of control, and the pain becomes a disease. And this disease brings pain to everyone that we touch. This is a vicious cycle; and we will never discover peace of mind or bring anything positive to ourselves or anyone else until we make a conscious choice to let go.

Whatever personal abuse we have experienced, at any level (either physical or mental) we don't deserve to continue punishing ourselves for someone else's ignorance. Nor do we deserve to become so ignorant ourselves, blinded by anger, and frustration, that we submit our loved ones to that which we would have gladly never experienced in our own lives.

These words are not just for you and me to understand. They are also meant for all of those who have abused us. Because they are no different than you and I; this isn't really an issue of "us and them". There is only us. There isn't one of us on the face of the earth that hasn't been mistreated by someone, and not one of us isn't guilty of mistreating someone else. Therefore, we all deserve forgiveness from each other and the right to move on. Anger has its place. It can result in good and can bring out our best. But, almost everything I am writing here is coming from the worst of me, my frustrations, my anger and my loss of control. Anger is the cause of these words I write. There is a place for everything in life where the very emotions that bring a person down will lift him up. But you shouldn't allow anything but love and understanding dominate your life.

When we are hurt emotionally by someone else, we may think we are angry at them. But really, we are angry at ourselves, and punish ourselves, thinking there is something wrong with us. We begin acting as though it was our fault. It never occurs to us that we don't even understand what happened. So, we become insecure. We begin doing demeaning things to ourselves; constantly beating ourselves up mentally with negative self-talk. Day after day, training ourselves to accept the opposite of what we really want. Convincing ourselves what we want can never be, because we are not worthy. All this time, we are demanding very little of ourselves, and accepting little or no responsibility for our actions because we believe someone else caused us to feel this way.

I can guarantee that this mentality doesn't punish the ones who hurt us. It punishes us. Not just once and it's over, but every single day for the rest of our life. We will learn to dislike ourselves more and more, losing sight of who we really are as we become consumed by our own anger. We strike out at anyone or anything, just as we were trained to do by those memories we have played over and over in our mind for so many years. We are now what we dislike the most; constantly reminding ourselves of the ignorant opinions and actions of others. Although it is no longer real, and completely blown out of proportion, we continue to keep it real in our imagination, until abuse becomes a way of life. We have succeeded in believing we don't deserve better. When the truth is consumed by lies, your life becomes whatever you dwell on and that becomes your truth. Let me tell you again; let it go! You deserve the best life has to offer you. You are equal to the person you admire the most. Your life is valuable. Would it be too much to believe that your life is a gift? You do not have to live rejected, sad, lonely, angry, or guilt ridden. Once you release all the things that hold you down, you will instantly feel the tension leaving your body and become free to realize your wildest dreams when you just-let-go.

I only wish that I had known this when I was 18 years old. But then, there is a reason for everything, and no matter how bad something appears to be, there is always something good to be found in everything. If all my pain and suffering, and all of the pain and suffering I have caused, is for a greater good, then who's to judge what should have happened? For me, I will be very pleased if I can help just you understand so that you can go on to live a beautiful and peaceful life.

Back in Minnesota

Let's rejoin my story, as two 18 year old brothers hitchhike from Texas to Minnesota.

It took us six days, and we were with each other most of the way until we were a few hundred miles from home not getting picked up because there were two of us and we looked pretty rough after a few days on the road. We decided to split up and meet closer to home. We met again less than 100 miles from home and Wally came to pick us up.

Besides myself, my brother was definitely one of those people who was filled with anger and rage. In the short time that we were together, I never was aware of anything he was subjected to that caused him to be so violent. He had his biological mother and father, and while they were not perfect, neither of them were abusive. If anything, it appeared that he was just spoiled. As I recall, I remember being told that he had always been in trouble, and dad always bailed him out. When I showed up, he saw me as a rival. There was only room for one older brother, and one oldest son. I believe that's why we never stayed together for long; we were both playing the same attention game. I haven't seen or heard from him, or any of my other brothers and sisters on my dad's side, for several decades now. But we did get together again when one of the twins died, when dad died and the last time when I went back to Texas in a stolen pickup truck with the intentions of staying. More about that later on.

While I was happy to be back in Minnesota, my brother wasn't around very long before he got homesick. On the farm, everyone is expected to pitch in and do their chores. My brother didn't necessarily like work of any kind; in fact he would say, "I like work- I could lay down and watch it for hours."

By this time Willie had been discharged from the Navy. I think he got a general discharge but I never asked him about it. Willie, my brother, and I went out on a few drunks together before my brother finally called home and asked dad to wire him money so that he could head back to Texas. The money came, and then Wally and I gave him a ride to the bus station where we sent him on his way back to Waco.

On the way back from the bus station, I was talking to Wally about my biological dad and all of my brothers and sisters. Wally sat there very quietly, just listening. All of a sudden, out of nowhere, he said in his deep thundering voice, "What did your dad ever do for you?"

I knew the answer. My dad did very little for me, so his question didn't hurt me. Actually, it was a very special moment for me. Wally was actually jealous. I never brought my biological fathers name up again in Wally's presence. Wally was the only dad that I ever really knew, and it was always him I wanted to please more than anyone else. Like I said before, we had a great relationship at the end of his life. I remain very grateful to Wally for all that he did for me. I know he loved me.

Man, was I happy to have Willie home! There's a hundred stories I could tell you, and even more reasons that I considered him my best friend. We just understood each other. He and I were more like brothers and we pretty much picked up where we left off before we joined the Navy. Except now we could only get together on weekends because he was working out of town, and I worked for local farmers.

I was also good at fixing cars. It wasn't unusual to see a nice looking Pontiac or Oldsmobile sitting in someone's backyard with weeds growing up around it. I used to buy them for next to nothing, spend under $30 for a timing chain and gears and within 45 minutes to an hour have them running like a top. Then I'd sell them for top dollar.

Burning Oil

It was in the fall of the year and we needed transportation. We got on the old John Deere D and drove at full speed, 3 miles an hour, over to Willie's house which was about 2 miles away. We hooked up to his old Ford and pulled it all the way back to my house. We proceeded to pull parts off of my old '50 Ford and transfer them to his, replacing all of the parts Willie's dad and I had taken off the car. We closed up the floorboard that I had ripped up when I pulled the transmission out and hammered it out to where it was unnoticeable when the floor mats were in place.

After a few days of work, it was ready to roll. Away we went. But that old '49 Ford still burned more oil than gas. We'd recycle used oil that came out of the tractors on Willie's uncle's farm. The oil was usually sitting out in open buckets in a shed. Sometimes there were bees floating on top. We poured it into the engine, bees and all. I can't tell you how many times we ran out of oil and overheated the engine before we finally seized it up. We had it towed into Fertile where they gave us $15 for junk. We put that cash towards the $49 we paid for a 1950 Dodge. It looked like it had been painted with a broom, but it ran like a top. We put a lot of miles on that car before a rod started knocking and I traded it even up to a kid for a 1955 Chevy with disengaged push rods.

First Love

About this time, Willie was getting pretty serious with his girlfriend, Avis. They were good together and I was happy for them.

I believe it was the summer of 1963 when I became serious about someone. That someone was Angela. She was one of the sisters to my stepdad. We were close when we lived together at age 8 on the farm with grandpa and grandma Leines. As Angela and I got older, we became even closer. I suppose it was pretty tacky, considering that Angela was actually my aunt through marriage. But, we really didn't stop to consider that and certainly didn't let it stop us from falling in love one summer when she was 16 and I was 17.

Our romance pretty much came to an end one night when I was out drinking with my dad's brother-in-law. I let it slip and said something about the relationship between Angela and me. He immediately told his wife, who then told her mother, my step-grandmother. It ended when Angela got off the school bus with my brothers and sisters one evening after school and came to see me instead of going home like she was supposed to do. Her mother had warned her to stay away from me. When Angela didn't come home from school, grandma knew where to find her and walked across the field to our house. She walked in, grabbed Angela, and without a word, left for home.

It was for the best that grandma intervened, but it still broke my heart to see. I believe I really did love her. I also knew it was never going to work out for us.

To make it easy for everyone concerned, I left for California a few days after that incident. I received one letter from Angela after I got to California. I didn't answer it. When I came back to Minnesota, she was seeing someone else and so it ended. That was really heart breaking. She remarried a wonderful man who she is still with today.

I'll always have a special place in my heart for her. Right or wrong, she was the first girl I ever loved. I'm happy she found a really good man. Together they have made a wonderful life for themselves.

I guess if you really care about someone, the best you could possibly ever want for them is their complete happiness. I believe Angela has that now.

I e-mailed her the other day and asked if it would be all right to include her in my book. She gave me the okay and I sincerely hope that I have not said anything offensive or threatening to her or anyone else.

As another human being, I hope you remember back to some of those times so many years ago when your common sense was blinded by emotions. I trust you to be understanding of my intimate relationships and cut me a little slack as I share my most vulnerable moments.

The Lost Years

Out West

My trip west took me to my Aunt Florence and her home in Gardena, California. Aunt Florence was a cleaning fanatic. After removing your shoes and walking into her house, she would follow you with a vacuum cleaner. I remember the carpeting in the house was blue and when she emptied the vacuum cleaner bag, there was nothing but blue fibers in it.

She had one room in the house that was always locked. She humorously referred to that room as Fort Knox, because it was loaded with all sorts of stuff that she valued and didn't want anyone to touch. Part of the reason that she locked it up, was because of her son, Donald. He was in his 20's and still lived at home because he was mentally handicapped and had the mind of about a five-year-old. Donald and I got along great. He was like a really good, well mannered, really big five-year-old. There were three other kids in their family and all of them lived fairly close. I stayed with Aunt Florence for about a week and then was invited to stay in Harbor City with my cousin, Dolores, and her family. She had been divorced for some time, and was raising three girls. Another cousin, Pat, (the girls were sisters), lived within walking distance, so I chummed at both places. Pat's husband was in the Navy, yet he came home every night after his duties were finished in Long Beach.

Dolores had a 1954 Buick that she let me use to go back over to aunt Florence's to pick up my clothes. This was Los Angeles. I wasn't used to city driving as most of my driving had been done out in the country. I didn't know the city either and found myself in a right-hand lane needing to make a left hand turn. I made the turn and got stopped by the police. I didn't even have a drivers' license, but they let me go with a double ticket. One for driving without a license and the other for making an illegal left-hand turn.

I stayed at Dolores's for about a week and then I was invited over to Pat's to stay. Dolores has since passed away, but I will never forget her and that week that we spent getting to know each other. Pat was about seven to eight months pregnant with their second child. Her husband, Leslie, and I hit it off pretty well. He was cheating on Pat with a girl across town who was a senior still attending high school in Torrance. I had hooked up with a girl in the same area, so Leslie and I often hitchhiked from Harbor City over to Torrance where we met the girls. The girl I was seeing was also seeing someone else, but that didn't bother me because we weren't serious about each other.

One evening, Leslie and I were hitchhiking to Torrance when this kid pulled over and picked us up. As we got closer to our destination he asked, "Where are you guys going? I'll drop you off." Now what do you think the chances are, that on a busy Los Angeles freeway, with thousands of cars coming and going, that the one car that would stop and pick us up would be driven by the other guy that was seeing the same girl I was? He didn't say a word after we gave him the address. He just dropped us off a few blocks short of her house. We finished the short walk to the girl's place and soon discovered who we had been riding with. But it didn't do that guy any good to get there first, because the girl picked me for the evening anyway.

I got along really well with Pat and Leslie. I only had one run in with Leslie. Pat asked me to help her move one of those old-time, round washing machines with a ringer mounted on it. We could wheel it because it had casters for portability. Those washers were very heavy and there was a patch of grass we couldn't roll it over followed by a flight of steps that had to be negotiated in order to get it into the house. Having just come off the farm, I was in very good shape and very strong, so I picked it up and carried it across the lawn, up the steps, and into the house.

When Leslie got home, he wanted to know how the washing machine got there and I told him. He insisted that Pat had helped me which made him angry because Pat was pregnant. A little guilt thing there on his part at my expense. He finally ordered me to pick up the washing machine and carry it outside and then back inside to prove it. I'll spare you the foul language that I used in telling him where he might consider putting that washing machine. I believe that was the last time that he ever thought of telling me to do anything, because there definitely was going to be a fight the next round. I don't think Leslie was afraid of me but I don't think he wanted to fight with me either.

Riding The Rails
I think Leslie finally got tired of being tied down to a pregnant wife and naval orders. One weekend, he didn't report back to the base for duty which made him AWOL. By now, I had a warrant for my arrest because of that traffic violation and the fact that I hadn't paid the tickets. With the shore patrol knocking on doors looking for Leslie, he and I decided to get out of town. We left California with nothing but the clothes on our backs and $.35 between the two of us. We were heading for Texas.

We did all right getting rides as far as Albuquerque, New Mexico. Then the traffic thinned out and we couldn't get a ride to save our souls. We walked for about 25 miles, before someone finally picked us up. We certainly didn't get a limo, as we climbed into the back of a dump truck loaded with barbed wire and all kinds of other unpleasant building materials to cope with on the ride. The cab held three Mexicans; they must've passed us coming and going five or six times before they finally gave us a ride. But, who's complaining? At least we got a ride. It turned out, that there had been some murders in the area and the local radio stations were warning motorists not to pick up hitchhikers. The dump truck crew got us fairly close to Tucumcari, before they let us off. We walked for a few more miles before it started getting dark. We walked off of the highway to a thicket of brush and laid down on the ground and went to sleep.

As soon as the sun came up, we were back on the highway headed to Tucumcari. After a few miles of walking, we got a ride from a nice guy. He gave us a dollar and a quarter to buy food. He was also the one who told us that we probably wouldn't get very many rides, if any, all the way through New Mexico because the radio stations were warning motorists about hitchhikers. He then suggested that we go to the railway yard and ride a box car to Texas. He told us that if we found someone working in the yard, they would tell us which train goes where. Before saying good-bye, he dropped us off at a grocery store where we bought milk and baloney with our money. We hadn't eaten for two or three days! The little bit of food we got for a dollar and a quarter certainly helped, but we were still very hungry.

From the store we walked several blocks to the rail yard. Wow! There were so many trains going every which way. We took the advice of the man who told us to ask someone working in the yard what train to take. Surprisingly, there were no objections at all to telling us what train to get on and where we would find empty cars with open doors. The train that was pointed out to us, was a very long train with empty boxcars towards the very end. We were told that it would go right straight through to El Paso Texas without stopping. Then, we could get off and jump another train to San Antonio. We were officially going to be hobos.

The train didn't leave for a little while, which allowed us enough time to prowl around the yard. We found this little shack where the railroad workers must have gone to eat. We found lockers with lunchboxes and stole a little food out of each one, then returned to the boxcar with our stolen goods. One sandwich had thick pieces of meat loaf on it. Man! That was the best meatloaf I have ever eaten. I was sorry right away that I hadn't taken the whole sandwich. We weren't exactly full but we certainly weren't hungry anymore.

The boxcar that we got into was empty and relatively clean. At one end there were clean sheets of plywood that were about three quarters of an inch thick, with holes the size of a softball about every 6 inches. There may have been three or four sheets stacked atop of each other. And that is where we made our bed for the night.

Riding in a boxcar at the end of a long train is not exactly a smooth ride. Besides being bounced all over the place, every time the train went down a hill, the slack would be taken up between the car connections all the way to the very end. Once the train was on level track, or possibly going up a hill, all of the slack was let out between the cars connections. When it got to the end, it was like the crack of a whip. It jarred every bone in our bodies. Fortunately, for the most part, the track was fairly level so we didn't experience a lot of jerking.

I had just fallen asleep when Leslie shook me and asked me to get up so that he could maneuver the plywood sheets around to where the holes matched up. He had been laying on his stomach trying to sleep, but kept bouncing because of the rough ride. He said it felt like he had been kicked in the testicles. Maneuvering the boards around to where the holes matched up allowed him to position himself to where his privates no longer were in contact with the board.

Well, this certainly sounded like a good idea in theory and it did work pretty well for a number of miles until we came to one of those hills that I mentioned. When the jerk came to the end of the train, one board went one way and the others stayed in place. All I can tell you is that I am very grateful that I don't sleep on my stomach. Leslie screamed in pain and I thought for sure he had lost his package between those boards. But, it turned out that he had only gotten pinched and nothing was as damaged as his dignity. If I were writing fiction here, I don't think I could make this stuff up.

Daybreak came and we were still bouncing along the track wondering when in the world we were going to stop in El Paso. Later in the day we finally did stop in a rail yard. We jumped off and asked someone in the yard where we were. You can imagine our shock when they told us we were in Denver, Colorado. It turned out that the train had gone to El Paso; in fact right through at full speed. We asked the Denver yard man which train was going to El Paso or San Antonio. The man pointed to a train that was already moving very slowly. We ran alongside it and I got on between two boxcars in one spot and Leslie got on between two boxcars in another spot. We rode four hours between the cars before the train finally stopped. I jumped off and started looking between the trains for Leslie but he wasn't to be found. I thought maybe he had missed the train, or worse yet, fallen off the train. It wasn't easy standing on the wrung of one of those ladders. It was especially tiring after four hours of hanging on for dear life.

It turned out that Leslie had gotten off on the other side of the train and was thinking the same thing about me when we finally saw each other.

We found someone and asked them where we were and, of course, it wasn't El Paso. For the third time, we were directed to another train that would be going into El Paso. This train didn't have any empty open boxcars so we had to settle for a gondola. Riding in that gondola couldn't have been any better than riding in a refrigerator. Man, it was cold at night! When daylight came a few hours later, the train stopped and we got off. Everything looked a little familiar but then all train yards looked the same. We found someone and asked where we were. We were told, "Tucumcari, New Mexico." Well, now I know why everything looked familiar!

We inquired as to which train we could take that would be stopping in El Paso and we were assured that the train he pointed out was a hot shot to El Paso and that would definitely stop once it arrived. Fortunately, this one had empty boxcars that were, of course, at the end of a really long train. And this time we had company. There were three or four hobos on the train with us. The train did not leave right away so we had a chance to get acquainted and learn some hobo terminology. We learned what it meant to "shoot a snipe." That was the name they gave to the process of picking up cigarette butts from the ground to be divided evenly and smoked later.

It's been so long ago that I don't remember any of their names, but they seemed to be good people. Maybe we were foolish but neither of us had a fear of them. Besides, I don't think they could have overpowered us without weapons. And why would they want to? We had absolutely nothing of interest to them.

The train finally started to move after several hours of sitting in the yard and we were on our way to Texas ... again. By this time, we had been on the way to San Antonio for six days. We all settled down for the night. The hobos at one end of the boxcar and Leslie and I at the other end. We fell asleep when suddenly we were awakened by a commotion in the boxcar. One of the hobos had gotten up to take a whiz out the door of the boxcar. He had opened the door just a little way so that he could do his job without letting too much cold air into the car. The train was going up a hill and gave one of those jerks that

I mentioned. The door of the boxcar slammed on the hobos thumb cutting it almost completely off. He simply put a glove on his hand and held his thumb together with his other hand until it stopped bleeding. We urged him to see a doctor as soon as we stopped, but he said that he would be all right.

Finally, the next day, we arrived in the rail yard of El Paso, Texas. As we pulled into the yard, we were moving very slowly and I was sitting with my bare feet dangling out of the door, when we passed one of those little lights with a visor that sits alongside of the tracks (they stand about 3 feet high). I whacked my feet on one of those darn lights. I didn't break anything but it sure did hurt. When the train stopped and we all got off, the hobos led us to the Salvation Army, where, after listening to a sermon, we received a bowl of soup and a sandwich. Then we went back to the rail yard and asked which train would go to San Antonio. Later that day we arrived. It had taken us seven days to get there. And we came in smelling like last weeks' garbage.

We walked to the nearest service station and asked to use a phone. I called my uncle Otis and told him where I was. It turned out that we had gotten off the train right in back of his house. I should have known that, because he had always lived close to the rail yard, and his next-door neighbor worked for the railroad. My uncle asked us if we were hungry. Other than the Salvation Army snack, we hadn't eaten since we stole that food in the rail yard in Tucumcari. He said that the two of us had to clean up before we could eat or do anything. That suited us just fine because we felt pretty much like we looked.

Outside Looking In

I think it's time to put my story on pause again, and tell you what was going on inside of me. I was rambling from place to place trying to find a place to belong. I think back to the chain of events between when I joined the Navy at 17 and when I arrived in San Antonio. Believe it or not, my self-esteem was worse than ever. All I really wanted was to find a place where I felt that I belonged. I thought the Navy could be that place because I could handle all that was required of me, except for those darn tests. While I wasn't a complete failure because I really knew all the answers to the questions on those tests, it still wasn't enough. I was sent home because I didn't tell them that I couldn't read fast enough. I was too proud to speak up. So, in the end, it looked like I wasn't good enough and I felt that way.

I wasn't confident enough to just strike out on my own and find my way in life. I thought the answers I sought could be found somewhere other than where I was, at any given time. At the first sign of resistance, I always found it necessary to move on. I never seemed to be welcome in any one place for very long, causing me to become depressed and even more insecure and more desperate. No matter where I was, after a while I always felt like I was on the outside looking in. It always felt good at first, to visit people who hadn't seen me in a long while because they were always visibly happy to see me. They asked me to come in and stay. For just a little while, I could experience that good feeling of belonging. The feeling that provides confidence and security. But then all too soon, the newness would wear off and I was once again on the outside looking in.

Nothing ever seemed to work out for me. My relationship with Angela ended because it wasn't acceptable for us to be together because we were related through marriage. Funny reason, because I never felt like I was part of the family except for those few months I lived with Grandpa and Grandma Leines so long ago. That very first year I was in Minnesota was the most security I ever experienced. But like everything it came to an end. I had 12 brothers and sisters in two separate families, but I still felt unaccepted and alone because all of them were half-brothers and sisters. The connection that makes us truly family was never evident. I could clearly see that all twelve of them were treated different than I was. I was never made to feel like I was one of them.

So far, my biological father disowned me at birth. My grandmother, who was more like a mother to me, died. My next father was killed. I was bounced around from relative to relative for about six years. I was moved in and out of a multitude of schools for eight years. I was shunned by my stepfather, Wally, even though for many years we awkwardly tried to connect. And finally, I was again turned away by my biological father when I was 18.

Bad habits were mounting up fast. I never stayed in any one place for very long. I was stealing to get by at times. I never completed anything that I started. I couldn't hold a job for very long. I had absolutely no direction, no goal, or even a desire to do anything because I was convinced that I was incapable of anything. I was completely and utterly lost. Living from day to day, responding only to the moment, chained to the past, always skeptical about today and fearful about tomorrow. But the worst was yet to come.

My guess is that the way I was feeling at age 18 is pretty close to what many teenagers today experience. At this point in my life, all it would have taken to turn me around, is to realize what I know today. I know people are reading this and thinking that maybe my life wasn't all that bad, considering your personal hell stemmed from physical abuse, fighting for your life day-to-day, or living in a neighborhood where murder, rape, and robberies, were common. Or possibly, you think your life was not nearly as bad as mine because someone has always provided for you… except for the one thing you needed most of all.

Whatever your background is, I can assure you that emotional wounds don't heal as fast as physical wounds. The pain we inflict upon ourselves is far worse than anything anyone else could ever do. It doesn't matter what brought us to this place of despair, because when you're there, the devastation is the same for all of us. And the way out is always going to be basically the same.

It would have been nice to have people around me that encouraged me and made me feel like I belonged. But if that were the case, I would have never had any reason to become aware of what I am telling you now. This only substantiates the fact that there is a reason for everything. The fact is, things for me were less than ideal.

You may see yourself or someone you are trying to understand in similar situations. The answers are pretty much the same. They are found in the same place for all of us. Happiness, security, peace of mind, and all good things are the personal emotions that we have always been searching for. While they can be enhanced by others, it is only after we find them for ourselves that we feel secure and embrace the freedom we deserve. In other words, the responsibility of these things that are very personal to us cannot be provided by someone else. Our emotions and how we handle our life's experiences are our responsibility to ourselves. There is great power inside each of us; to give up and remain chained to past failures or pain is absolutely self-destructive. Often it goes back to what I said before. We have become so convinced that any effort is futile and we hold onto that thought at all cost. Rather than let it go and be free, we are even willing to fight and die to protect something that is killing us inside.

I have lived in poverty. I have lived in some of the worst parts of town where killings, muggings, and rapes were daily events. A way of life. The majority of the people around me in these places never even entertained the thought that a better life may exist somewhere else. Other than to resent the people who lived a better life somewhere else, they put zero effort into becoming the dream they wanted. I will tell you this: whatever it is that you think about the most is what you will become. The power of your thinking patterns are beyond comprehension. If you change the way you think, you will soon act differently, and as you act differently, you will find life's positive possibilities are endless. Things that were beyond your reach before will just fall into your lap. Yes, you will have to extend some effort, but the point that I am begging you to consider, is that thought patterns will bring you down one road or the other.

Purposely activate patterns that bring you peace, goodness, and well-being. While you may feel that I am harping on the same strings, I unashamedly am! You have the right to choose a good life! You have the power to be what you've always dreamed of! What do you really want? Who is stopping you? Will you walk away from this book and say, "My, that was a good story," or will you hand this book to everyone you care about and say, "You need to read this! There is a change in my life because I finally realized that I can live the rest of my life exactly how I want too!" Yes, it is just that simple! One sentence that you believe in can be the catalyst to a fresh new life that you endeavor to live.

Choices

I walked away from horrible situations and so can anyone else. Right here I think we need to briefly discuss grief and guilt.

There's often grief over what we missed out on in life because of what someone else did to us. Then there's guilt over what we did to innocent bystanders in our life. Often we are not healthy in our reactions to either guilt or grief, or both. I believe my personal journey to all that I've gained started when I realized that I needed to take authority over every choice in my life. You might think that taking authority over present choices is the key. You would be partially right. However, the greater gain, is when you accept responsibility for all previous choices. Even the most painful ones. Once that happens, your present situations will become less challenging.

The choices we make are not always the right ones and we can't always clearly see what the right choices are. But they are always personal choices. Often, we try to place blame for our circumstances rather than change the circumstances. Whatever we choose to do, or not do, is a personal choice. It always has been, and always will be, a matter of personal choice. When we are on top of things, the view is great; we can clearly see many choices and almost inevitably know which one is right. But as we get closer to the bottom, our vision becomes obscured, as our choices are very few and unsure. When we hit the very bottom there are only two choices that are clear. One is the end. The other is the beginning.

I want to quickly defuse any notion that what I am saying will not apply to your life because I do not understand our culture as it pertains to your generation. That's just an excuse. You are never too old or too young to apply truth. The truth will work for everyone. The young people of today are no different than the young people of yesterday. People my age look at the younger generations around them and blame their shortcomings on the fast pace. But it's all irrelevant. It may be difficult for someone my age to keep up with the pace because we have to continually give up old ideals for new ones. Many of us won't even consider touching a computer. Young adults were born into this fast-paced, constantly changing world and really can't imagine anything else, having never lived in our time.

Some things never change; especially the emotional components that we are all reacting too. We complained in my day about authority the same as kids do today. We rebelled against anything that represented control. Yet we were allowing ourselves to be controlled by our emotional differences towards authority to the point of surrendering our physical freedom to the system we complained and rebelled against. Anger and resentment are not things that we control; they are instead, things that control us. Our anger and resentment towards authority is at the controls from one generation to the next. This provides us with very few alternatives. It's kind of like being stuck in quicksand. The more you struggle the deeper you sink.

From my generation to yours, I can plainly see that nothing has changed in this respect. If anything, this situation concerning teenagers and authority has gotten worse. The thing we've feared more than anything is having to answer to our parents. We rebelled against them and did everything they told us not to do. When it came right down to it, we did not respect them.

I turn on the news and hear about a teenager that killed his parents because they were having a bad day, or their parents wouldn't let him have his way. It's a sad thing to know that a kid was so neglected that they were never given parameters or taught the value of choices and consequences. It isn't the fast pace of the world today that is screwing up our children. It's us not paying attention. It's about us not giving them parameters and teaching them the respect we hope to get from them.

At five years old, I knew right from wrong. When I put that dirt clod in that cotton sack, I knew it was wrong. I assure you that I am not unusual in that we actually start learning right from wrong the day we are born. When children are very young, we parents make the choices for them but as they grow older, they may be less likely to rebel if we give them choices and hold them accountable for the choices they make. If they make the wrong choice it's not a bad thing. We all make mistakes as we grow. I believe we should focus less on the mistake and more on what we have learned from the mistake. Focusing on the mistake makes us all feel rotten.

Let's practice learning. So now, we take what we learn from our mistakes and move on to a better place. This process is a choice. Start making a positive change!

Looking For A Place to Belong

We didn't stay with Uncle Otis and Aunt Eunice for very long before we hooked up with Aunt Marie and Uncle Bud. By this time, Aunt Marie and Uncle Bud were still married, but Uncle Bud rarely came home because he had a mistress. Everyone knew about it, and knew he was with his former secretary. Why Aunt Marie didn't divorce him I don't know. Why Uncle Bud didn't divorce Aunt Marie was obvious; I think she would have taken him for everything he owned and he knew it. We stayed with Aunt Marie for a couple of weeks doing some work around the place, along with taking care of the yard and the apple orchard. Leslie and I met a couple of girls at the San Antonio mall, so we'd make plans with them sometimes. The girl I was "dating" was only thirteen. She was as tall as I was and seemed much older. Both of the girls were "jail-bait" but we kept the relationship clean.

After a couple of weeks Leslie decided to go back home. I never saw Leslie again and no one in the family knows what ever became of him. I stayed for a few more weeks seeing the girl that I had met at the mall. She didn't live far from Aunt Marie's and walked over to see me often. Some days Aunt Marie would take us to the public swimming pool in San Antonio and other interesting places. I enjoyed being around that girl a lot and really hated to leave her. But, I eventually wore my welcome out, again, and before I knew it, I was on a Greyhound bus headed back to Minnesota.

I was briefly home, when I got word that my little brother Danny, one of the twins, had died as a result of being given a wrong prescription by a doctor. So back to Texas I went.

I stayed in town with my cousin. Her husband was home on leave from the Navy at the time. One night, my 18-year old brother and I hooked up again, went out, got drunk, and landed in jail. Just like old times. My cousin's husband came down and bailed me out. I told my brother that I would come back for him. It took me a few days to scrape up the money, but I finally did go back and pay up to get him out.

I had the chance to visit some of my other relatives on this trip. Remember my cousin, Patsy, who was considered a slow learner back when we were in kindergarten together? She had been missing for a few years and was now living in Waco with her husband. I know that he made a living by towing cars and while I can't remember what his name was, he treated my cousin like a dog. They had one little boy about 18 months old and he was neglected.

Aunt Kate, Nancy and I went over to visit Patsy one day and after no one answered our knocks at the door, we peeked into the house through the window. There weren't any curtains or shades and we could see the baby all by himself crawling around on the floor. A few minutes later, my cousin Patsy came walking down the street saying that she had been over to a friends' house for just a few minutes. While she still wasn't the sharpest knife in the drawer, she did want to get away from her abusive husband. She didn't know how to go about leaving him, so she asked her dad to help her. Uncle Louis picked her and her baby up one day and brought them out to his house and said, "Don't go back." Her husband showed up once, but Uncle Louis ran him off with a gun and he never came back again.

It wasn't very long before I wore out my welcome there too, and my relatives moved me on to Grand Prairie, Texas, where I could stay with my uncle MD and his family. They said I could stay until I found a job and got on my feet. There weren't a lot of jobs available at the time but after inquiring around, I found one working with a local chain link fence contractor. I really liked the job. It was almost like working on the farm doing custom bailing. The work was hard and physical. The job involved digging a lot of holes with hand-operated scissor type post-hole diggers, heavy lifting of cement sacks, shoveling and mixing gravel with cement in wheel barrels, setting steel posts in the cement, installing chain-link fence, and attaching it to the steel framework with wire ties. The ties were installed by hand with a pair of pliers using a special wrist action that had to be learned. I was doing all right on the job. I was getting along great with my boss and looking forward to every morning when he picked me up at the house for work.

I was beginning to feel real comfortable when I was asked to leave my relative's house. Right about that time, the guy I was working for hired another helper from Louisiana. The new guy needed a roommate, so I moved in with him. He had this black and white '55 Dodge that he told me he had bought from a dealer in

Dallas with no money down. I needed my own ride, so one night after work, we went to that dealership where I purchased a 1956 Oldsmobile Holiday 98. Because of my age, my roommate had to co-sign for me.

My new car was cream color and salmon, with every option imaginable that was available on cars in those days. It had leather interior and even a leather headliner with chrome bars running across the top. It felt good to be independent again.

Up until this point, I never ventured very far away from family or people that I knew. I really never once thought that I was taking advantage of anyone. I was kind of on my own looking beyond my immediate family for that place to belong.

Between age 18 and 32, my life changed drastically for the worse. Previous to this, my little trips in and out of county jails were no more than the growing pains of a troubled kid. But soon I would experience a whole new level of mayhem.

My job with the chain-link fence company started to take a turn for the worse when I started to develop an attitude because I thought the new guy was being treated better than myself. I had been there longer and was more knowledgeable. I thought I had earned the right to be in charge when the boss was away. But instead, the new guy seemed to be in charge of me. I became angry, argumentative and disrespectful to my boss. I suppose I should've been eternally grateful to my roommate for giving me a place to stay and cosigning for my car when he didn't even know me, but I wasn't grateful at all. In fact, I never really even thought about it.

I never paid my new roommate a dime towards the monthly rent. Aside from being irresponsible, I resented him for coming between the relationship with my boss and myself.

I was dating a 15-year-old girl that I had met one evening at the local drive-in where all the teenagers hung out. She had a lot of girlfriends who often rode around with us in my '56 Olds. I was beginning to become the envy of all the guys because I always had a carload of foxes.

I was still free-loading, when my roommate's younger brother, John, showed up from Louisiana. We were the same age and hit it off right away. We started to run around together. It didn't take him long to mix in with all those girls I was toting around.

Soon things started going wrong with my car. First a motor mount broke. I couldn't afford to fix it, so I just let it go. Then the brakes started to fail until they were grinding metal to metal. I finally replaced the brakes. Then the transmission started to slip. That's when I stopped making payments on it and let it go altogether. Unfortunately, the responsibility fell on my roommate because he was the co-signer. Right about that time, I got fired from the chain-link fence company. I completely deserved to get fired, but I was angry and denying any responsibility for my own demise. At this time, I was also kicked out of the apartment.

I found a job down the street at a service station. My mechanical experience from the farm enabled me to do minor repairs on cars and other services related to vehicles. For my living arrangements, I got a room at a boarding house in town. The whole place was run by this big heavy-set woman who reminded me of Ma Barker. She was as mean as a junkyard dog, but man could that woman cook!

Since I no longer had a car, my girlfriend began to lose interest in me. Before we parted company, we went on one last date. We decided to double date with her older sister. This particular week, her sister's boyfriend was coming home on leave from the Navy. Now what do you think the chances would be of me actually knowing her boyfriend from when I was in the Navy? Not only did I know him, he was one of the many that Willie and I flew to San Diego with from Grand Forks, North Dakota. We borrowed the girl's dad's pickup and went to the drive-in. We parked in the back row and backed in. We made a bed in the back and let the tailgate down so that we could watch the movie. But I don't think any one of the four of us could tell you what the movie was about as our concentration was definitely not on the movie.

I finally bought another car; a black 1949 Buick straight eight. It was the absolute ugliest thing you've ever seen but it was cheap transportation. It accelerated at the speed of moss. Once I got it rolling, I could bury the needle. Now that I had new wheels, I decided to see if my girlfriend was serious about our break-up. She lived in a trailer house, but when I got there, she had moved. With a little talking, I found out that she was in another trailer court just a little ways away. She looked real surprised when I pulled up in my piece of crap car. I could tell that the romance was gone. We talked for a bit. Then she told me that she was seeing another guy, a guy I knew, as he was always hanging around the house but couldn't make a move on her because of me. He had a really fast '57 Chevy two-door hardtop that turned this chick on. The last date and the very last time I ever saw this girl, was a few days later when the '57 Chevy guy took my ex-girlfriend out and I took her older sister out on a double date.

My buddy was back on duty in the Navy so I was keeping his girl warm and trying to get back together with my girlfriend. The older sister was a very nice looking girl. I can still see her face like it was yesterday but I cannot remember her name. Aside from being very pretty, she was very nice, and especially nice to me. But I couldn't enjoy her company when my ego wanted her sister. All because I had been dumped for a '57 Chevy. Ah yes, young love; it makes absolutely no sense does it? But it makes all the sense in the world when you're a teenager.

Things started heating up around the boarding house between me and Ma Barker. In the beginning she had kind of taken me under her wing and given me some clothing that had been left behind by someone else. We shared some stories and she confided in me about a situation with her daughter. The girl had run away with a border and this really bothered Ma Barker. I told her some of the things that I had been through, being in the Navy, and the places that I had traveled. I guess it wasn't so much about getting close as it was about business. She was feeding me and keeping a roof over my head and I wasn't paying her. That relationship came to an end when she started accusing me of lying about being in the Navy and some of the bizarre things I had done in places I had been. She claimed that no one my age could possibly have done all those things. Although I wasn't above telling a lie or running a line of BS, everything I told her was in confidence and the absolute truth. In fact, I held much of the happenings in my life back.

Instead of telling me to move herself, she sent this big burly guy by the name of Blackie. With a name like Blackie you just know he's a bad ass. Anyway this is who Ma Barker sent to tell me to vacate immediately. I left without hesitation since Blackie was the kind of guy that might take your life and drop you in one of the many abandoned wells found around Texas.

I had no other place to go. I talked my boss into letting me have the key to the men's room so that I would have a place to stay. Every night, I would take the back seat out of my old '49 Buick and place it on the bathroom floor for my bed. The room was about 6 feet by 4 feet. Smaller than a prison cell. It was kind of funny; my Uncle MD lived only a few blocks away from where I was sleeping in a service station bathroom every night.

I finally bought another car because I just couldn't stand that old Buick. This time it was a '51 Mercury with rolled and pleated interior, three deuces sitting on a flathead V8 with shaved heads. It was bronze with a white scallop paint job. The transmission gave up on me early on and I had to park it at the station. I owed a little money on it so it finally got repossessed. I really felt bad about myself when I didn't have a car. It was as though my identity was directly related to my wheels. In retrospect, I was longing for acceptance, freedom, and independence. I could get chicks if I had wheels and that was a big deal too. I don't think I consciously thought about it, but I was realizing that I felt I was worthless to the world unless I had something. Like a cool car.

I was still hanging around John, the younger brother from Louisiana. He had picked up a yellow and white '56 Dodge. I quit my job at the service station and John and I bummed around staying with friends we met.

We finally got a job through a car dealership owner who also owned some other resources. They took us way out into the middle of nowhere to a horse race track. To be exact, we were located in Grapevine, Texas and the track was Ross Downs. Our job was to walk the horses to cool them down after the races. Man, was that a bizarre bunch of people! All of the characters in all of the situations were like a movie I had seen that didn't really even seem real.

There was this little jockey, as most jockeys are little, who was married to this voluptuous blonde bombshell. She was sleeping with anybody and everybody except her husband. Everyone knew, because everyone was doing her. Her husband was suspicious but not sure or maybe really didn't want to know. Almost every night he would beat her up, accusing her of things she denied. It felt like the whole situation was a lit stick of dynamite with a slow burning fuse. We didn't stick around long enough to see it blow up.

We got a ride back into Grand Prairie with some Mexicans. We were each paid a lousy $20 for our hours of walking horses. We used the money to rent a motel room. We couldn't afford food, so we went to a busy restaurant and drank ketchup until we got thrown out. They say necessity is the mother of invention, so we got a bottle opener and broke it in half. Then we took a cup over to the soft drink machine and using our broken bottle opener, we opened exposed bottles letting them drain into our cups.

Maybe I should explain to you younger folks that it wasn't one of those electronic servo machines, but one of those old pop machines with exposed bottle necks behind a long glass door that opened to expose the bottles, but wouldn't allow you to extract one until you put coins in the coin slot. We got around the inserting money part.

We visited John's brother, you know, my old roommate, and discovered that one of John's cousins, Bill, had arrived from Louisiana. He was also our age. The next day the three of us found work at a place called David Hicks Trailer Manufacturing. We worked assembling trailer houses and shooting out lights with nail guns for excitement. It was a boring job. When we received our first paycheck, we cashed it, bought a case of beer and headed for Louisiana. We ended up in Shreveport where John's family lived.

We were all drifting and we needed a plan that would guarantee food and a roof over our heads. The three of us went over to John's uncle's house where we talked about going on down to the New Orleans area to see about getting hired on a fishing boat. We knew being a deck hand was hard work, but the money was good too. We were really tired so we thought we'd take a nap before heading out in John's car. But when the cousin, Bill, and I woke up, John and his uncle were gone. They had decided that four were too many and left without us. We were left without a ride, so we decided hitchhiking was our only option.

We got to New Orleans and a girl that picked us up told us we should go to Port Sulfur. She told us that there were always job openings there. She seemed believable. It was pretty late at night but she said she would take us to where they would be coming in to dock in the morning and gave us a ride to the parking lot by the pier. Then she left. It was dark and as quiet as a tomb. Not a soul was around. Bill started checking car doors until he found one that was open. The keys were in the ignition no less. He said, "I'm taking this car."

I didn't want any part of a car theft deal. Stealing a car was way out of my league and I didn't like the idea. But then, I didn't like the idea of being left all alone in a strange place with a missing car that I was sure to be asked about in the morning.

I jumped in and away we went. We were in a black and red 1961 Chevy Impala two-door hard-top with a six cylinder engine. On the key chain was a silver dollar holder that had, indeed, a silver dollar in it. At that time, you could almost fill a car up with gas for a dollar, which is what we did. We headed back to Shreveport where Bill lived. Bill was speeding, while I was sleeping in the front seat of the car, when the trooper pulled us over. Luckily, the car hadn't been reported yet and Bill only got a speeding ticket. I suppose that should have been some sort of indication for me to part company with Bill, since he was obviously an idiot. What kind of person speeds in a stolen car? But I think I was just too tired to even care anymore.

We got back to Shreveport that evening and slept in the car. In the morning we went to Bill's house where I met his mother for the first time. She seemed like a nice lady but reminded me of some haggard old lady who had been ridden hard and put away wet.

She was a big woman, overweight, and sloppily dressed in clothes that looked like she had been wearing them for the past month. She smoked homemade cigarettes. She had tobacco rolled up in pieces of newspaper and the whole works smelled awful. Her hair was long and stringy. It looked like dark gray wood clumped together in strands. She was indeed a sight to behold, but like I said, she was a nice lady.

That evening we hooked up with a couple of girls. I was with a foxy girl who was tall, and pretty and she was studying to become a model. We didn't have any money so we found a secluded place to park and make out. We took the girls home and pulled the stolen car into Bill's mother's back yard. We slept in the car again. In the morning, we washed the car and Bill dropped me off at my new girlfriends' house. Her brother was graduating and the whole family had left for some kind of rehearsal.

They left us to babysit her two younger siblings and then came back sooner than we had anticipated. They almost caught us in an embarrassing situation.

Bill was supposed to come back and pick me up, but he didn't show. So I got a ride over to his house where his mother told me that he had been arrested right in the driveway an hour ago. I really didn't know what to think about the situation. Now, I was deserted in a state where I didn't know anyone, I had nowhere to go and no idea of where I might sleep that night. I was penniless with nothing but the clothes on my back as everything else was in the car that had been impounded by the police. I went next door where a couple of kids my age lived and told their parents about my predicament. They told me I could stay there for the night. That was a big relief. I went back over to Bill's house and told his mom, "I have a place to stay next door."

That's when the police pulled up and arrested me.

Well, at least there was no doubt about where I was going to be eating and sleeping for a while. Since I wasn't even in the car when Bill was arrested, I didn't know how they could legally hold me for car theft let alone convict me of car theft. But this was the South in the '60s where the laws for minorities and poor people seem to be made up by law-enforcement as needed. I was told that I could get as much as 10 years in prison, but since this was my first time committing a felony, I might get a break. I suppose it didn't help much that everyone in Port Sulfur was related. It was a lot like the county in Minnesota that I grew up in. And it probably didn't help that the car that was stolen belonged to the sheriff's daughter.

I got to make my one phone call. I decided to call my mom. She told me, "You made your bed now sleep in it." All things considered, I believe that was really hard for my mother to say. I am ashamed now that I put her in that spot where she had to let me handle the consequences for my poor decisions. One might argue that Bill actually stole the car and left me in a situation where I had no choice. But there's always a choice to be made and I made the wrong one. When I got into that car and drove away with Bill, I was just as guilty as he was regardless of who turned the key in the ignition and actually drove the car away. My decision was made in desperation, but my desperation was born of insecurity. My personal insecurity was my fear of being left alone in a strange place.

You might argue that if you were faced with the same situation you might feel justified by doing the same thing, because who knows what a bunch of pissed-off Southern rednecks might do to a stranger? A Yankee no less. If you want to go back to where this all began, re-read the part where an overactive imagination caused me to misunderstand a chain of events, then you'll know where my paranoia came from. Then re-read about all the times that I was moved around. You'll realize I had many insecurities that were born of the fear of being left alone. Sure, when you lay it all out like this it all sounds justifiable. Let me assure you, that the law rarely, if ever, takes into consideration what your personal hang-ups are when they cause you to break the law. And there is absolutely no reason that it is right for you, me, or anyone to break the laws that were designed to serve and protect the innocent. It may not be a perfect system, but it is the one we have. The person we stole the car from didn't deserve to have her car stolen after a hard day of work out on the boats.

Chain of Events

Instead of looking at the laws of the land, Bill, or the guys who left us without a car, I'd like you to look at my own personal choices. If you were to go back just a few weeks in my life, you will realize where the real decision was made without a thought about consequences. The drifting and desperation were set in motion back when I started to disrespect my boss at the chain-link fence company. If I had continued the relationship that we had started, I would have never found myself in a compromising situation where I felt the need to make a decision in desperation.

When bad things happen, whatever the circumstances at the time, try looking a little farther back and you'll most likely discover where the chain of events began. I guarantee that your unpleasant experiences and troubles can always be traced to poor personal choices. If you understand what I am saying, you'll realize that as you accept more responsibility in your life, you will have more control over your own personal destiny in life. Here again, I would like to point out, as I will throughout this book, that if we continually blame someone else, or a set of circumstances for our poor decisions, we will continually relinquish the freedom of personal choice to something, or someone, that we have absolutely no control of. If you are in one of those situations right now, perhaps behind bars because of some set of circumstances of which you had no control, you need to ask yourself, "Where did I actually lose control?" Then answer this: "What can I do to be assured that I will never make that mistake again?" There is absolutely no way to move ahead in life without making mistakes, but the most successful people on the planet, are those who limit their mistakes by learning all that they can from each and every one of them. Then they let their mistakes go and move on.

Locked Up

Let's get back to my real life. Bill and I were sent back to Port Sulfur to stand trial for car theft. It went off pretty much like kangaroo court. I knew I was in trouble when the judge said "Send the Yank up next." I was asked to enter a plea. My plea was not guilty. Since I really didn't steal the car and wasn't even caught in the car, I thought I had a case. But the judge said "I find you guilty of grand theft and sentence you to one year in Plaquemines Parish Prison." I said to the judge, "I plead not guilty." The judge responded, "I said you're guilty." And that was it.

All of Plaquemines Parish was segregated. The black people had their own drinking fountains, their own bathrooms, and even the parish prison had black-and-white cellblocks. I was put in a cellblock that contained three cells. Each cell contained eight bunks.

I experienced a lot of things in the next few months and learned some things that would surely get me into more trouble later on. Since Bill snitched me out, we kept our distance. We barely even acknowledged that we knew each other.

One day they brought in three teenagers that were my age. The trio came to be known as the "Bubblegum Bandits" because one of the things they stole out of the hardware store they burglarized was a bubblegum machine. They received three years each for their criminal behavior. Soon after they came, we were all in the day room and the three of them rolled up on me and tried to strong arm me. (The day room was a large room where all 24 of us were let out of our cells early each morning until late afternoon. We used this time to exercise, shower, and eat our meals.) "Paul" seemed to be the ringleader since he was the biggest and the most aggressive of the three. I let them know that I was pretty sure that I would come out on the losing end of a fight, but I wouldn't make it easy for them. Then I invited them to make their move. Everyone else just backed away to watch. I was anticipating a brawl, when all of a sudden, Paul extended his hand in friendship. We shook and became close friends after that.

There wasn't much to do for excitement in the evenings when we were locked up in our eight-man cells, so we threw our mattresses on the floor and had tag team matches. One guy got hurt a couple of times and moved into another cellblock so that he wouldn't have to play anymore. The rest of us got banged up a little bit, bruises, black eyes, and things of that nature. But we had fun! Besides, it was a good way of getting exercise.

Once a week we got macaroni and cheese for supper. Paul and I loved macaroni and cheese but no one else seemed to like it. We'd get plenty of seconds since nobody else went for seconds and some didn't even accept the first plate.

One day, everyone on both the white and black side decided to protest by not eating the macaroni and cheese, except for Paul and me, because we loved it. When the sheriff heard about this, he wasn't about to lose control. The very next day Paul and I were called out into the hall between the two cellblocks. Usually, a cart of food was wheeled between the cells and food was passed through little trapdoors on either side of the corridor. As we walked into the hall, instead of the usual cart of food, a table had been set up with two plates loaded with unusually good food. Not that the food wasn't always good, but this was special. Paul and I were told to sit down and eat while everyone else from the two cellblocks watched us. They weren't offered a thing to eat. We were put into trustee quarters for the time being, and every day this process was repeated until, on the fourth day, macaroni and cheese was served to all. They served macaroni and cheese for the next week. No one complained or refused to eat again.

Plaquemines Parish Prison had its own set of laws. These laws weren't just, but were governed by the sheriff and his deputies. Black women had a cellblock across from the black trustees. White women had a cellblock across from the white trustees. Being a "trustee" was an earned position. You were higher up than just a regular prisoner and this came with privileges. The sheriff that was in charge just before I was incarcerated used to prostitute the white and black women to the trustees for anywhere from a dollar to five dollars. If any of the women refused to cooperate, every woman in that cellblock was denied food until they cooperated. The corrupt sheriff was dismissed without any charges, when a young girl from a prominent family was able to get a letter out to her family exposing what she was being forced to do. The girl was freed because she was only in on minor traffic charges and the Sheriff was replaced. That was all that became of the incident. Unfortunately, the Sheriff that took over really wasn't a whole lot better.

The prison systems are not a place you want to be. While we should be able to count on being treated with respect and decency, I am afraid that many in authority view criminals as expendable people and abuse their power. We will revisit this problem later on in the book.

Paul and I were made trustees, and sent across the river to Port Sulfur. We were boated out to some island where we worked on several projects. We were kept busy building piers, moving huge water tanks, painting buildings inside and out and the like. It was on the island that I got my first introduction to the chemicals used to preserve pilings. Paul and I were diving off the top of a boat after work one evening, when I decided to climb a piling instead of going around to the ladder. In order to climb the piling, I had to wrap my arms and legs around it and "shimmy" up it. That night I felt like someone had poured gasoline on me and set me on fire. Darn, was that painful!

If you like seafood, the place where we were working was the place to be. They stuffed crab into almost everything we ate. Man, was it good! There was a black guy there that must've weighed 450 to

500 pounds. We called him Tadpole. You would think that someone as big as he was wouldn't be able to get around very well, but Tadpole moved around with grace considering the weight he was carrying. I can still see him walking around in his baggy khaki pants with the legs torn off at the knees and a steamed crab hanging out of each pocket. He'd grab a crab, pull it apart, and snack on it for a while. Then he would simply go and get more.

Neither Paul nor I was looking for trouble. We were both trying to behave ourselves and get out of that place. We did, however, feel the need to defend ourselves against any threat. There was this one guy there we called "Boo-boo." I have no idea what his real name was, but Paul was convinced that Boo-boo had snitched him out one day after a visit from his girlfriend. The jail officials accused Paul of receiving drugs on that visit. They didn't do anything to Paul, but they terminated his visiting rights. To tell the truth, I don't think Paul was even into drugs. If he was, we never talked about it. I'm sure the subject would have come up because we had time to talk about everything. Messing with a guy's girlfriend is a major offense to an inmate, so Paul and I decided we'd have to bring equal ruin on Boo-boo. (Again, I want to assure you that what I am about to tell you I am not proud of, but it does show the level of care that I had for another human life.) Paul and I pretty much tried everything that we could think of to hurt Boo-boo and make his life hell on earth. I swear to God, he had nine lives in order to live through some of the stuff we did to him.

Our first opportunity presented itself when we had just set this big water tank into place. The tank held several thousand gallons of water. Paul, Boo-boo and I had climbed inside of it and coated the interior with some sort of grease to keep it from corroding. That evening a barge arrived, and I was told to pump water into that tank. A few hours later, Boo-boo was sent up to check on the water level. Boo-boo didn't have a flashlight, so the only way that he could tell, was to climb down inside the tank until he reached the water level. Once he climbed inside, one of us, and I am not saying who, shot up the ladder, slammed the hatch door shut and latched it. Hours had passed before Boo-boo was discovered missing by the boss. I don't know how it came about and if I told you I would only be guessing how he was discovered, but nevertheless, he was discovered when the water was about up to his neck. Boo-boo had no idea that someone was out to get him. Like everyone else, he just thought it was an accident and let it go.

After that project was over, we were sent back to Port Sulfur to do some work inland. One of the jobs required removing some old chain-link fence; the kind with the top cut off to expose spikes for discouraging people from climbing over. We rolled up about 50 feet of it. Paul and I were in the back of this utility truck pulling the rolled up fence up as a couple of other guys were at the bottom pushing. One of the guys was Boo-boo. His work partner stepped to one side to position himself. It was then that Paul and I looked at each other with a grin, then pushed the roll of fencing off onto Boo-boo pinning him to the ground with all those little spikes sticking in him. When they pulled the fence off of him, he got up with all these little holes in him. He looked like he had taken a shotgun blast from head to toe. Again, it was just considered an accident and no one, including Boo-boo, gave it a second thought.

Our last attempt was when we tried to electrocute him. We prepped an extension cord by cutting off one end, stripping the wires and leaving the wall end intact. Then, we filled a pan full of water, which just happened to be very hot. We went up to Boo-boo's bed and wrapped the stripped wires around each of his big toes while he was sleeping. Then we plugged him into an outlet. The idea was that Boo-boo slept sound enough to wrap his toes with wires but may awaken if we poured water on his bed, so the plan was to plug him in to an outlet first and then throw water on him. It worked out just like we planned it. Boo-boo came off of that bunk and started jumping around yelling when Paul threw the entire pan of water on his feet. We succeeded in shocking him and scalding his feet but nothing more. By the time Paul dumped the water on him, Boo-boo had pulled the plug out of the wall. Boo-boo snitched us out, but the jailers just laughed about it and didn't do anything to us. Gees, do you realize that if we had succeeded, both Paul and I would have been doing a lot more time in Angola, Louisiana State Penitentiary? Of course, being young and stupid we didn't consider that.

Having nothing much to do in the evenings after work now, since we were going back to the cells in the Port Sulfur jail, we decided to give each other a tattoo. These were my very first tattoos. Paul thought it would be cool to put a cross between our thumb and pointing finger. A cross was supposed to represent membership in a notorious gang. There were three more marks above the cross that were supposed to represent rape, murder, and robbery. There are no marks above my cross although I earned one for armed robbery later on.

Here's a thought; gang members were actually doing this, yet everyone, including the law, knew what the tattoo with those three marks represented. Now, you have to ask yourself, how smart can it be to advertise the laws you break?

The other two tattoos I got that day were the model girl's name on my left arm and my name on my right arm. Nowadays guys and girls alike are having huge tattoos put on their bodies and I wonder why? Are they as bored as I was when I first had my tattoos done, or do they just think it's cool? My personal opinion for myself, is that it was a stupid thing to do. I have often wished that I could undo it. Maybe you'll feel differently about your tattoos when you're my age. But my question is, why find out? The statements we make today may be totally different than the statements we wish to express tomorrow. Think about it before you make a statement you can never erase. I sure wish I had.

One morning when everyone was let out for work, Paul and I were kept behind in lockup. Later on that day we were told that my car theft buddy, Bill, and the other two Bubblegum Bandits, had made trustee status and were out in the driveway washing cars when they decided to take one and leave. I'll give you three guesses whose idea that might have been! There was only one way besides the ferry to get across the Mississippi river, and that was to go back to New Orleans which was 50 miles on a two lane narrow highway. Needless to say, they were caught before they reached New Orleans. They locked Paul and me up because they thought we were in on the escape plan.

Shortly after that, Paul and I were sent back across the river to Plaquemines Parish Prison because all the work had been completed in Port Sulfur. Since Paul was doing three years and I was only doing one, Paul was made "turnkey" which meant he had the keys to every door in the prison. This included segregation and the "hole" where Bill and the Bubblegum Bandits were now being held in a 6' x 6' padded cell with a drain in the center of the floor. No water, no toilet, and absolutely no light other than a slit at the top of one wall that was there for ventilation between the two cells. There was the occasional light that came in through the trap door where food and waste was passed. The food consisted of water, spinach, and cornbread, once a day to sustain the three of them. Newspapers were given to them for the purpose of defecating. They were to roll the feces up and pass it through the trap door before they were allowed food. It was like a trade; feces for food.

I honestly believe they made Paul turnkey because he would be tempted to help his buddies. The jailers seem to love putting us in crappy situations. But, Paul stuck to his duties, no matter how his buddies begged and pleaded for food, cigarettes and water. He knew if he helped them in anyway, he would soon be trading his feces for food.

On the other side of the padded cell, where Bill and the boys would be kept for the next 90 days, was a segregation cell where a man by the name of Collagen was being kept in protective custody after almost being killed by cell block inmates. The incident happened while Paul and I were still in the cellblock. Collagen stole some personal property from another inmate; it wouldn't have made any difference who he had stolen from, because the law in the cellblock was that you don't steal from each other. Collagen was appointed a jailhouse lawyer, a judge was elected, and the rest of us were the jury. We found Collagen guilty of theft and sentenced him to near death by hanging. We hung him in the shower and let him hang there until he passed out and went limp. We let him hang just a little bit longer, then took him down. (Snitching us out would have normally done him no good, but Collagen was a member of the community, and he was only in for 90 days after getting drunk and trying to flee the police in his old straight eight. He was burning high test fuel. I guess he led them on quite a chase before he got stuck in the marsh.)

So for his own protection, after the hanging, the jailers put him in a cell by himself which was next to the boys. On the other side of Collagen, was a black man all by himself by the name of Clark. He was on death row for the rape and murder of a white woman. At the time, they had what they called "the traveling chair" and it was just a matter of time before the chair came around for Clark. There were a lot of unanswered questions concerning Clark's guilt. Both Paul and I talked to Clark a lot. He claimed that he was innocent, and that he had only ran because he heard he was being accused of the murder and black people in Plaquemines Parish were always presumed guilty of anything and everything and if a crime needed to be solved they could always find a black person to take the fall. They claimed he was guilty because the dogs led them to where he was hiding. Which makes sense to me; if they went to his house and got some clothing that belonged to him for the dogs to sniff, I suppose the dogs would lead them to him. But, it doesn't prove his guilt.

The thing is, back then, they didn't feel the need to prove guilt. I can't tell you whether he was guilty or not, but I can tell you that everything I heard from him and all the circumstances that led to his arrest, were not in the least bit substantial enough to prove his guilt in a true court of law. We can be very thankful for forensics and the sciences that now prove a persons' guilt, instead of having a man on death row for no good reason except to close a case.

Getting back to Collagen. During the months of June, July and August the cellblocks were like ovens. There was very little ventilation, and absolutely no air conditioning or fans. The boys discovered that Collagen could pass them water in a Styrofoam cup through the 4 inch slit at the top of one wall between the two rooms. But Collagen wasn't so obliging since these were three of the people who almost killed him. Collagen would make them do things, like say the rosary 10 times each before he would give them enough for a sip of water. Sometimes, depending on what mood he was in, he would send them hot water. The next time, he would pee in the cup and send it over. They would almost always drink it before realizing what it was. The jailers never came back to that part of the jail unless they were bringing someone in, so one day Paul and I beat the living crap out of Collagen with a promise of more beatings if he didn't give the boys cold water when they asked for it. He cooperated after that.

Back in the trustee quarters, both black and white trustees were allowed the freedom of the hall where we usually watched TV. Paul, being turnkey, was allowed the run of the prison until about 10 or 11 o'clock. He was also allowed one assistant, which was always me. We got to do things like watch color TV in the jailer's quarters, walk around outside, or fix snacks in the kitchen.

There were certainly some bizarre people in that prison. One of those people was a black man we called "The Iron Man." He got his name because he was so strong that they had to put two sets of handcuffs on him because he could break one pair with hardly any effort. Another black man was serving time for shooting his girlfriend in the groin with a shotgun because she touched him with a broom. It had something to do with his superstition.

Then there was Canary who got his name because he served time in Angola. Canary was our cook and a darn good one at that. And who could forget Reggie? Reggie was about our age. Paul and I didn't like him much. He was a smart ass who thought he was tough. I broke arms with him once and took him down without even straining. Paul and I were out one evening and Reggie asked if we would make him a sandwich. Bad mistake. I won't go into the gory details about what we put in his sandwich, but it had to do with a syringe and a couple of body fluids. Reggie thanked us and said that it was the best sandwich he had ever eaten. Another time, Reggie was just outside the office sitting on the top rail of a guard rail with his feet locked behind the back rail so that he wouldn't fall. As I walked by him, he made some wise crack. I spun around and knocked him cold. He fell backwards and hung there with his feet locked behind that bottom rail until someone helped him up.

There were a couple of 17-year-old black boys that were serving a year for having voluntary sex with a 15-year-old black girl. I told you they have their own laws in Plaquemines Parish. They were really good kids and certainly didn't deserve to be incarcerated on such a weak charge. Even the girl was placed in a juvenile center somewhere. I'm surprised they didn't put her in Plaquemines Parish Prison. The boys were made trustees almost right away. One of the officers, who went by the name of Mr. Luke, didn't like the boys. I suppose because they were black.

On one visit, family members left the boys a sack full of food and personal things like underwear. I was in the kitchen when Mr. Luke searched the bag and placed a butcher knife in with all of the other stuff. Then, Mr. Luke placed the bag back with the other items to be searched. The standard procedure was that your name was called and you came forward to receive your goodies and they were searched. This bag was left for both of the boys, so they came forward together. As planned, at the bottom of the bag, Mr. Luke pulled out the butcher knife. Other officers were called in and the boys were escorted to the bullpen. I thought at first it was just a joke, but then I realized this was no joke and that Luke was actually going to frame those innocent boys. I was in the office when they were talking about putting them back into the cellblock. I said, "Did you look at the knife real close? It came from our kitchen; Mr. Luke put the knife in the bag, I watched him do it." Mr. Luke gave me a dirty look, smiled at the other officers, and said that he was just joking. They released the boys and it wasn't too much after that, when Mr. Luke was kicked back in his chair with both his feet on the edge of the desk and I was standing in the doorway looking at him, he said "What are you looking at, boy?" I said, "You remind me of a gorilla sitting there…only smaller." I know I should have kept my mouth shut, but I didn't, and the next thing I knew, I was in the bullpen. Paul stayed away from me, which was a smart thing to do because he would've been right there with me if he did anything for me. The people who did do something for me, were the two black boys that I helped out of their predicament. They made sure I had plenty of food and cigarettes. After about a week, the sheriff who liked me, reinstated me as trustee.

The mortuary for Plaquemines Parish was also located in the prison. Whoever of the trustees was available at any given time, was required to assist in the pickup of dead bodies. Most of them were no big deal. But I hated floaters and burnt bodies because of the stench. The jailers and officers really enjoyed messing with people. The mortuary was right next to the fingerprint room where everyone was photographed and fingerprinted. Every now and then, they would have a body out on a slab. They would send some poor black fellow in the room which was totally dark, lock the door and then they just waited around until they heard a click, which was the sound of the light switch being discovered. The click of the light switch was usually followed by a loud scream when the prisoner discovered what was in the room with him.

Sometime before I was incarcerated, a man crashed a stolen automobile and was burned to death leaving no way to identify the deceased victim. They cut his fingers off and sent them to Washington for identification. Once Washington identified the man as a Mexican serviceman on leave, they sent the fingers back to Plaquemines Parish. When they came back, no one knew what to do with them, so they kept them in 10 little jars that they placed at the fingerprinting station. Then they kept a meat cleaver in a top shallow drawer to intimidate people (mostly black people) who didn't relax their hands while being fingerprinted. Mr. Luke was usually the person doing the fingerprinting, so he used this trick and could roll their fingers without any problem.

These things were not right, but the poor or black person didn't have a voice back in those days. There wasn't a place to complain or ask for a retrial, or fair treatment. Again, my best advice, is to obey the laws of the land and avoid prison. Don't get desperate and do dumb stuff. Once your life is under another's control, you can only survive their ego and whims.

Mr. Luke thought of himself as a cowboy of sorts. He had coffee can lids hanging from trees all along the highway. As he drove along, he shot at these lids through the window of his patrol car with his pearl handled 44 revolvers. He was quite the piece of work.

I turned 19 in Plaquemines Parish Prison. Although sentenced to a year, I was released within six months for good behavior. The day I got out, I got a ride across the river to Port Sulfur. The guy who gave me a ride took me to this bar where we had a couple of beers and then he left. I still had a few dollars on me, so I continued drinking until I passed out on the bar stool. Somewhere during my drunken stupor, I got up and walked the distance from what would've been my bed in my cell to the toilet. This put me right in front of a pinball machine which I proceeded to urinate on. The bartender tapped me on the shoulder; he gave me a box of rags and told me to clean up the mess. He told me to go home and I explained to him that I didn't have a home. He felt sorry for me and directed me to a shack in back of the bar with a bed in it.

The next day I hooked up with someone I knew who had just recently been released from prison. I called my mom and dad and asked them to wire me money so that I could come home. While waiting for it, I was invited to stay at my friends' house. When the money came to the post office a couple of days later, I bought a ticket on a Greyhound bus and was on my way back to my home in Minnesota.

Gloria

By this time, mom and dad bought the tavern in Bejou that they once rented and moved into town and were living in a little three-room cottage next to the tavern. My buddy Willie was married to Avis and they were somewhere in South Dakota where Willie was working in a gold mine. Everyone was moving on, yet I was coming home wishing it could all have stayed the way it had been before joining the Navy.

I needed a car, so I traded a record player for a 1955 Mercury which I got from a guy that was now married to one of my old steady girlfriends. My cousin, Conrad, was in college at North Dakota State University majoring in aeronautical engineering, He came home on the weekends and sometimes we would get together but we really didn't have a whole lot in common any more.

I helped out at the bar and bummed around for a while. The Mercury had some bad valves and didn't run very well so I took it to a dealership in Mahnomen and traded it for a '55 Buick Super. I was dating a girl that lived east of Bejou about 10 miles out into the country. Her name was Windy and she was a stone fox. I liked her a lot. In fact, we were going steady when I decided to go to Fargo and look for work. Commitments didn't mean much to me back then. I just figured nothing good ever lasts for long. I found a job at Kmart as a bag boy. My cousin Conrad had an apartment in town and he let me stay with him.

I came home on weekends and spent time with Windy, until one evening, when I was back in Fargo, a friend of mine and I were cruising around in my Buick. His last name was Venom, but we all referred to him as "Snake Poison." Anyway, I ran a red light and was pulled over by a police officer. I told him the usual story that my foot feed was stuck and I couldn't stop. He bought it and let me go with a warning. Just as I was about to pull out into the street, we spied these two girls walking along and asked them if they wanted a ride to wherever they were going. They declined and we left.

A bit later, we were cruising down the same street in the opposite direction and came across the same two girls. I pulled over and asked them if they wanted to ride again. This time they got in. I can't remember the other girls name or even what she looked like, but the one that I was interested in I remember very well. Her name was Gloria. We went to one of the local hangouts in town and talked a bit. After that, we took the other girl home and then I dropped Snake Poison off. Gloria and I were sitting in Snake Poison's driveway swapping spit when we decided, out of the blue, to get married. I think we had known each other about two or maybe three hours.

Once we decided, we didn't waste any time. We then headed for South Dakota where we knew there wasn't a waiting period for a marriage license. I didn't have any money, but I did have a set of tools that I sold for gas money to get us on the road. Once we were in South Dakota, we were required to show proof of our age. Gloria was 18 and I was 20. By South Dakota law, Gloria was old enough to get married without anyone's consent but I was not. I needed a parents consent because the legal age for a man to get married was 21. I had no choice but to call my mom and ask for her consent. The date was April 1, 1965. Mom thought it was an April fools' joke, but when the man came on the line and asked for her consent, she gave it. Then we had to take a blood test and pay for the marriage license. We didn't have a dime, so we borrowed money from the Justice of the Peace who married us. We were also given $10 for gas to get home.

We had slept in the car the night before and by the time we stood in front of the Justice of the Peace, Gloria looked like I had punched her in both eyes because they were ringed black with mascara. But we were married. Even though we both looked like crap, now it was time to go back to Fargo, meet my new family and to explain to Conrad why I had a roommate.

Gloria had a lot of sisters and brothers. Her sisters were very protective of her since she was the youngest of the girls. She had one younger brother, but her sisters were the test I had to pass, as their mother had passed away a few years earlier. The first thing Gloria's sisters asked for was the marriage license. They wanted to make sure that we were really married. Well, we were really married and there wasn't anything anyone could do about that fact now.

My job as a bag boy at Kmart wasn't cutting it so I applied for work at a concrete company and was hired. Gloria's dad, one brother and a brother in-law already worked there. It was a union company, small in size, and dead against hiring family because of union voting issues. They didn't know that I was related to three people that already worked there and I didn't tell them, until after I was in the union. The foreman was not happy with me about that situation, but I was a very hard worker and I know he appreciated that.

We got a little two room apartment down the street from one of Gloria's sisters and now I was just a couple blocks away from the concrete company where I worked. We were about to get blasted with real life. Let me tell you, it doesn't take very long when you don't have a plan and neither of you had very good life skills.

The first major problem began when the transmission in my Buick started to go out. I let it get repossessed. We talked Gloria's dad into cosigning for a 1959 Ford convertible. Now we had wheels again, but my concrete job was seasonal and I wasn't getting any unemployment benefits. I had to find work elsewhere. I worked for a little while delivering feed bins out in the country, but that didn't pay very well, so I quit and went to work for a laundry company picking up and delivering baby diapers. Wow! What a crappy job that was. I quit the laundry job, then went to work delivering bakery goods. At least the bakery goods smelled better than the diapers. I didn't get along very well with one of the guys there, so I worked at a service station for a while. From there, I went to work for the Holsom Bakery Company doing janitorial work, baking, packaging, delivery, shipping and receiving. Holsom was another union company that paid rather well. I always worked hard, caught on fast, and moved up the ladder everywhere I worked. But, I never stayed long enough to really do well.

As I was bouncing around between jobs, we spent a lot of time with Gloria's family. They loved to drink and fight usually with each other once they were inebriated, I wanted to fit in so I began to seriously drink. You can just imagine all of the details.

I had unreasonable expectations of marriage. It seemed like one night I had found Gloria and I remember thinking, "Now I have found a place to belong." The next thing I knew, I was in way over my head. I didn't realize the responsibility that came with being a husband. Nine months after our wedding day, my first son was born. We named him Tyrone. Now I was a father too. Ten months after Tyrone, my first daughter was born. We named her Charmane. By this time, I was beginning to discover that when you marry someone in Gloria's family, you married the whole family. Gloria's sisters were in all of our business. We were beginning to have marital problems.

I thought the best thing to do for our family would be to get Gloria away from her sisters. We rented a U-Haul trailer and filled it with our belongings. Then Gloria, Tyrone, Charmane, one of Gloria's brothers, his wife, and a friend, Kenny, all headed for Minneapolis. The night before we left, Kenny and I went out and burglarized a car dealership in Fargo and got a few hundred dollars so that we could afford to make the move. Obviously, we did not have a good plan.

I was once again operating out of desperation. It felt like I could not be the man of our home with Gloria and her sisters all over me. I was self-destructing with alcohol, and marriage was a lot more work than just "a place to belong." We had two babies in under a year. There were a lot of bad habits, baggage, and lack of life skills kicking our rears on a daily basis.

A Painful Past

I look back and just shake my head. So many things could have been different. So many things I wish I could go back and change.

I have mentioned how I have learned to forgive others, because I look back on the destruction I have caused in my loved ones lives and I can only hope for their forgiveness. I didn't intentionally hurt them. I look back to those days with my first wife and those two babies. I was not a man that valued any of them like I do now. Those old lessons I learned early on that caused me to feel worthless could not be overcome by creating a family that I couldn't care for properly. I loved them as much as I could, but unfortunately I was driven by the fear of losing those I loved rather than caring for their needs. I brought my painful past and habits to innocent children who didn't deserve any of the hell I was about to put them through.

Part of the reason that I am writing all of this down, is to bring hope and healing to my children, grandchildren, and now, my great grandchildren. I want to leave a legacy of honesty and truth. Just knowing the truth isn't enough. Each of us has to apply this knowledge to our lives, and be honest with ourselves. I especially want my family to know how sorry I am for the sorrow I caused them. I'm not asking for their forgiveness, forgiveness is something we do for ourselves before we can move on with better intentions than before. It may feel good to be forgiven by someone you have wronged, but no one can change the way you feel about yourself but you. The scars that have been the toughest for me to handle have been the ones that I created in my children and now cannot erase. I see the cycle continuing in my grandchildren. I feel very responsible. My mistakes still pull at my subconscious and they are a poison to my present life. If I do not control them and put them in their proper place, they would consume me with guilt and grief. In the first 32 years of my life, I was a master at avoiding the pain in my life, self-destructing and creating a worse situation than what I was previously in. I was toxic to everyone... including myself. My fingers type out these words slower than I am thinking them. I have so much to tell you!

My greatest joy would be if you could feel the intensity with which I want what I have learned to affect your life in a positive way. I want you to see how miserable and awful I was. Whatever your situation is, I want to bring you hope!

Dreams

It is probably time to tell you a little about my life today, as I write this I have come to grips with who I was and why I did what I did. I have consciously decided to live a different life, and be a different man. I do believe in God. I believe there is more out there than chance and a destiny that we have no control over. I refuse to fall into the "victim" category. I am tired of hearing people hang their worst problems on that word. It is just an excuse to avoid personal responsibility. I don't care what someone else did to you. I care what lies you are believing and what you are doing today to take responsibility for exactly where you are at. I believe we have choices and free will to change what we know is damaging us. We can leave a life of destruction behind us and with purpose and meaning rekindle the dreams we once had, but gave up on.

Remember when I told you that I used to dream on the tractors? Remember the dreams I told to Willie? What I wanted when I was a grown man? I bet you thought I'd never have a chance at those dreams coming true. I had said that I wanted to be true to one girl and have nice cars? Would you believe that I am happily married to a beautiful lady, and we have been married for over a quarter century? She is more than I ever dreamed a lady could be. We retired early and have zero debt. We just bought a brand new vehicle we paid cash for. I have had any and every nice car I have ever wanted. We live in an exceptionally good neighborhood and have healthy relationships with our family and friends. It just doesn't seem possible, does it?

Minneapolis

Let's rejoin our little family as we headed out of Fargo, North Dakota. All three of us men applied for work at a foundry in Minneapolis. My wife's brother and our friend, Kenny, flunked the physical, but I passed and was hired. We then went to a place where they sold trailer homes for next to nothing down. I was able to get an almost new three-bedroom trailer home which we parked in Rogers, Minnesota.

Kenny and I went out again and burglarized a gas station in Rogers. We thought nothing of it and never considered the consequences of getting caught. We'd burglarize a business one night and act like regular, law-abiding citizens the next day.

The morning after we burglarized the gas station, we went out looking for a car for Kenny. We ended up with a slightly rusted out

'59 Chevrolet Impala convertible. The next weekend, he went back to Fargo to visit his girlfriend. While there, he did one more burglary and got caught in the act. When he tried to run, the police shot him in the back. He lived, but he was sent to prison in Bismarck, North Dakota.

Gloria's brother and sister-in-law finally moved back to Fargo because he couldn't find work around the Twin Cities. That left us alone and without the family pressure that I was certain was affecting our marriage. I worked nights at the foundry.

One morning I came home to an empty house. There was a note from Gloria telling me that she and the kids had gone back to Fargo with her sisters. I went after them. I managed to get her and the kids back, but I started missing work and lost my job at the foundry. I went to work for another foundry, but blew the engine on the way to work one evening. With no transportation, I lost that job too. With the bit of money I had coming from my last check, I bought a '59 Pontiac. It was total junk inside and out. We rented a trailer, loaded up our belongings and headed back to Bejou.

Back In Bejou

Once back "home," we rented a little house on a corner lot that was fully furnished. It was a cold day in spring when we moved in. The water lines were frozen. We couldn't get running water and couldn't flush the toilet. I removed the faucet in the kitchen in an attempt to dislodge the ice in the lines, but wasn't having any success getting the water to flow.

Then, the next night, as we slept, a thunderstorm rolled through shaking the entire house. I was awakened by this hellacious noise in the kitchen. Turns out, it was water spraying on the ceiling. The ice in the lines had broken free. I managed to cap it off after a few minutes, but was soaked and freezing. Cold and wet as I was, it felt so good to have running water. Finally, we could flush the toilet.

I found work in Mahnomen working at a Chevrolet dealership. I was adjusting everything on new cars before delivery, doing minor warranty repairs and detailing used cars. I was really having a problem with my back around that time but no one believed me.

Knowing that my wheels were about shot, I dumped the '59 Pontiac and traded a TV set for a 1955 Chevy. It had too many problems so I brought it back and traded it for a 1937 Ford pickup truck.

Hitting a Bridge
I pulled up in front of Mom's tavern in Bejou. Gloria came out looking really mad. I put the truck in reverse, floored it and took out the transmission in the process. The junkyard was 7 miles away and parts were falling out of the transmission. I barely made it to the junkyard where I sold the truck for $40.

Mom took me into Erskine the next day to look for another car. I had $50 to my name but I knew mom would help me out if need be. I found the car of my dreams; a 1957 Ford two-door hardtop. It was rusted out to no end, so I took a pass on that one. I was about to leave the car lot when the salesman told me that he knew of a car a few miles out into the country that was for sale for $200. He said it was supposed to be in fairly good shape. We went out to take a look at it. It turned out to be a 1956 Chevy Nomad station wagon in excellent condition. Mom cosigned for the remaining $150 at the Erskine Bank. The car didn't have license plates on it, so I couldn't drive it home yet. I got the plates the next day and got a ride out to the farm where my new car sat. My ride was from a friend in town who drove a brand new 1967 Buick GS which just happened to be the fastest car in town at the time. On the way back to Bejou, we decided to race and I beat him really bad. Man, was that car fast!

I finally got fired from my job at the Chevrolet dealership. I'm not saying I was completely at fault this time for losing my job because there were days when my back was so bad that I could barely stand. I would most likely have found another excuse for quitting if it hadn't been for my back. Quitting was my answer to everything. We packed up and headed back to Fargo. I went to work for a chemical company after trying out a few other odd jobs. The problems between Gloria and I kept growing and I knew she was seeing someone else. We were living with one of her sisters, at the time, when I decided I'd had enough and left her.

My good buddy Willie, his wife Avis and their son were living close to Fargo. I was rooming with a friend in town. One evening, a bunch of us met out in the country just west of Fargo, as we often did, to drink and party. We all decided to go into town and meet at the taco shop, which was the local hang out. Everyone took off and I decided to take a different route to see if I could beat them to the shop. I was doing all right until I came to a barricade on what is now Interstate 29. I had been drinking quite a bit, so I thought "What the heck! I'll drive around the barricade and be on my way." I was doing a hundred or better when I saw the reason for the barricade. Interstate 29 was under construction and they were building a bridge over the railroad tracks. There was a 1½ foot high concrete slab across the road at about a 20 degree angle. I hit the brakes, sliding in the dirt leading up to the ridge. The impact turned the whole front end of the car under. How I lived through that accident was a miracle. I was cut and busted up, but was able to walk away from it. I walked for a few miles to a motel just off of University Avenue. The person at the front desk took a wide-eyed look at my bloody face and disappeared into the back room to call an ambulance. I must have been in a state of shock and awfully drunk because I didn't even wait for the desk clerk to come back. I turned and headed towards my sister-in-law's house, where Gloria was staying. It was after midnight when I got to the house and knocked on the door. Gloria came to the door in her nightgown, half asleep. It had been a month or more since I had last seen her. She took one look at my bloody face and said, "You've been fighting again, huh?" Then she turned around and went back upstairs to bed, leaving me standing alone in the kitchen.

With all that walking I should have been completely sober, so I can't tell you why I did what I did next. For some reason, I called the police and told them what had happened. I think I was concerned about my car but I really don't remember what my reasoning was. The squad car arrived and took me to the accident scene to determine if anyone else was involved. Then they arrested me and took me to the Cass County Jail. The next day I went before the judge and got 45 days for destroying public property. I guess I did some damage to the bridge when I hit it. My car was totaled.

After a few days in jail, I began to experience severe pain around my nose. They transferred me to the hospital where they discovered a serious infection as a result of my wounds. I was hospitalized for a couple of weeks and somewhere in that time, Cass County dropped all charges on me so that they wouldn't be stuck with the hospital bill.

In the time I was in the hospital, I didn't receive a visit from anyone. When I got out I stayed with my good friends Willie and Avis and began seeing Gloria again. We got back together and moved into a little house that was owned by a brother-in-law. Right about that time, my buddy Kenny was released from the Bismarck State penitentiary. He had nowhere to stay, so we let him stay with us.

You'd think we'd have learned by then. But we were repeating patterns and not breaking through anywhere. We were trying the family scene. I was going to get a job. We were trying to make it work, but nothing had changed. As for the kids, they were just an after-thought, so I don't have much to say about them, as they weren't our priority in any way. How sad is that?

I went back to work for a concrete company with the understanding that I would be laid off every 30 days so that I could not join the union.

Cheating
The relationship between Gloria and I wasn't getting any better. I would work all day and when I came home, she would leave me with the kids and stay out until morning when it was time for me to go to work. I would have had to be brain dead not to realize that she was seeing someone else. We had kind of decided to separate, but since neither of us had anywhere else to go, we lived together. Sometimes we acted like husband and wife, but most of the time not.

One weekend we had a little party at our house where I met another girl. She and I spent a little time making out and getting to know each other that night, while Gloria was making out with another guy. The girl and I decided to go out on a date together, turned out to be another double date with Kenny and his girlfriend. I had an Oldsmobile just like the one Willie had years ago. It had the same symptoms; it would rarely start. We went out into the country and parked just off the gravel road on one of the approaches to someone's field and began to suck down some brews in between making out. We were just about ready to get down to business when a patrol car pulled up behind us. It was too late to ditch the booze. Luckily, we were completely clothed, but since it was my car, I was charged with open container and hauled off to jail where I spent the next 30 days. The girl I was with came up to visit me a couple of times and much to my surprise Gloria even came once for a few minutes.

By the time I got out of jail, Gloria had taken our kids to my mother and father in Bejou. This was in the best interest of Tyrone and Charmane, as neither of us were stable enough to provide a healthy life for little kids. While I didn't protest about the kids, I never really knew what to make of the relationship between Gloria and me. After all of these years, I guess I still don't have it figured out. Sometimes Gloria acted like a devoted wife and other times she acted like she didn't want to have any kind of relationship. I chose to think that maybe we had a chance and I was clinging to that hope until one afternoon when we were over at her sister's house visiting. Gloria just disappeared. I asked everyone where she had gone, but no one knew or at least they weren't telling me if they did.

I decided to walk back to our house which was about 3 miles away. When I got there, all the doors were locked from the inside. She and Kenny were in bed together. After beating on the door for a while, Gloria let me in, and gave me the usual story. This affair with Kenny just happened by accident. Like she was just lying there in bed naked, minding her own business, when Kenny walked in the room by accident. This whole scene was more than my ego could handle. But I couldn't really blame her because I had cheated on her as well. She just didn't catch me in the act. She knew, because one of the girls I cheated with was her younger brother's girlfriend. (The girl eventually became his wife). What is really ironic, is that the one and only night that this girl and I were together, was a double date with Kenny and the girl he was seeing at the time. So, no matter what I make this sound like, I was no better than Gloria.

I think our relationship was doomed from the beginning. We were both looking for something and thought we had discovered it in each other. Gloria was looking for an escape. I was looking for a place to belong. I really did love her or at least what I thought was love, and I know that she really loved me. I was sure that she would eventually be gone from my life like everyone else. Sometimes love isn't enough. We didn't really have any good role models, or for that matter, anyone encouraging our relationship on a day-to-day basis. We didn't have the discipline and skills needed to survive life alone, let alone support each other and our two kids.

I'm not excusing Gloria's behavior. I'm just saying there were circumstances that caused her to develop poor standards. These poor standards motivated her to make poor decisions in relationships. There was constant cheating going on throughout her entire family. Cheating was just a way of life in her family. I on the other hand had no excuse for my actions. I was never subjected to the things she experienced while growing up. Cheating for me, was just a selfish, thoughtless, inconsiderate, insensitive, and immature act, fueled by lust and desire for the taboo. I really believe that if I had been strong and true to Gloria, we would have fulfilled the emptiness in each other and discovered the security we sought in all of our cheating relationships.

A Bad Place

The relationship between Kenny and Gloria escalated. I really didn't do anything to discourage it. Instead, I went into a deep depression and played the part of the wounded spouse that was treated unjustly. I couldn't seem to find the strength within myself to move on or give our relationship just one more chance to survive. I wallowed in self-pity. Your ego will do that to you if you allow it to.

When I went to jail, I lost my job because it was a seasonal job and at the end of the season. It was about the second week of December in 1967 when Gloria took off to Minneapolis with Kenny, one of her brothers, and his girlfriend. I didn't have any money and no means of transportation. The electricity had been turned off in the house, the furnace stopped working and all the water lines froze up in the house. For nine days I had nothing to eat and the only way I could get water was to make a hole in the half inch of ice that had formed in the reservoir of the toilet. My wife had run off with my friend. My kids were with my parents in Bejou. I didn't have a job, heat, wheels, or food. Finally, I became so depressed that I decided to take my life. I got into bed and piled all the blankets I could find on top of me. Then I took a propane tank, opened the valve and put it under the covers with me. Every time I pulled the covers up, the propane tank would stop. When I pulled them down, the propane tank would start leaking gas again. I thought, "Oh great! I can't even kill myself right, what good am I?"

Then I thought, "Well, if I wait long enough, I will just starve to death or die of dehydration." But on the ninth day, another one of Gloria's brothers showed up. He convinced me to go along with him to a bar, where over a beer he bought for me, we discussed the possibilities of burglarizing a lumber yard. Another one of his brothers and Kenny were the safe crackers, I was to be an inside look out and he was to be the driver. I thought, "What the heck? What do I have to lose?"

Unbelievable, right? Once again, I was at a place of such personal misery and despair that I was desperate and about to self-sabotage and take myself even lower. When you are ready to take your own life, there isn't much rational thinking going on. I was starving and now drunk. Numb is what I was looking for and I didn't give a second thought to what this would turn into if we were caught. I didn't care about my kids or my family.

Sounds stupid doesn't it? I was out of control, exhausted, and desperate. Please look into my situation and ask yourself if there are times when you are just as foolish with your life. Does it feel like you are in a blender with all of your personal problems circling and spinning into one big mess? Does it all look hopeless and beyond repair? Do you feel that there will never be another happy day? Are you so destroyed by personal pain that you no longer have any identity other than that pain? I have been there so many times!

Burglary Gone Wrong

It was now January 1, 1968. There was a blizzard that night and the temperature was way below zero. We broke into the lumber yard without any trouble. The safe crackers went to work ripping at the safe with hammers and chisels while I kept watch up front. I sat watching out through the display windows. Our get-a-way car was parked about a block away.

Depending on the safe, it usually takes 30 minutes or so to get inside with hammers and chisels. The tools are used to spread the framework from around the steel door until the locking pins of the door separate and clear the side frames. This is done by using bigger and bigger chisels until the gap is wide enough to use a crowbar to pop the door open. Or, sometimes using hammer and chisel, the front of the door is chiseled and peeled back to expose the cement or brick that is used for a fire and heat insulator. At this point, the material is easily removed to expose the back panel of the door. Then it's just a matter of chiseling through the back panel. It's a lot of work and unless you know your safes, there is always a possibility of tripping an alarm system or running into tear gas or sometimes both. While the boys worked on the safe, I was upfront stuffing my pockets with some bright gold self-adhesive letters and numbers I found. Why did I want those letters and numbers? I was drunk. At the time, it made all the sense in the world to me; although I couldn't explain that rationale to you now.

Somewhere during the process of opening the safe, a silent alarm was set off. The safe crackers got the money out of the safe and we were just about to leave when the police pulled up in front. I warned them and out the back door they went with me following close behind. We were in blizzard conditions and couldn't see two feet in front of us. The boys disappeared somewhere ahead of me. The police were hot on our trail, so I crawled behind a piece of material that was leaning up against a lumber shed. I didn't know at the time, but the boys were pulling the money out of their pockets as they ran.

Unfortunately for me, they ran right past where I was hiding. I had taken all of those shiny, little self-sticking letters and numbers out of my pockets and placed them near the opening where I was hiding. I was trying to empty my pockets of everything I had stolen. When the police followed the trail of money that led very close to where I was hiding, I was discovered when the light of their flashlight was reflected by those little letters and numbers that I had taken out of my pockets. I was cuffed and placed in the squad car and hauled off to jail, again. The boys were picked up in a heavy equipment lot about two blocks away.

I was dead in the water and I knew it. The police had a good case on me. I was caught right on the premises with a trail of stolen money leading to my hiding place. Those darn little reflective letters and numbers! It would have taken one heck of a lawyer to convince a jury that I had no part in the burglary. Kenny and my brother in law, on the other hand, had a really good chance of walking as long as they didn't break down and admit to anything. The getaway driver got away clean and never was arrested. The three of us were put into a cell block together with some other criminals.

One day, my dad came and I was taken out of the cell block and taken to the courthouse where they made me an offer of freedom on probation if I would testify against Kenny and my brother in law. My dad urged me to cooperate but I told him that I couldn't. Right or wrong I wasn't about to roll over on anyone to save my butt, not even Kenny. No one twisted my arm to go along. I was caught, they had a chance and I wasn't about to give them up. I was sent back to the cell block where I told the guys what had happened. Even Gloria came up and so much as ordered me to cooperate with the prosecutor. Figure that one out; she was asking me to roll over on her boyfriend. The guy she had chosen over me.

I was the first one to go to court and the first to be sentenced. I got one to three years and was sent to the Bismarck State Penitentiary.

I can only guess about what I am about to tell you next, but I am pretty confident that I will be right. I think one or both Kenny and my brother in law were told that I had turned state's evidence against them and they were given one chance to come clean for a reduced sentence. That's usually the way the game is played. Either one rolled over on the other or they both rolled over on themselves. Kenny had just gotten out of prison for burglary and he received only one to three years, the same as me. My brother in law had also been recently released from Bismarck State Penitentiary after serving five years for his second burglary offense. This was his third burglary and he only received five years. I personally think they both told on themselves. When Kenny came to prison, he came in telling everyone that I had snitched him out. You see this is the kind of crap guilt will cause you to do to innocent people. Nothing happens without a reason and I presume I was just getting back some of what I was sending out.

Bismarck State Penitentiary

The Bismarck penitentiary was pretty regimented so we couldn't really get to each other except at yard time. Kenny was sending me notes accusing me of snitching. Whenever I would get within hearing distance of him, he would call me a snitch. At one point, he degraded me by telling some inmates, right in front of me, that he had taken my wife from me, had his way with her, then, kicked her to the curb.

Now I understood why Gloria wanted me to cooperate with the prosecutor. I could have easily killed Kenny and I most likely would have if I thought for one moment that I could have gotten away with it. I thought maybe just a friendly whipping with a baseball bat would be in order, but the way the system was set up, I would only get more time added on to my sentence for assault or possibly attempted murder. Thank you, but no thanks.

Fortunately, I didn't let my ego take over my life long enough to flush it down the toilet, yet I couldn't stand the thought of someone walking around falsely accusing me of being a snitch and telling everyone that he had stolen my wife. Don't think for one minute that I didn't spend a lot of my time thinking about how I could take Kenny out and get away with it. In the yard, Kenny would spend a lot of time jacking iron with the big boys. He was getting pretty muscular and must have thought he was invincible. I just kept thinking, "You're freaking muscles won't do you any good when I put a baseball bat alongside your head, or a shank in one of your eye sockets, fool." I was angry at Kenny on many levels and he was the target of my very violent mental retaliations. As angry as I was I still couldn't connect with hate. Maybe that's what saved him from me and me from myself.

I did get a chance to talk to my brother-in-law and he said that he had never thought for one minute that I had snitched on anyone and that this was all Kenny and had nothing to do with him.

Somehow I believed him and he and I were on good terms with each other.

There is not a lot I can tell you about my stay in the Bismarck State Penitentiary. This was my second prison experience and as you can imagine this place was filled with some pretty bizarre people too.

The first few months, I worked in the twine plant. Then I transferred to the kitchen where I washed dishes. No one ever approached me about Kenny's accusations and I got along with everyone. That is to say, they didn't mess with me and I didn't mess with them. Kenny died of a heart attack a few years back. Gene my brother-in-law died of a lung disease close to the same time.

I learned to play drums while I was there and I even participated in a country band. Once in a while, we would play out in the yard. Most of the time everyone would go about their business and keep doing whatever they were doing out in the yard. That is, until I started singing.

Inmates actually stopped and began to listen to me. I thought that was pretty special because these people were the rudest people on earth. If they didn't like something, they would not hesitate to let you know in no uncertain terms exactly what they thought.

On Parole

After serving close to a year I was released on parole. I was paroled to an uncle on my dads' side of the family. He, his wife, and their five children lived just outside Fertile Minnesota. He worked for the local hatchery as a mechanic/backhoe operator. My uncle got me a job as a mechanics assistant. The hatchery had several portable feed mills that were sent out every day to grind various types of feeds like corn, grains, hay, and other livestock related products. Because of the nature of what the mills were used for, they got a severe beating every day and required a lot of servicing and preventive maintenance. That's where my job came in. When everyone else's day ended at six o'clock, mine started.

The year was 1968 and I was 24. Since my uncle lived out of town, it was difficult for me to get home each night without a vehicle. After a couple of paychecks, I had enough to purchase a 1956 Plymouth. When my parole officer found out that I had bought a car, he had a fit and threatened to send me back to Bismarck. Technically, I was violating the parole rules, because I hadn't involved him or asked permission. He finally calmed down and let me slide when he came to the realization that I didn't have a lot of options under the circumstances. I got away with that, so I traded the Plymouth for a '59 Chevy Impala. My parole officer got mad about that too, but I was so close to being off parole that I didn't care what he had to say. Good attitude, huh?

Finally off parole, I quit work at the hatchery and got a job as a janitor at the Mahnomen high school, and moved back home with my parents. They were running the tavern in Bejou. Gloria had our kids and I could see that my brothers and sisters were growing up. I saw that I needed to get my own life together, again. One of the first night's home, I went into Mahnomen, hooked up with an old friend and got stinking drunk on whiskey. A guy about my age that was living with his parents, let me come home with him and spend the night in town. It was really a nice house. I was in an upstairs bedroom and sometime during the night, I got up and walked the distance that I would have walked to get to the toilet in prison. This put me right at the top of the stairs. Yep. I whipped it out and peed all the way down the stairs before my friend woke up and stopped me. That was another fine, embarrassing moment just like when I got out of prison in Louisiana and peed on the pin ball machine.

The next day mom came into town and took me home. She could still smell the whiskey on me as I was sweating it out of my pores. Mom asked me if I had been drinking and of course, I denied it, being the liar that I was. I was a little hazy as to where my car was.

People didn't like me very much around Bejou. My reputation was pretty well messed up. Now everyone knew that I was an ex-con. I dated a few local girls but the relationships didn't last very long when they were ordered, by their parents, to stay away from me.

Gloria and I were still married but one day she called me up and told me that she had filed for divorce. My response was "Good! That saves me the trouble. Thank you." She surprised me when she said "You mean you don't even care?" I said "No, I don't care." Then she started crying and acting as though I had called her up and told her that I was getting a divorce. The next call I got was from one of her sisters, calling to let me know that Gloria had had a nervous breakdown and that I should be ashamed of the way I treated her. I just really never could figure that woman out. Sometimes it seemed like she wanted to get back together and other times she didn't. If she would have just said, "Let's get back together again," I really do believe that I would have agreed to another try at it. But divorce was where we were headed.

Chick

Shortly after the phone call from Gloria, there was a going away party at the tavern for a young man that was joining the service. He was a Chippewa Indian and he had 8 sisters and one brother. The whole tribe was there that night when I spotted an attractive young girl and inquired about her from my sisters Joyce and Kathy. They told me the girl was only 15. She looked as old as me. She was a pretty girl, about 5 foot eight, with long straight auburn hair that fell to the middle of her back and had a golden complexion.

When I heard how old she was, my response was "Bummer". But, then it was brought to my attention that she had an older sister that had a two-year-old kid and was unmarried. The sister was pointed out to me across the dance floor. She was a beautiful girl about 5 foot nine, well-built, with long black naturally curly hair, a dark complexion, and beautiful deep dark brown eyes. Her name was Mary and her nickname was "Chick." It was love at first sight.

I sent my sister over to let her know that I was in love. As she received the message she looked in my direction and we were drawn to each other like moths to a flame. We met half way across the dance floor. We talked for the rest of the night, went out into my car and made out for a little bit. She asked her mother if I could take her home, but her mother said no. Where there's a will there's a way. I couldn't forget her.

Through my sisters, I was able to get a phone number where I could reach her that weekend. I called her and she directed me to where she was staying with a cousin. I got there late and we just went out and parked for a while and then I took her home. After that, we saw each other every day at school because she was attending school where I was working as a janitor. I started going out to her house and sometimes it was late, so I spent the night. Chick's mom and I got along fine. Her dad worked somewhere growing and cutting Christmas trees, so I didn't see him very often. With her brother off to the service and now stationed in Vietnam, Chicks other older brother, "Sunfish" and I became very close friends.

One of the reasons I stayed overnight a lot was because my car would never start. Something was wrong with it that caused rotors to break. Sometimes it wouldn't run at all. One day it crapped out about halfway home. Of all the people who could have come along, I got roadside assistance from my old girlfriend, Windy. Man did she look hot. She pulled in behind me, matched her bumper to mine and pushed me all the way into Bejou. I was tempted to make a move, but was in love with Chick and took a pass on that opportunity.

It wasn't very long before Chick told me that she was pregnant. When Dad found out that I had another girl pregnant, planned on marrying her and that she was a Chippewa Indian, he kicked me out of the house. From there, I moved in with a friend in Mahnomen and continued to see Chick. I got some funding for school and decided to take up the welding trade. I had to go to Minneapolis a few weeks before school to enroll. Chick and her mother came along since Chick had two married sisters living in Minneapolis. Right next door to each other in fact.

The guys that the girls were married to were brothers. One was a dwarf and a miserable drunk; he was married to Chick's older sister who was an absolute knockout. The other brother was married to another sister; he was a bar fighter who fancied himself as the area bad ass. These two guys had two younger brothers that lived across town with their dad. There was yet another younger brother who was married to another of Chick's sisters. Three brothers in one family married three sisters from another. I swear I'm not making this up.

When we got to Minneapolis I was introduced to all the brothers and their wives and was invited to a poker game. Poker was secondary to the drinking, lots of drinking. I got stinking drunk and somehow managed to win all of the money. I later heard that one of the guys had planned to beat me up, take the money and have his way with Chick. I guess he could have, since I was dead drunk, but it never happened.

Chick's brother, Sunfish, lived fairly close and was working as a machinist. I got together with him while I was in town and he invited me to stay with him and his wife when I returned for school. That would give me a place to crash until I could find a place of my own. They lived over on West 15th across from Loring Park in Minneapolis. This area was otherwise known as "The Den of Iniquity."

A few weeks later, I did return to Minneapolis and move in with Sunfish. It wasn't long before I was kicked out of school for poor attendance. I became caretaker of a building on West 15th and received a free apartment. I was working for a scrap metal yard. I was barely surviving and not working on anything positive.

Every weekend I tried to make it back up north to visit with Chick. Being unfamiliar with city driving, I ran through a red light and broad sided a station wagon. There was a young woman in the other car, a small child and an elderly lady. They got hurt a bit. The front end of my car was totaled out. I had absolutely no insurance whatsoever. I ended up losing my drivers' license because I couldn't pay for the damages and doctor bills for the occupants of the other vehicle.

When had I ever let the law stop me from doing what I wanted? I had met some good people in the Minneapolis area. One guy was a cousin of Chicks by the name of Joe. What a character! Joe often visited Sunfish. I never really knew him to ever have a job, but Joe was handy and talented. He was left-handed and played the guitar upside down and played pretty well, I have to say. Joe once dismantled a whole car with a pair of vice grips and a crescent wrench. Joe and I went to a wrecking yard and found a front end for my car. Between the two of us, we replaced my front end and put me back on the road. Of course, without a drivers' license. Oh well, I just figured I'd have to be careful.

The Burned Car

After I had put in a lot of hours one week and was really tired, Joe and another buddy, Johnny, who was the younger brother to Sunfish's wife decided to make the trip up north together. I didn't have a lot of gas, but I had a two gallon can of gas in the trunk for emergencies. I was dead tired and I told Joe that I was going to take a nap while he drove and that he should stop at a service station soon. I also let him know that if he ran out of gas, he could use the gas in the trunk to get us to the nearest station.

I went to sleep and was awakened by a horn going off. I raised my head to see what was going on and saw smoke pouring from under the hood of my car while Joe and Johnny just sat there, as if in a daze. I think they had been sniffing gas. The horn was blowing because the wires were melted together. We were in the town of Staples somewhere in the suburbs. Someone heard the horn blowing and came out of a nearby house with an extinguisher. By then, I had the hood up. Flames were a couple feet high. The homeowner put the fire out and I thanked him and he left. I got back into the car and asked Joe what the heck happened. He said that he had run out of gas, then went to the reserve in the trunk leaving a little bit to prime the carburetor. He had accidentally poured gasoline all over the engine which ignited when he turned the engine over. Well, it was late at night and the car wouldn't run, so I suggested that we get some sleep and deal with it in the morning. I went to sleep and was awakened a little while later by the police who arrested me for car theft. It seems that the boys got restless and had stolen a neighbor's pick-up truck.

Now just what I could have had to do with that I didn't know. It was pretty obvious that I certainly didn't have a stolen pickup truck in my pocket, but it still didn't stop them from arresting me. They just didn't have anyone else to arrest so they took me to the county jail, where they said they would hold me until the missing truck was found. Three days later they found the truck out of gas about 2 miles away from where it had been stolen.

The sheriff talked about detaining me for the summer because they needed someone to mow the grass, but couldn't think of anything to charge me with. It was much like my experience in Louisiana. I told him that if he let me outside to mow the grass that I would run away. The sheriff said that he would handcuff me to the lawnmower. I told him that he would be missing a lawnmower as well. The next day, I was not only released, I was also given a ride back to Minneapolis where I could get the parts I needed to restore my car back to running condition. Most of the damage was burned plug and ignition wires. The damage looked a lot worse than it was, but it did require a complete new wiring harness and plug wires.

One of my friends had an old '56 Oldsmobile that looked like crap, but ran well enough to get us up north and back. With my two buddies, Tom and Wayne, we headed out. When we got to Staples with the parts, the first thing I noticed was that some stuff was stolen out of my car. I asked about it and the police played dumb. I installed the parts and started the car. In the meanwhile, Tom had gone to get gas. When he didn't come back, Wayne and I went looking for him. We found him just as he was being handcuffed and put into a police car. He had decided to show off while coming out of the gas station by spinning his wheels and burning some rubber. Unfortunately, Tom didn't see the police car that he almost ran into. He didn't have a license and neither did I for that matter, so when they asked him for his drivers' license, they said he could go if he didn't have any prior charges. Unfortunately, he gave them his brother, Bud's name, who had some priors that Tom was unaware of, which meant Tom was going to jail. He was not completely doomed however, as we had just enough money to bail him out.

Back Up North

The next weekend we made it up north and it was good to see Chick again. She was 16 years old and I was 24. She was pregnant with my child and already had a 2-year old. I knew enough to leave her 15 year old sister alone but the fact that Chick already had a kid put her into a completely different category, in my mind. Rational thinking, right?

My mom was also pregnant at the time and she was having some complications that caused her to be hospitalized in Mahnomen. When I got home, Chick and I went to see her. Of course, on our way out of town I stopped for a 12 pack. I let Chick drive, while I sucked down some brews. We were on a gravel road doing about 60 or 70 when Chick lost control of the car. We hit the ditch sideways. I grabbed her and pulled her down in the seat as we rolled over a couple of times and then flipped end for end. We landed right side up with the top pushed down almost level with the seats.

She was hanging halfway out the door with a look of horror on her face. I asked if she was all right. She said yes and then started crying and she pointed to my face. I had a few cuts that were kind of deep but not serious. A lot of blood can make a head wound look worse than it really is. Strangely, I was still holding the can of beer.

We got out of the car and started walking down the road while I finished my beer. About a mile or so down the road, someone stopped and picked us up and gave us a ride to Chick's cousin's house. I got into the tub and she cleaned up my wounds.

I sold my car for junk and bought a '55 Oldsmobile with a conversion stick shift and a bad clutch, but what can you expect for $25? The next day we were on our way back to Minneapolis. I had Wayne drive since Wayne was the only one with a drivers' license. The problem was, Wayne didn't have a very good sense of direction, so when I woke up, we were about 100 miles off in the opposite direction. But once I got him back on track, we made it back home without further incident.

On my next trip up north, I asked Chick's mother and father if we could get married. They gave us their blessing and we headed for South Dakota to get married. I had an ex-wife and two children in Fargo, North Dakota. I now had a pregnant second wife in northern Minnesota, a two-year-old stepson and a large family network.

Chick's two-year old son's name was Oscar, named after her dad and her brother. Man, was he a brat! I couldn't wait to get him to myself so that I could whip him into shape. I think for the first few months I was very mean to him, but it wasn't very long until I loved him just like he was my own. He was a good kid; he just hadn't been given any parameters.

Bill and Rollin

Our new little family headed to Minneapolis, where I met two of Chick's cousins, Bill and Rollin. They would turn out to be a very big part of the next few years of my life. When I met Bill, Rollin was in the workhouse doing time for assault.

The assault happened one afternoon up north when Rollin, Bill, and this white guy they called "Brown" walked into a bar in the small town of Lengby. Understand that Rollin and Bill are Chippewa

Indians. They were playing pool, when four or five of the local redneck white boys came in and wanted the pool table. Rollin calmly told them to wait a minute as they were almost finished. One of the guys walked over and started pushing the balls into the pockets. Then he placed both hands on the edge of the table as he leaned towards Rollin with a smirk on his face that said "I dare you to do anything about it." The story goes that Rollin smiled at him, then broke his pool cue into three pieces as he smacked the kid in the mouth with the heavy end of the pool cue. The kid went down and the fight was on.

Brown was a little on the yellow side and took off out the back door to get the car while Rollin and Bill cleaned house. They were out-numbered six to two, but those boys could fight. They got away but were picked up later and arrested for assault. Brown and Bill got off, but the judge felt sympathetic towards a kid with mangled lips and a wired jaw and gave Rollin workhouse time.

There was another brother, Steve, doing time in St. Cloud, I don't remember for what. Chick was very close to Bill so we saw him quite often. I heard a lot of things about Rollin from Bill before I finally got to meet him. From all the stories I had heard, I sort of expected Rollin to be an intimidating bad ass. I was surprised when he turned out to be a clean-cut, slightly overweight, highly intelligent, good-natured person. I liked him.

When Rollin got out of jail, he teamed up with Brown and Bill again. The three of them were living quite large off the spoils of burglaries around the neighborhood until their brother Steve, who had just gotten out of jail, got busted and sent away again. About that time, Brown just disappeared.

Chick and I were not doing so well. I was having trouble holding down a job between the drugs I had started using and the booze. I did very well everywhere I worked; I caught on to things but just got bored real fast. Then there was the fact that I kept waking up with hangovers depending on what drugs I was using. Sometimes, I hadn't been to bed all night. We were living in a crappy apartment in a crappy part of town and I was working in an even crappier part of town as a service station mechanic. I was making just above minimum wage. By now, Chick had given birth to another boy who she named Randy Jr. We didn't have a bed or a refrigerator and cooked on a single burner hot plate. The place looked pretty much like a trash can. Our sleeping quarters consisted of a beat-up couch that pulled out into a bed. That was what I provided for my 17 year old wife, our infant son, and a two year old.

Once again, I was getting desperate and tired of my current situation. Can you guess where this is going? I think the phrase "Some guys never learn" applied directly to me at this stage of my life. While I had previously blamed Gloria and her family for our marriage troubles, I was now in the middle of another mess that looked exactly like the last one. I still wasn't ready to look at why this dysfunctional pattern was happening. I was numb. I was trying to survive life the only way I knew how. I was into drugs, sex, and alcohol. Those three things consumed any common sense I might have had. Every day was hopeless and rolled into the next. Pretty soon my life was such a blur that I didn't care about anything or anyone. Including myself.

Processing Pain

One of the misconceptions that healthy people beat "losers" with, is the selfish stick. How many times have you heard someone referring to a horrible situation and make some comment about how selfish the offending person is being? While it does appear selfish, I guarantee you that the "loser" doesn't even possess enough energy to put it to purposeful selfishness. The worst of situations are born out of desperation and the despondency of complete personal worthlessness. There isn't enough "self" left at the bottom, to even know how to benefit yourself. You are only trying to survive anyway you can. I am not suggesting that this behavior is okay, or that it doesn't completely destroy everyone in its wake. What I am trying to do, is give you some understanding and insight into the facts of why selfishness isn't the motivating factor when someone is completely out of control.

Beating the selfish stick on someone will produce feelings of guilt and shame, but I guarantee you, it will not suddenly snap them out of their funk. The problem goes a whole lot deeper. The foundational problem for me, was that I didn't have a clue how to process my own pain. If I couldn't handle my own pain or put it into words, or seek help, what do you think the chances were that I had a consciously selfish plan to abuse others and gain from their pain? I am not suggesting that we calmly look at all of the pain we have caused and say, "Well, I couldn't help it. What was I supposed to do?" There is always a right thing to do, and we need to take responsibility for the wrongs we have brought to others.

At this point however, our subconscious is driving our lives and completely overpowering any conscious efforts we might attempt. I am only sharing this insight because it took me years to understand this.

If you are truly trying to help someone scrape themselves off the bottom, look for the pain in their life and help them address that pain. Most likely this pain will be buried very deep, and its source was in years past. Pointing out all of the people they have selfishly hurt will not further their healing. (They will come to that themselves when they are strong enough to handle the emotions it brings.) The first step is to realize that old habits have to go and help this hurting soul believe that they have the power to change their situation. As long as any of us believe we are a victim of a situation that we can't change, we will never change it. The power for change is when we diligently pursue facts. Be ready to fight hard; you will no longer be able to numb your pain with any of your former vices. You will stand against the greatest pains in your past and present life.

You will need a lot of help and that is to be expected. There are many good resources, programs, and people to help you. In fact, if you have come to the place in your life where you realize that you have been going the wrong way and that you can do better, just think about having the life you want and then pay close attention to the people and opportunities that present themselves to you.

When you begin to excel, the people in your life who contributed to your misery will no longer have anything in common with you and will stop coming around as they are replaced by people who will inspire you to unimaginable achievements. What you cannot allow are any of the old habits to kick in. When you are closest to triumph, you are also the most tempted to return to whatever it is that you self-destruct with. You will come to the place where two choices exist. They will take you in two different directions. Choices always exist before you. Action that leads to good habits or bad. They never go away. They are with you forever. You have to find something to believe in that will carry you through to consistently make right choices.

I should know, as I was about to go lower than ever before with no idea, or thoughts of anything, but the bad habits that drove me.

Stealing

While my life was once again in shambles, I still wasn't close enough to the bottom to be honest with myself.

Rollin and Bill started coming around encouraging me to go out with them. I really didn't see where I had much to lose so we started prowling around at night breaking into cars, stealing whatever was of value in them. From there, we progressed to "bull rushing," which is the name of a robbery technique used to gain entrance into a motel or hotel room.

Here's the way it works; one person knocks on the door of any given room, pretending to be the building manager, messenger, UPS, or whatever fits the situation. When the door is opened just slightly, the other person takes a four or five foot run at the door, hitting it with his shoulder, putting all of their weight into it. This sends the surprised person behind the door flying across the room. From there, it's pretty easy for two people to overpower almost anyone, especially if they're dazed and confused.

Besides bull rushing, we would also go out and roll people that were coming out of the bars at the end of the evening. We burglarized motels stealing television sets. None of these things provided enough money to support one person, let alone two or three plus our families. It doesn't take a rocket scientist to figure out that our efforts, at this point, provided far below minimum wage at the risk of 5 to 20 year sentences for burglaries and robberies. If that isn't criminal insanity I don't know what is.

Consequences of Stupidity

It certainly isn't what I would call intelligent, would you? If you are into this kind of crap this may be a good time to rethink your current situation and consider some other alternatives before you forfeit your freedom for next to nothing.

If you're a family person, it would be a good time to consider the burden you will place on your family while you are behind bars, not to mention what it's going to do to you. I hope you don't think that your woman, or man, is going to wait for you, or that your children will remember you if they are young, or that they will respect you if they were old enough to understand that you considered your criminal behavior more important than their security.

You will think of all sorts of alternatives to the poor choices you made until it's tearing you apart inside and driving you crazy because you can't do a thing about the new circumstances you have created for yourself.

You will blame everyone and everything for your shortcomings.

You will become angry and frustrated and then you will tell yourself, "If I can just get through this one, I'll change my ways. I'll treat my family with love and respect if they will just hold on while I get through this."

Meanwhile, the love of your life starts making excuses why she can't come to visit and you know it's the beginning of the end, you become depressed and eventually accept the inevitable. Then you begin to teach yourself to become hard and callused to free yourself from the pain and the embarrassment of the foolish decisions you made and the consequences of stupidity.

The process I just described is actually the five phases that people go through before death. Denial, anger, bargaining, depression, and finally acceptance.

If you're out there breaking the law, I don't care how good you think you are at what you're doing. Don't think for one moment that you will never get caught. Because no matter what you think, the odds of never being caught breaking the law on a daily, or even weekly basis, are not very good.

Of course, if we were smart enough to figure that out, we wouldn't have put ourselves in that position in the first place, would we?

Christmas Hold Up

One evening while Rollin and I were out looking for scores he said, "Let's try something new." I asked him what he had in mind and he said, "Just follow me." We were driving Bill's car that night, which was a 1967 RT 440 Magnum convertible. It was yellow with a black top. We pulled up in front of a motel, parking about 50 feet beyond the front door. We left the car running and went into the motel. At the front desk, Rollin pulled a gun on the girl behind the desk. We demanded all the money from the safe. While Rollin was in the back room cleaning out the safe, a guest came in. I pulled a switchblade on him and relieved him of his wallet about the time Rollin walked back into the lobby with the girl at gunpoint. The guy I was robbing said, "Come on guys, it's Christmas!" I responded by taking all of the money out of his wallet, then handing it back to him saying "Merry Christmas."

We tied the two of them up in the back room. We're about to leave when someone else came in. This time it was a cop. We got the drop on him and handcuffed him to something in the back room, took all of his money, which was not much, and left.

When we came out of the motel, I thought for a moment "How did the car get in front of the door?" But we were in a big hurry and I didn't give it much more thought as I jumped in on the passenger side and Rollin jumped behind the wheel. He put the bag of money between the seats on his side. Then we realized that the car we were in was a four speed. Bill's car was an automatic! We were in the wrong car. In a panic, we looked over the hood to see an exact same model, right where we had left it running. As we jumped out, the sack split open and money spilled out between the seats. We grabbed as much of it as we could, ran to our car and left. It was a scene from "Dumb and Dumber." I have no idea how much money we left between those seats, but the car no doubt belonged to the guy who I had wished a Merry Christmas.

This new career choice seemed to be much more profitable. We started robbing hotels, motels, and bars as though it was a regular job. Rollin and I robbed as many as nine motels in one night. There was one motel that we use to rob fairly often because we always knew how much money we were going to get. For some reason, it was pretty much always the same. We weren't smart enough to figure out that the larger part of the money was probably hidden somewhere and the $300 that we usually got was a diversion. The motel was run by an elderly man and his wife. One night we came back to rob them and there was a chain-link fence around the motel and a sign on the locked gate instructing people after 8 p.m. to register at the police station across the street. That was the end of that "job."

Each time we went out to rob people, we spent a couple of hours drinking to steady our nerves and increase our confidence. Or you might say, increase our stupidity.

After a few robberies, Chick, the kids and I moved into a better part of town and into a nicer apartment with a bed, stove and a refrigerator. Right after I moved, Rollin and Bill were picked up for burglary. Rollin got a year in the workhouse, and Bill was out on bond. With Rollin serving time, I stopped my criminal activities, and went to work down the street from where I lived. I was again a mechanic in a service station, but this time I made better money.

One evening Bill and his wife came over and offered the title to his '67 RT convertible for all the money I had on me, which was only $52. He wanted to leave town because he had to appear in court the next day on the burglary charge that Rollin was already serving time on.

He took my $52 and left town on a Greyhound bus.

Now I had a nice car. But then Chick ran a red light and T-boned a taxicab. I had it repaired and even repainted it black with lace and web, diamond dust and flames. It was a sight to behold! It kind of reminded me of the Bat mobile with the top down. Not that my senses were all that keen, as I was drinking a lot and doing a lot of drugs too. True to form, my job didn't last long at the service station before I was canned.

There was a guy that lived down the hall from me by the name of John J, who had just come back from Vietnam. John had been a sergeant in the Army and was highly decorated including the Purple Heart and Bronze Star for bravery. His platoon was charging up a hill under heavy gunfire and John was hit in the shoulder. He stopped to pick up a wounded soldier and put him on his shoulders to carry him up the hill to safety. John's shoulder wound was so severe that he was discharged and sent home. The way John tells it, he stopped and picked up the fallen soldier to protect himself from the hail of bullets. He said his Purple Heart was certainly warranted, but it was of little comfort, since they were being given out for blisters on soldiers' feet. Still, he was an interesting character and I remember him well.

John and I teamed up on a few jobs, one of which was to burglarize the service station where I used to work. Knowing where everything was, John went in through a window that we broke and came out with some money and a Colt 32 automatic, which we used to pull a job up north.

I did a couple more jobs with John before I realized that he was a real loose cannon. He wanted to hurt people, to shoot them needlessly.

I stopped running with him. I was doing some real bad things, but I had no desire to have part in cold-blooded killing.

One night, he came to me wanting me to go on a job. It was a good thing I declined. He found someone else to go with him and got busted just like I predicted. He got 20 years and was sent away to Stillwater State Penitentiary.

I pulled one job with one of Chicks brothers and a brother in-law but that didn't net us much money and I never worked with them again.

Shortly after that job, Simon Lee (Chicks brother) was home from duty in Viet Nam. He and I went out looking for a score, when he side swiped a car. Instead of stopping, he floored it and the guy took off after us. We skidded around a corner, plowed into a tree, jumped out and started to run. The Colt 32 automatic that I had stolen from my old boss at the service station was under the dash board of the car, but when we hit the tree, the gun flew onto the floor. It was confiscated and returned to its rightful owner, good old Fred. Simon's wrecked car was impounded.

I was badly in need of money at the time, as my car needed brakes and an alternator and I couldn't afford either, so I offered to sell Simon my car for $1000. He gave me $100 down and then borrowed it to go up north for the weekend. I had a new job at an ammunition plant and needed the car back by Monday so I could go to work. Monday came and went and no Simon.

Four days later, at about two o'clock in the morning, Chick's sister and brother-in-law knocked on my door. Through the peep hole I could see something was wrong because of the look on their faces.

They had found Simon and his girlfriend out in a clover field in the backseat of my car gassed to death.

We all went up north and buried Simon. Then I went out into the field, picked up my car and drove it back to Minneapolis. Shortly after that, I traded it for a Buick Electra 225.

Becoming a Mean Idiot

At this point, Rollin got out of the workhouse and we teamed up again drinking and doing robberies. Once in a while, we would drink to the point where I felt mean and I really did want to hurt somebody. We usually robbed bars just before closing time when everyone was inebriated. Drunks can be counted on to be stupid and do stupid things in the face of danger. We generally got to pistol whip a few people or kick the crap out of someone who tried to play the hero.

By this time in my criminal career, I was obsessed by the feeling of power with a 357 Magnum in my hand. We were living fairly well. I always had a nice car and lived in a decent dwelling. I had a constant supply of dope and booze so there were friends dropping in to get blitzed and listen to the loud music of that time. It was 1970. The popular albums were Cream, Led Zeppelin, Frank Zappa and the Mothers of Invention, Chicago, Crosby, Stills, Nash and Young, Grand Funk Railroad, and Santana, just to mention a few. Pretty much anything I wanted. If I didn't have the money for it, I would go out that night and steal it or rob for the money to buy whatever I wanted.

By this time, my daughter Jody was born. I was almost completely and utterly lost between drugs and alcohol. I didn't have any consideration at all for all five of my children or Chick. Chick said something to me one day and I pulled a gun on her and held it to her head. I did mean things to her and said mean things to her often. I didn't treat her with an ounce of respect or consider the safety and security of my children for a single moment. I was a selfish, self-centered, irresponsible, drug addicted, drunken, angry mean idiot.

I had become a loose cannon.

One weekend, I had been playing in a country western band in a low class dive bar in Minneapolis. I couldn't fit all of my drum set into my car at the end of the night, so I left part of them until the following Monday. When I came back for my stuff, some of my equipment was missing. I lost my temper and pulled a gun. When I fired a shot, everyone in the bar hit the floor. I ran out the back door, jumped in my car and left.

Rollin came over one evening, and wanted me to go with him to do a job but I declined because I had other plans. The next day, I was informed that Rollin had been caught in the act of robbing a motel by himself and was in jail. I felt pretty good about the fact that everyone around me was getting caught and I wasn't. That was short lived.

Busted

It all came to an end for me one morning when I received a call from the main office to the complex where I lived. The manager wanted me to come down and straighten out some discrepancy concerning my rent. I had paid a month or two in advance and I thought maybe that was the confusion, as he wasn't used to people paying in advance. As soon as I pulled up in front of the office, I knew something was wrong. But, it was too late. A man stepped in front of my Buick Electra 225 and pulled a Dirty Harry 44 magnum out and pointed it at my head telling me to keep my hands on the steering wheel.

A few days before we were arrested, Rollin's wife was laying up in bed with another man. Rollin walked in, jerked him out of bed and threw him out into the snow without any clothes. His wife retaliated by telling the police what Rollin and I had been up to in the past year. He was being watched until he made his move. They didn't know who I was, but they had my name and told him that they already had me in custody and that I had already told them the whole story some of which they repeated. Only it wasn't my story. It was his wife's story and he bought it thinking it was me. Rollin got 20 years for aggravated robbery and I got five years for simple robbery. I guess that's the difference between getting caught in the act, or after the fact. Then it was quite obvious that Rollin had a longer criminal history than mine in Minnesota.

We did get around to talking, one day, about how he had fallen for an old trick that landed me in prison with him. I know he felt bad but I let him know it was okay.

I had done time before, this was somehow different. I think a lot of it had to do with Chick and the fear of losing her. I became very depressed and ended up on thorazine and valium in the intensive care unit of the Stillwater State Penitentiary.

Stillwater

I used to hold my breath every time a name and number was called for visit, hoping it would be my name and number called to visit with Chick, it rarely ever happened and before long, she didn't come to see me at all.

This may be a good time to mention that I have a very dark complexion with kinky, curly dark brown hair. The Mexicans mistake me for Mexican, the blacks mistake me for black and though I have blue eyes I can pass for Native American. I am not at all sure what my true nationality is although I know I am part Indian on my mothers' side and German on my father's side. There may be some black somewhere, I don't know, or possibly even Mexican. All I know, is that I can easily pass for four different nationalities. It suited my needs to be Indian at this time. This enabled me to be a part of the Indian folklore group in prison. It also meant that Chick and I could actually meet unsupervised for an unauthorized conjugal visit. I think Chick made it up to see me once.

Losing Chick

I should have known this would be the case. I treated her like crap and yet I expected her to care about what I wanted. When I was in the county jail, a friend gave her money to bail me out, but she spent the money on something else, and left me in jail. I'm sure it wasn't very long before she found someone else to sleep with and that thought was destroying me. She never once brought the kids up to see me in the seven years that I was in Stillwater.

Looking back, as I do today, and remembering the hardships that I put her through, and the way I treated her when we were together, not to mention leaving her with three children to raise at the age of 18, I should be thankful that she ever came to visit me at all. I've never been the type of man to physically abuse a woman, but I obviously had no problem with mental abuse. Chick was really a good kid and didn't deserve a loser like me to come into her life, shake her up and then leave her without a crumb. Is it any wonder why she kept those kids away from me? What possible good could I have been in their lives while in my present state of mind? Maybe her motives were nothing more than revenge. If that indeed is the case, then I'm very sorry that I caused her to be consumed by such an angry emotion.

There are many things that I would change, if only I could go back in time and change them. But Chick and her children were unfortunate victims of the collateral damage I caused along my destructive path.

I am not excusing her part in our relationship; I am only taking responsibility for mine and offering this statement as an apology, so that I might become free of the guilt that I have carried for all of these years.

I would hope that this is also a good opportunity for Chick and my children to find forgiveness in their hearts and become free of some of the animosities that restrain them from the pursuit of their own peace of mind.

I knew so little about true love at the time. I am sure it was my ego causing most of my depression when I first got to prison.

In fact, being apart from Chick and the kids was a situation I had become used to. The fact that I couldn't imagine life without them was actually some sort of selfish insecurity. I don't doubt that I loved them. Love and relationships that are not built on a strong foundation are overpowered by selfishness. Part of me knew that I deserved this prison stay, as I was completely responsible for my present circumstances. I punished myself severely by surrendering to emotions I did not fully understand. I started by sinking into a deep depression for several months. Finally, I found the strength and courage to change my mind and go on without Chick. I fully realized that we were done as a couple. She didn't want anything to do with me and I was ready to let her go and move on with my life.

Prison Life

While in ICU, I was introduced to another girl by the name of Pat. She was introduced to me by another inmate and although Pat was white, she was still welcomed by the Indian folklore group. When she visited, she provided drugs for me. She brought me both speed and weed. We also had a couple of conjugal visits before we parted company.

I was no stranger to prison life, and was soon assigned a job in industrial welding. I welded parts for manure spreaders and grain wagons. In no time at all, I became very good with a stick welder; then I moved up to wire feed welding. I learned that very quickly and operated other pieces of equipment used to make parts in our shop. Wire welding doesn't produce nearly the intense flash of stick welders so I was able to use a welding hood with a large glass just slightly stronger than sunglasses. One day, someone on the other side of me was trying to burn a hole in a huge piece of steel with a carbon arc rod and he wasn't having much luck. I offered my assistance and took over. I didn't have a problem getting the job done.

However, that evening it felt like someone had set my eyeballs on fire! There was a red square area on my face that had a second degree burn caused by the flash of the carbon arc rod which had burned me through the weak wire feed helmet lens. The next day my eyes were matted shut and I was unable to see at all. The pain was terrible. I was admitted to the prison hospital and given synthetic morphine for pain.

Being an addict, I liked that. I didn't care what they gave me as long as it took away my pain. I think a lot of medical training was done at the prison hospital and that we were used for guinea pigs. They used prisoners for experiments of a new technique, new medications and training. After all we were expendable.

Nose Job

Ever since that car accident on interstate 29 when I was back in Fargo, my nose had been flat and wide, causing me to look blacker than ever. Not that appearing black was a problem for me, as it actually gave me the opportunity to experience some of the hardships that minorities experience. My only regret was that I had to experience the hardships of minorities without being able to cash in on any of the many benefits that minorities receive. However, it may be a good thing. I really needed to learn how to depend on myself.

I didn't like the way my nose looked, so I made it my mission to get it fixed. My main reason for a nose job was because I did look better with a straight nose. I managed to convince the prison doctor to schedule a plastic surgeon to fix it.

A week later, I was scheduled for surgery where the idea was to operate on me while under sodium pentothal. By removing a bone from my hip, they would replace the bone in my nose. When I woke up, I was surprised to discover that I really couldn't walk very well because of the bone removal from my hip. All in all, the operation went alright, and I recovered without any problems, although the operation didn't really change the condition of my nose all that much.

My buddy in crime, John, was still serving time on that 20 year sentence when I got to Stillwater. We got together a few times in the weightlifting room and in the band rooms where he, a few other guys and myself, harmonized singing Motown songs.

A couple of times I got on the Stillwater stage and did some country-western that the audience seemed to like. I played drums now and then but I really wasn't very good compared to a lot of other people who were there. I had always loved music though and it gave me something positive to do with my long days.

Test Scores

I still attended groups and programs that were popular at that time, trying to find a way to better myself. I was always fascinated by the psychologists, psychiatrists and other group leaders who ran the programs. I envied them and their intelligence and wished that I could be like them. They were always saying clever things that helped people to understand their problems and how to make them better. I wanted to do that too. But for someone as illiterate as me, that seemed not very likely to ever happen.

Part of the orientation for new inmates is to be given an IQ test. My IQ score was in the low 90s. Average is 100, so yet again, I was below average. I could read but not very fast. My spelling was then and is now, atrocious. I can't spell atrocious without Spell-Check. My vocabulary is actually above average, but what's the use if the people you wish to communicate with can't understand what you are saying? On the other hand, if I were ever to be tested for common sense and you scored it like an IQ test score, I would have tested in the genius level, although I hadn't displayed much evidence of it in my early years.

It still bothered me that I was considered below average, so in 1972, I took the GED test. I was absolutely shocked when I came in from work one evening and found the test results lying at the foot of my bed with the rest of the mail that had been delivered to me that day.

I was afraid to open the envelope and reveal the results that I was sure that I would find. I had to muster my courage up to open it. I discovered that I had passed. The first word I read was "congratulations." I was in absolute disbelief and thought there had been some mistake. The next day, I checked with the education department and they assured me that I had, indeed, passed the GED test. The first person that I thought of was my sixth grade teacher who put me down in front of the entire class by saying that I would never amount to anything. The feeling wasn't, "I guess I showed you." The feeling was more of an apology for being such a poor student. Teaching was her life and I wanted her to know that I remembered her when I achieved something great and that she was a part of my success, even though her statement years ago helped to convince me of something that was not true.

I continued on with my educational pursuits and in 1973, was awarded an actual high school diploma from the Grace Fridley High School in Minneapolis. You must realize the importance of this accomplishment for me. It was a very motivating step in the process of changing my subconscious self-image.

Work Release
Eighteen months had passed and I went before the parole board and was released to a work release program. They set me up to stay in the Hennepin County Jail at night and work during the day at a Midas muffler shop installing mufflers and brakes on vehicles.

I had an Amicus sponsor by the name of Duane Olson. Duane had a wife and two young boys and worked for Univac at that time. Duane helped me secure work and get adjusted. The first weekend that I got off I went over to see Pat, the girl who visited me in prison.

It seemed the safest place to go. We smoked some pot and had hours of sex and then she kicked me out the next day. We really didn't have anything going together, we just liked sex with each other, so it didn't bother me when she asked me to leave. From there, I went over to my sister-in-laws to see my kids. It was really good to see them again. They had grown a lot. I wasn't there very long before Chick showed up. Man, did she look good! She had always been a knock-out and I was still attracted to her. We were still married, but I really didn't know what to expect. We talked a little bit about superficial things. I think it was just as awkward for her as it was for me. She had some reefer, so we smoked a little bit and talked some more.

Then she invited me over to her house where we had sex a couple of times. When we were finished, it was time for me to report back to jail. Before I left, she told me not to tell anyone that we were back together again. I really didn't know what to make of that, but we made a date to meet again the next week, when she would let me take Randy and Jody to spend the night at my Amicus sponsor's house.

I no longer had a driver's license so I took a driver's test and passed. I asked my parole officer if I could use one of my Amicus sponsor's cars the next weekend. He said that I could, only if I had insurance. Well, what was I going to insure? I didn't even own a car. I don't remember what my parole officer's name was, but he was a pain in the butt. It seemed like he went out of his way to make things difficult for me.

I ended up walking about 5 miles one day, in subzero weather, to an insurance company so that I could procure a copy of an insurance policy that covered me driving someone else's car. Reluctantly, my parole officer gave me the okay to use one of Duane's cars. He saw something in me that I wasn't aware of. Because the way things eventually turned out, I could have avoided trouble if I didn't have transportation.

The next weekend I borrowed Duane's '64 Chevy and went to pick up Randy and Jody. I took the kids over to the house and Duane's wife watched them while Duane, his boys and I went to his curling club.

I have to tell you that is the most boring game I have ever witnessed! Just watching it was pure torture! I would rather have had a root canal! Before the game ended, I was just about to ask somebody for a can of gas and a match. Seriously, it wasn't that bad but I really didn't enjoy it.

The next day I took the kids back to Chick. She told me to meet her at an Indian bar over in north Minneapolis the next week. That was a big mistake.

More Criminal Insanity

The next week came around, and I borrowed Duane's car again to go over to the bar to meet Chick. It was about six o'clock in the evening when I got there. I sat down and drank a beer real slow while waiting. About seven o'clock an Indian, teenage band showed up. At about eight Chick showed up with her cousin Bill, a friend of his and an Indian girl that I had never met. After a few beers, I got up and sang a couple songs with the band and danced a few dances with the girl they had brought along. I was getting the feeling that she was there for me and that Chick was with Bill. Then I thought, "No, that can't be, they're cousins."

The guys and I made occasional trips from the bar out into their car, where they had a quart of whiskey that we were sucking on. It didn't take much of that stuff before I was blitzed. I have no recollection at all of leaving the bar. I vaguely remember waking up in the car thinking that I had been locked out of the house. I punched out a window and in the process almost cut my thumb off. The next thing I remember is being picked up by some Indians who took me to the hospital where they sewed my thumb up and put my hand in a cast because the tendon in my thumb had been severed. I don't know how I ever found Duane's car, but I did. The keys were in the ignition, so I started it up and headed for Chicks house. When I got there, she was in bed with someone I had never even seen before. She told me that it was her new boyfriend. At this point, I really didn't give a crap about Chick and her relationships. I was more concerned about the damn cast on my hand. If I couldn't work, I was going to be sent back to Stillwater prison again. I got a hold of Bill and his buddy Chuck and had them follow me over to Duane's where I returned his car. He had been good to me so the least I could do was return his car. From there, I went to my place of employment at the Midas muffler shop to see if there was any way that I could continue working. The answer was as I expected. No. My next stop would be prison.

Take a look at my situation. I was heavy into alcohol and was doing drugs when I could get them. I was putting all of the same old toxins back into my life. I was feeling desperate.

I did not want to go back to prison, at any cost. While we can all take an accurate guess as to the path I was about to choose, do you wonder why I didn't stop to make the right choices. I can only say that I wasn't yet ready to bring to mind the dark, painful moments of my past and face them. I was still self-medicating. Sabotaging my own happiness with bad habits. I had some really good things going for me, yet, I wasn't focused on them. I had skills and had gained an education. Why couldn't I see that? I was so used to being a failure. I couldn't handle being healthy. I didn't even know what that would look like.

So, I continued on with what I knew best of all, the negative people and all the crap that comes with those people I knew that I didn't want anything to do with prison. I thought that I had no power to stop what was happening. It seemed to me that my life was happening to me, instead of the fact that I was creating it.

With escape being my top priority, I was about to get myself into another bad situation as I progressed in the world of criminal insanity.

On The Run

Chuck and Bill had just burglarized a gun shop up north and had a trunk load of weapons and ammunition.

As if performing some type of ritual, they presented me with my very own, brand-new Smith & Wesson 357 Magnum. I had Bill cut the cast off of my right hand, so that I could handle my newly acquired weapon. They each had the identical weapon to mine. We were ready for action.

I had not reported to the county jail, so now I had to live on the run. I couldn't stay anywhere the police might look for me, so I stayed close to Bill and Chuck. I had my suspicions about Bill sleeping with Chick, but since he also had a girlfriend he was living with, I let it go for the time being. Chick also had a boyfriend, so between the two of them I couldn't prove anything. Besides, I needed a place to be and with Chuck dating Chick's sister, the four of us piled into Bill's girlfriends house.

We'd hide out during the day and go out at night doing robberies.

One of the robberies was a bar where we robbed the ticket stand. A slightly inebriated kid in the hallway was arguing with his girlfriend when he got into Chuck's face. Chuck was not a person to trifle with whether he had a gun in his hand or not. Without a gun he was downright mean and could hold his own in any fight. With a gun in his hand, he was deadly and he would bust a cap on you in a heartbeat. Knowing this, Bill stepped in between the two of them and backed the kid off before he got himself killed.

The next job we did was a motel in Carver County. We not only robbed the front office, we took the keys and robbed everyone in the units. It was on this job that I got to experience first-hand some of Chuck's rage. There were two guys and a girl, all in their late 20's, in the manager's room when we pulled our guns. One of the guys tried to run. He made it to the window when Chuck leveled off and fired a round at him. Fortunately, Chuck was not a very good shot with a pistol and missed. The shot hit the window frame which caused the glass to shatter. The kid hit the floor and didn't make another move after that.

Seattle

That robbery gave us enough money to buy another car. We got an Olds 442 and left Minneapolis for Seattle, Washington. We paid for our trip by doing robberies all along the way.

We were just outside of Seattle, when Chuck asked me what a synchromesh transmission was. Bill was sleeping in the back and rather than explain the clutch system to Chuck, I thought I'd demonstrate. At about 85 miles per hour, I stepped on the clutch and shifted into a lower gear to show him that the gears wouldn't scrape. When I did, the clutch engaged by itself and exploded, scattering pieces of the clutch all over the highway. The back pressure was so great that it blew the oil stick out of the engine block and oil all over the top of the engine. Fortunately, the only thing destroyed was the clutch. So much for my high degree of common sense, huh? We got towed to a service station where I replaced the clutch with my sore right hand. We were on our way again.

Chuck had a sister living in the area and wanted to go and see her. Bill thought it was a bad idea and that we should stick to ourselves for the time being. There was an argument at one point so heated, that they stopped the car got out in the middle of the highway and started fighting.

So much for keeping a low profile. They finally made up and got back into the car. We went to a motel and the next morning Chuck took the car to pick up some cigarettes. He never came back. We were running out of money so we had to vacate the motel room. Bill called Chuck's sister and demanded to know where Chuck was. She said she didn't know, but Bill knew better, so he started telling Chuck's sister about some of the things that Chuck was in to. He told her about a guy that Chuck had shot in a robbery. (This was before I got into the mix.) I was totally unaware that Bill was saying anything to Chuck's sister as he just kept coming back telling me that he hadn't gotten a hold of Chuck yet.

Later that evening, we talked to a guy in a local bar and got a ride over to Chuck's sisters' house. When we pulled into the parking lot, we spotted our car. The guy dropped us off and we got into the car and tried to start it. It wouldn't start. The problem was the starter. My guess is that some wires were loose as the starter was removed in order to replace the clutch. Being a four speed stick, we could have still started the car if Chuck hadn't driven the car over the curb so that it couldn't be moved. We both laid down in the car waiting for Chuck. After a while Bill became restless and decided to go and knock on Chuck's sister's door. Again, I was totally unaware of what he was saying and doing. When she refused to tell Bill where Chuck was, he made threats on her life and then on Chuck's life.

The next thing I knew, I woke up seeing police with guns pointing at us from every direction. I was in the habit of sleeping with a 357 Magnum between my legs with my finger on the trigger. Bill had told me that if the cops ever cornered us that he wasn't going to prison. He would rather go down shooting. I said "Okay" because I really didn't care if I lived or died anyway. When I woke up and saw all those guns, I thought, "This is it." But then Bill started pushing guns in my direction like he had no intentions of dying. That changed everything. If he would've started shooting like he said he would, so would I, because I was certainly in the "I don't give a crap" zone. But instead, we gave up without a fight and were taken to the Snohomish County Jail, where we learned that Chuck had also been arrested after being given up by his sister.

After the smoke cleared, it was obvious that Bill had single-handedly caused all of us to be arrested because of his temper.

Back In Jail

I didn't have anything better to do, so I decided to get high and stay high for as long as I could. How do you do that when you're in a county jail where there are no drugs and you don't know anyone who can get you some? You pretend like you're strung out and they will give you drugs so that you won't die while coming down. I managed to stay high for a couple of weeks before they cut me off.

We spent about another week in Washington State before we were extradited back to Minneapolis to stand trial for a number of aggravated robberies. My get high scam worked so well in Snohomish County that I decided to try it in Minneapolis. This time it worked even better. They put me on the methadone program where I really got high.

The first charge was for the robbery at the bar where Chuck almost shot someone.

All the witnesses fingered Chuck and Bill but never said a word about me so the charges were dropped on me. The police officers who escort you to and from your cell and into the courtrooms, do not know the circumstances of your charges. When the charges were dismissed on me, the officers thought that I was free to go and didn't bother to handcuff me when we left the courtroom. I could have easily excused myself, saying that I needed to use the restroom and just left the premises. But I didn't. I didn't have anywhere to run or any means to get out of town without committing more crimes. I just let it go, thinking that maybe all I would get is a little more time on my five-year sentence for escaping the work release program. Unfortunately, Carver County had a hold on me and came to pick me up within a few hours after my victory in court. Carver County was where we had robbed the motel and all their guests.

Past experience reminded me that the best thing to do was to keep my mouth shut and not admit to anything. I would let my fate be decided by a jury.

The year was 1973. I thought it was kind of strange that the jail was full and yet I had a cell-block all to myself. I later discovered that I was alone because they didn't want to expose any of their local citizens to my violence. At the time, I didn't think of myself as violent although I know better now. (Definitely in a state of denial). What did they think I was going to do to someone? After all, I was not Hannibal Lector. I was just a young man that was self-destructing.

A Little Paperback Book

Then to add insult to injury, no one came to see me. No one wanted anything to do with me anymore. Not my mother, not my father, sisters, brothers, wife, kids, or people I once called friends. I was, for the first time in my entire life, all alone, becoming more and more depressed with each passing day. This was agony for me, as I had a deep rooted fear of being alone. Although it was an irrational fear, it had proven its hold on me through previous experiences. I didn't even have another inmate to talk to. Then, to make matters even worse, the crappy TV set self-destructed, leaving me with nothing to preoccupy my mind. My depression became worse and I begin to think of different ways of killing myself.

I finally got a visit from Duane, because he had a check from Midas for me. I asked him if he would buy me a television set with the money and he did.

There was a set of bars at one end of the cellblock where visitors were allowed to visit with inmates through the bars. Right in the center against those bars is where I set my new television.

One Sunday a clergyman came by to deliver the "word." I had absolutely no interest in anything he had to say, but I tolerated him anyway, right up to the point when he put his hands through the bars and accidentally bumped a paper cup full of water onto my television set shorting it out.

I became very angry and probably pretty violent. If I could have gotten my hands on him, I would have choked the living crap out of him. I called him every rotten word I knew and I knew a lot. To make things right, he offered to take the television set and have it repaired. My new TV was taken away.

Once again, I was all alone without any way to escape my depression. The sheriff became aware of it and started to do things like take me out of my cell and walk around with me outside. He said he realized that I could overpower him at will, but he trusted that I wouldn't actually try it. The thought never crossed my mind until he mentioned it. But, I really had no intentions of escaping.

He got a hold of someone from AIM (American Indian Movement) who came out to see me once and brought a carton of cigarettes. We talked a little, but I never saw him again. I think he didn't believe that I was an Indian, at least not a registered one. Finally, the sheriff had a psychologist visit me.

The psychologist was probably about my age, and he asked all kinds of stupid questions, to which I gave him stupid answers. All things considered, even though I was in desperate need of company, I didn't need this crap any more than I needed the clergyman's crap who destroyed my television set. Before the psychologist left, he pulled out a small paperback book. He handed it to me and asked me to read it between now and the next week when he would return. I thought, "Oh great. I have to endure another hour or so with this idiot." I said I would read it and tossed it aside as he left.

I went about my business the following day. I had nothing to do, so I spent my time thinking of clever ways of killing myself. One of the ways required waiting for my television set to come back. With it, I would be supplied an extension cord that would be plugged in to an outlet located outside of the cell block. If I stripped the wires and dumped water on a blanket on the floor I could easily electrocute myself.

So, that was the plan I was going with, and now all that was left to do was wait for my television set to come back.

There wasn't a soul to talk to and absolutely nothing to do. I kept picking up the book and looking at it. It looked boring so I threw it back on the table. I did this many times, until I finally picked it up and thought, "What the heck! I don't have anything better to do until that television set comes back, so I'll read a little." The name of the book was "Psycho Cybernetics," by Maxwell Maltz. He was actually a plastic surgeon, who had become fascinated by personality changes after surgeries that altered the appearance of his patients.

I can't remember just how much of the book I read, but one important paragraph helped to change my life forever, making things possible that I had only dreamed of.

Imagined Reality

The paragraph said, "The human nervous system cannot tell the difference between a real or an imagined experience; whatever you think or believe to be true, your nervous system reacts accordingly." In other words, you really can convince yourself of almost anything. It's a matter of what you think. Thoughts change your mind and eventually your reality. The more intensely you think about something, the more intensely it will change your life. With this knowledge I thought, "I don't really have to serve time here in this cell. I can actually be anywhere I choose and experience what I want."

There were so many possibilities that I couldn't wait to try them all.

I was like a kid in a candy store for the first time and I have been this way ever since. I had been reacting to real and imagined experiences my entire life. It had never occurred to me that what I thought about actually worked its way into my reality. What if I was able to control my life and have it be what I wanted?

It never occurred to me that I had control over my future. For whatever reason, I was living as though I wasn't making my own choices. I had believed that my life was just happening. What a discovery to actually glimpse the knowledge that I could get out of life what I wanted if I put the right things in. I am still thrilled over this just as much as I was back in 1973. I still can't get enough knowledge! And as I focus my thoughts, my understanding seems to become simpler all the time.

But I had only just begun a journey in a new direction. I had a long way to go and many obstacles to overcome before I was to come to these simple understandings.

This certainly wasn't the end of my hardships, but this did have a promise of becoming the beginning of a better life. It appeared to be a step into a new direction that could eventually lead me to where I wanted to go.

I believe that nothing happens without a reason. People make things happen. I also believe that people are connected to each other telepathically and are compelled to rescue one another when called upon. I think this happens a lot and on a level that is too deep to put into words. My suicide attempt was a call to a power much greater than any one of us, yet a part of all of us. Although I did everything I could to prevent my recovery from happening, something more powerful than me was at work making it possible for me to pick up that book and read it. The kind sheriff, Duane, the clergyman, and the psychologist were all directly involved with me reading that book. Years previous, Maxwell Maltz, authored it. The line of people getting those pages into my hands is remarkable.

I want to stay away from things that I can't explain and some things just can't be put into practical words. So I will ask you to do some of your own quality thinking to draw your own conclusions. It is also important that you test what I am saying, whether or not it is true.

There is no formula for life. But in a way, I'm offering you a way of formulating your thoughts. You can try and see if it works for you. This may stretch your mind. Because of habits you may resist it. Or you just may not understand. But because you don't understand something doesn't mean that it's not true or that it doesn't work.

Think about it.

In order to experience what you desire, you have to look for it and then believe it once you see it. It's sort of been there all along, just on a different level than you are used to understanding. Good things will happen. Help will come. You just need to keep looking in the right direction.

I believe that we are all connected to each other in a mind blowing circle. I bet you have a ton of questions for me, such as, "Can this happen to us when we don't know anything about it?" Yes, we don't have to completely understand something, although we do have to be willing to learn something new.

Another thought that will make you scratch your head, is "How does this happen when we are not aware of it?" Most often, another human being will bring truth into our path. As mysterious as this may seem, I can assure you, that there isn't anything mysterious about telepathic communications at all.

We do it all the time with each other on a subconscious level. The really interesting thing, is that every time we are in need and send out an SOS, it is someone else's goal to come to our rescue. In fact, this book is my mission and may very well be the answer to your SOS. If that is the case, then you can rest assured that this book was written just for you.

Now consider for a moment, everything and everyone that has been involved in the delivery of this book to you. It would most likely take years of research to uncover just how many people might be involved in just one small request and it would be equally as time-consuming to determine how long ago the solution began to move towards us. We could guess or spend our time analyzing our lives. This much I can tell you; the answers to all of our questions, and the solution to all our problems have been available to us long before we become aware them. The answer to everything is all around us all the time, but we need to ask a question before the answer can make itself known and our minds have to be open to any way the answer may appear. I often say that people who are looking for something specific will always find it, because they will recognize it however it appears to them as they keep an open mind. In this respect, patience is required. Not that it takes so long to come to you, but because it may take some time for you to see it.

When you finally "see", you may realize that it's been there all along but you were not aware of its presence. This experience should be sufficient evidence that we all have the answers to every question we have now or will ever have and that we need each other to remind us of where and how to find the answers. Tangible things that we want, need, and desire, in our lives, come to us the same way, but on a different level. Whatever it is in life that you want, or want to become, you can set out to discover, but I can guarantee that you will not find what you are looking for if you never look. I can also guarantee that nothing new will come to you if you are not ready, in some sense, to change your perspective of things right now. You have always had the ability to accomplish anything that you desire without harming another living soul. I want to be very specific in the fact that I am not proposing any of this for you to hurt others or for you to abuse anyone. I am trying to show you how you can completely revolutionize your life and make choices that bring peace and purpose to your life.

I know how hopeless and bleak life can look. I lived many years in the dark under lies and misconceptions. I didn't look for help, nor did I recognize the good people who had tried to help me. There are many more good people out there than bad. In fact, there is a whole network of people out there whose purpose in life, at any given moment, is to be instrumental in making those things happen that will assure your success. By doing so, they are realizing their own personal goals. I'm not making this stuff up! This is really and truly the way everything works and why we all need each other.

Mistakes? They are just part of the process of moving forward in life. Maxwell said our mind works much like a computer that gropes its way to a given goal by a series of trial and errors in order to reach the goal of your vision.

For instance, when I learned how to juggle three balls. I can't tell you how many times I dropped the balls before I was able to train my brain to release that third ball into the air and actually juggle them.

The only mistakes that are not very beneficial are the ones that you don't learn anything from, the ones you repeat over and over without progress.

I am quite certain that there are a few things we just have to take on "faith," even though we do not understand them yet. Life is a wonderful mystery.

Some of you may be thinking that God is behind all this. I do believe in God, but maybe not the way so many different religious beliefs and books like the Bible describe God. I believe God is the Truth behind everything. Certainly, my view of life must line up with what is true, right and just. If these ideas are just human inventions and imagination and not based on the real truth, then they are not worth much.

When Things Go Wrong

When things in our life are going horribly wrong and we can see no way out, we still long for something to change and make it all better. We ask for help and pray. Or we get depressed and wallow in our misery. We take positive action or negative. Either way, people show up to help, don't they? I don't believe that's a coincidence.

We don't need to understand this to believe it. I don't fully understand. But I've found it to be true.

When we are really down, we tend to drive some people away. But at the same time, other people are drawn to us. They are motivated to help. They show compassion. The ones we push away may cause more depression and frustration. But when we pay attention to those who show up to help us, we have the opportunity to be rescued if we open our minds and accept who and what comes to us. I fought everyone and everything for years until I was at the very bottom of my life with no fight left wanting my life to end. It was then that I found myself in the deepest, darkest place of my life with nowhere else to go, my mind empty of any thoughts, good or bad, that I acquired the capacity to discover then as I discover each and every day since that moment, that there are only two simple choices that we are always free to make. Either we give up and let the facts of our circumstances predict our destiny or we subscribe to the limitless world of possibilities that are yet to be imagined by each of us and begin to create from those possibilities the world we choose. We don't need to know the chain of events that will cause our dreams to come true. We just need to believe and trust that what we need to realize our desires will show up in our reality when we choose to pay attention to our desires in place of our circumstances. Isn't it the worst disasters that often bring out the best in all of us? We are not bad people. We are people who sometimes do bad things. If it were not for those undesirable things, we would not know the difference between what we want and what we don't want. Once you know the difference it's up to you to choose your own personal way.

Our struggles and hardships are usually the result of false information that we have taken in, digested and made part of our lives. The world is full of lies and false information. With effort, however, we can rise above it.

It's not something that we can work on now and then when it's convenient. That's an important point I'm trying to emphasize here. It's a way of life that we work at for all of our life, striving for perfection while discovering that unlimited happiness is a choice. We either choose to be happy or unhappy with every passing second. With all the noise and confusion of the world we often get lost. But in your heart there is a compass. Dig it out and look at it. Where does it point? It points to the true dreams of your heart. Keep your eyes on it. Pay it close attention. It will keep you on track. I still get distracted and pay attention to things that serve no greater good, but not like I once did. It's a work in progress that I have yet to overcome. I still get tangled in the negativity of the world. I am certainly better than before and I get better all the time, but I am still struggling with many of the same things as you.

The real difference is that I know that no matter what negative thing happens it will pass and become positive again. I also know to expect that things will happen both positive and negative as every cause has an effect. Understanding this gives me a feeling of security. Life isn't a matter of chance. It's about choices.

This Journey

My hope is that you will begin to take charge of your world by taking control of your thoughts. Peace of mind is only a thought away.

First you need to take responsibility for your own actions. This was the first crucial step for me. I realized that I would never be free to move forward and create the life I desired if I didn't take full responsibility for myself and my actions. I had to admit to myself that I had come to this place in my life alone and that it was my poor choices that were responsible for my troubles. I cannot blame anyone or anything.

With your next step and every step that follows, you can begin to create a better tomorrow. By the choices you make you can realize unlimited possibilities. And you are not alone in this journey. There are many people who are drawn to you to help point you in the right direction. Receive their help with gratitude, because they have been sent for your benefit. But as you know, people can let you down. So always be ready to land on your feet. Stay with what is true for you. The Truth will never let you down.

This journey of life is not an easy one. You don't need me to tell you that! My life has been a lot like that box of crackers, all crunched and torn with crackers scattered around. Some of those crackers were lost forever. But here I am today, whole and mended. Scars are still there. But negative things did not keep me from seeing my dreams fulfilled. The same can be true for you. With your compass set on what you know to be true in your heart, you will eventually get to where your dreams are. Like me, you may have a piece of scotch tape holding you together here and there, but that's OK. Scars just remind us of how far we've come. For the most part, we are whole and content as we move in a positive direction.

In Prison

Nothing Glorious

After several court appearances and being fingered as one of the people that robbed the motel by three witnesses, two of which could not have possibly ever seen me and the other who had me confused with Chuck, the jury was sent out to deliberate. While I waited in my cell for the jury to come in, I wrote a letter to the sheriff and his wife thanking them for the way they treated me.

A copy of that letter appeared in the Pioneer Press in August of 1973. My last words were, "I don't know what the jury is going to decide my fate should be, but whatever they decide, I want to thank you for your kindness."

I was found guilty of aggravated robbery and aggravated assault and sentenced to 10 years for aggravated robbery and five years for aggravated assault. These sentences were back to back, meaning that I had to serve the time on one sentence before I could be paroled to the next. But first, I had to finish the time on the five years I was already serving for simple robbery and then I would serve time on the next two sentences. This was a lot worse than getting a 20 year sentence where I could actually be paroled within a matter of months. Chuck and Bill had also received their time, which was zero to 20 years.

Maybe I should have been more depressed than ever, but somehow I felt like I had been freed from a prison much more debilitating than the one with brick walls and iron bars that I faced. While it doesn't make much sense to anyone who is not an addict, being addicted to anything is the lack of control in that area. I was out of control and hated myself for it. So, even if my personal freedoms were taken away, it also meant that I wouldn't have to struggle with my own bad habits. I wouldn't have many choices to make and that was a relief.

Back in Stillwater, I was put in the "shoot" which is a holding area where they put you as they assign you to a cell. I was sitting there when the main prison psychiatrist walked by. He shook his head in disappointment and said that he didn't really think that I would be returning to prison, least of all within weeks of being paroled. I told him that I was ashamed of myself and that I was looking forward to learning something from the experience this time around rather than just doing time. He nodded his head as if to agree, but with obvious reservations.

I have thought long and hard about how I might describe the next four years of my life in the penitentiary without encouraging people to do something wrong. I find myself almost wanting to say "but don't try this at home." There is nothing glorious about being in prison. I had some terrible days there and those days forced me to deal with some of my demons. I came out a better man, but I want to be very clear with you about the fact that it would have been better to learn those lessons as a free man.

A Dangerous Place

People are intrigued by prison life. Dramatic movies are made about it. But no one seems to be able to make sense of it. Not even the people locked up there can really tell you accurately what it's like. They are constantly studying the system in order to gain an advantage and salvage the best possible outcome for themselves. And the people who run the prisons don't seem to have a handle on it. That goes from the politicians on down to the officers that walk the hallways. They don't really know how to deal with criminals. The whole prison system is a kind of failed system, in my opinion. It seems to be a breeding ground for exactly what it's intended to prevent.

And it is different from prison to prison and state to state. The changes come from outside the walls, beyond the chain-link fences and coils of razor wire. Whatever is happening on the streets of the free world is happening on a smaller scale in prison. The same racial conflicts, addictions, greed, mental illness, loneliness, ignorance and class struggles go on inside. Only, it's more intense because of the tight quarters. All these problems of society close in on you in prison.

Each prison is different, but one thing seems to remain the same: it's full of danger. Since it's all about locking up people who are dangerous to society, when you confine these people in a small space, people are going to get hurt. Some inmates are inside because of non-violent crimes and some for terrible violent offenses. Some are weak and some massively strong. Some wouldn't hurt a flea and some can't wait to bust your head. This mixture in this confined space means trouble. One guy with a hatchet will make a lot of chickens very nervous. When you're locked up with predators who are skilled at taking advantage of the weak, everyone is constantly in survival mode.

On the outside, in your quiet little neighborhood, you have your own space. You can establish a comfort zone and stay inside it. You stay out of certain neighborhoods and stay in the safety of your own crowd. In prison, however, dangerous predators live just a few feet away and are in your space and in your face every day

Even if you are not doing something that would cause you to need protection, if you are young and good looking your kiester is not safe from the predators in prison. Heck, you don't even have to be young and attractive, just being unprotected will get your butt ripped. I don't know how many times I have heard some young wana-be bad ass say that no one will ever have their way with them. Ha! They are always the first ones to be abused because they aren't smart enough to know that everyone needs protection.

When I first came into Stillwater it was extremely regimented. We stood with our hands on the bars at count and moved in single file where ever we went, quietly. Even so, it was a dangerous place. I saw a prisoner killed over a pack of cigarettes he was unable to produce after losing at a card game. Right there, I decided to never gamble in prison, even if I could pay up. You never know who will get pissed for whatever lame reason. So part of remaining safe is to stay out of potent situations.

When some inmates were threatened, they met violence with violence.

I have known a situation where a big bad ass was taken out by a skinny little runt who drove an ice pick- like weapon into his ear while he was sleeping.

Most of the people in prison are extremely dangerous. Not necessarily because they are aggressive, but often because they are scared. Even a coward will fight for his life when cornered.

Hodo

One of the many dangerous ones was a fella by the name of Hodo. On the surface, he would be the definition of a model prisoner. But underneath the calm exterior was a monster. My buddy El and I smoked dope with him on occasion and enjoyed some special food he smuggled from the kitchen where he worked. He'd prepare it in his cell using a prison issue, converted one-cup coffee pot for a hot plate. He didn't talk a lot but he did tell me that he was serving time for robbery and attempted murder. That was part of his sentence but not all of it. The part that he didn't tell was the part about the young girl he molested and murdered by stabbing her to death. Apparently she told the police about something he did. He also shot his robbery partner in the gut because he was going to go to the police and confess some things. He left his partner for dead.

El warned me he was dangerous and that it wouldn't take much to set Hodo off. But I thought El was over reacting. "No," El said. "I was doing a Tarot card reading for him and the death card kept turning up. The card actually fell out of the pack onto the table!"

OK, I know it sounds like hocus pocus, but what happened next might make you wonder.

There were several groups in prison that allowed people from the outside to attend. Hodo met a lady in her forty's who had three kids: a boy who was the oldest and two girls. After meeting Hodo, the woman fell in love with him, as some women with certain tendencies are prone to do, and they were married in prison. Hodo got out of prison about three years after I got out.

It was 1980. I was living in my new home in North Minneapolis. I was picking up some snacks at a convenience store in my neighborhood when I looked up and there was Hodo standing at the counter with a bag of chips in his hand. We had a good laugh, exchanged phone numbers and promised to get together soon. I left wondering if he had gotten his life together.

I got my answer two days later. I picked up the paper and saw his grizzly face in a mug shot under a headline. I read how he had shot and killed his twenty-one year old step son and an eleven year old step-daughter who had tried to hide. Then he raped and stabbed to death his sixteen year old daughter. He was more sick and more dangerous than when I knew him in prison. El, being the insightful person he was, figured that Hodo had been molesting the sixteen year old for some time when she finally told her brother who confronted Hodo. That set off the murderous rampage. Hodo's wife was not home at the time or she would have been killed as well. When she did come home she found Hodo sitting in a chair with the gun in his hand. She tried to talk him into putting the gun down but when she realized it wasn't going to happen, she made a break for it. Hodo scrambled from his chair and shot her as she ran down the sidewalk trying to get away. Luckily she was only hit in the hip. I shouldn't say she was lucky in any way. She had brought a violent child molester into her life who had robbed her of her innocent children. He took from her the dearest persons she had in this world. After that Hodo jumped in his car and fled. He was pulled over by Highway Patrol in Iowa, I believe. As the Patrolman unsnapped his firearm and approached the car Hodo shot himself in the head. It was a sad ending to a sad life.

Duane

One of the most unusual people I knew was Duane. He was one of the guys I made my attempted escaped with. He stood about 5'6"and weighed in at only 135 pounds, but it was all muscle. In a weight lifting contest he bench pressed 405 pounds! He was about twenty one and good looking. He reminded me of a modern-day small-sized Conan. He was doing twenty years for robbery and it looked like he was about to get out in 1975. He was head of one of the prison groups that invited outside guests. One of the guests was a Channel 4 television personality named Carlson. He met other members of the Carlson family and they sort of took him under their wing. He was pretty proud that he had a celebrity friend.

Duane was granted a furlough just before his parole board hearing that would determine the details of his release. While he was out he was invited into the Carlson's home where all went well. He returned to prison on time and went before the board thinking he was in good shape to get out. He had done what he could and we all were confident of his release. But parole boards have their own way of looking at things. He was turned down.

That didn't sit well with Duane. His patience had run out. He had always been a rebel, but after working so hard to change his direction, the board decision royally pissed him off. He spent most of his time in segregation after that because he was trouble. Twice he actually took hostages while in segregation.

In segregation there were three cells in each room that were let out for showers two times a week, one at a time and were brought back one at a time. On one particular day Duane woke up mad at the world. He was taken out of his cell for his shower and led down the tier. There was a steel guard rail along a stairs that led down into the showers. There was a small, glassed-in room we called the "bubble" where the guards could safely watch the shower area. Duane bounded over the rail with a shank clamped between his teeth and grabbed one of the guards before he could enter the bubble. Two other inmates who were showering tried to grab the other guards but they locked themselves in the bubble behind the thick glass window. Duane looked around and spotted a floor fan with a heavy metal base. He picked it up and started beating on the bullet proof glass of the bubble which was about six inches thick. The guards thought they were safe until cracks began to open up into a hole that Duane widened with each crashing blow of the fan. Afraid for their lives, the guards opened a hatch in the bubble floor and pressed themselves into a crawl space. Duane then entered and grabbed the security phone. He wanted the warden to know he had taken control of segregation, again. Then he found a couple gas canisters and began giving the guards down in the crawl space a taste of tear gas. They had to come out and face him.

Of course it didn't end well for Duane. He agreed to let the guards go if he could have some drugs. The officials finally gave him the drugs, but instead of releasing the guards, he passed out the drugs and some gas masks to the other inmates. Then he kept tormenting the guards with gas while he and the guys did drugs until they passed out.

The warden had reached his limit with Duane and had him transferred to a federal joint. On the way he over-powered the Marshals on a restroom break. Somehow, he had hid a sharp weapon in his butt. He grabbed the Marshal's gun and keys to the van. He was caught down the road after a shoot-out. After a short time in the federal joint, he got on the bad side of someone and was killed.

When a man like Duane gets to the point where he feels he has nothing to lose, he's a danger to others and to himself. To me, the Carlsons and to others who knew him, he seemed like a guy who could have had a future. But when the parole board took that hope away, he lost it.

The Kid

I know of another situation where a new young inmate in his twenty's was approached by a big, ugly predator who was about 6'5" and two hundred and seventy pounds. With a shank (a knife) and some gold teeth that he showed, he smiled and demanded sex from the kid. The young guy was smart enough to buy some time by not resisting, then suggested they go down and shower together first. The big guy smiled showing those gold teeth and said, "OK I'll get my stuff and meet you at the showers, kid. Remember punk, there is nowhere to hide in here that I can't find you and hurt you!" Then he left feeling good about his prospects.

Another inmate noticed that the kid was stressed about something. The kid nervously told him what his predicament was.

Fortunately this guy had been around for a while and had a solution.

He said, "OK. You have two choices. Give him what he wants and keep on giving until yours or his time is up. Or you can take him out." He pulled a six-inch shank from his waist band and handed it to the kid. "Use this on him. If you do, get rid of the shank. If you choose the other option, I want my shank back."

Scared as hell, the kid took the shank, wrapped it in his towel and headed for the showers.

The ugly one was already stripped down and standing in the shower. The kid came over and began to slowly get undressed as the big ugly one began to soap up his hairy torso. He looked over at the kid, smiled real big showing those gold teeth, then started to lather up his hair. He put soap on his head that ran down onto his face, so he closed his eyes under the shower. Seeing his chance, the kid made his move pulling the shank out from under the towel and began stabbing the unsuspecting, soaped up, blinded ugly predator. The shank was slippery with soap and blood. But the kid worked fast. The big guy was still on his feet when the kid ran from the shower. Blood mixed with soap ran across the slippery shower floor.

Whether it was fortunate or not that the big ugly one lived, it was a statement to everyone who knew what had happened that it would not be wise to underestimate the kid. The big ugly one never bothered him again and kept his distance.

That kid got a reputation that gave him some safety. But new guys came into the prison and had to learn for themselves.

He had a little drug dealing business going on when a group of these new unaware inmates decided to take his drugs, money and gang bang him in the process. The kid knew what was going on. He had given a snitch some free drugs just to find out such things.

The thing about snitches is that they seem to know everything that is going on all the time. The last thing they want to do is loose their free drug ride so one of them told the kid about the pending robbery and rape. If you have money and drugs you can buy almost anything in prison. So the kid spent some money on a meat cleaver stolen from the mess hall. He taped it to his hand and walked right up to the doorway of the cell full of would-be robbers. He had the nasty weapon inside his jacket. He asked in a confident voice, "Hey, I hear you're looking for me. Is that right? I hear you want my drugs, my money and my ass. That right?"

The guys looked around at each other and then before anyone could move or even answer the kid opened his state-issued jacket, showed them the drugs, the money and the cleaver securely taped to his hand. They backed up in shock, afraid to breathe. Then the kid broke the silence. "Well, here we are come and get us." Not one of the five of them dared to move.

Then one of them, the instigator, said, "Oh, there must be some sort of mistake. We wanted to buy some reefer from you. That's all."

The kid responded, " When would that be? Before or after you rape me? Make your best move or die."

The next ass-kissing words went something like, "We're sorry. We don't want any trouble."

The kid said, "What's my guarantee that I won't find you at my back at a later date if I let you go?"

They didn't have an answer, but they never bothered him again except to buy some reefer pretty regularly.

The kid kept sliding by on his own surviving without any real protection other than his own guts and reputation.

Another incident involved a pan of lighter fluid, a lighter and a couple of inebriated idiots. They were pissed at the kid because he wouldn't front them some reefer. They managed to get at his reefer supply at shank point. The kid caught up to them in a cell passing a joint back and forth. He lifted a pan he had filled with lighter fluid and doused them, lit his lighter and said, " Give me my drugs."

What you can always expect from an idiot is that they will do dumb things. One of them pulled a shank. The kid just flipped him his lighter setting him on fire. While running around trying to get through the door, he bumped into his buddy and set him on fire. The kid left with his drugs in hand. Two more guys, lucky to emerge with minor injuries, learned the hard way not to under estimate the kid.

Now I don't know about you, but I can see the kid's luck running out sooner or later. He obviously wasn't a bad ass with the physical size and strength to defend himself. He used the strength of intimidation because he learned early on that only the strong, or really crazy, survive. But how long can the kid keep pretending? Eventually, he'd get his.

Getting What You Want

Perhaps this would be a good time to become familiar with the laws of cause and effect, which is life's unfailing boomerang. What goes around does eventually come back around. I was just becoming aware of a whole new way of thinking, but I had some serious debts to pay in the consequences department. The knocks I took brought me this wisdom. I am giving you a gift here. With the knowledge I am about to awaken in you, you can become a master at anything that you can imagine. Consider this for a moment: why would anyone want to continue being a criminal when what they really want, from another, can be brought to them and surrendered with a "Thank you!"? Imagine getting what you want without the unpleasantness of treating others and being treated without respect. I know you're probably saying, "Huh?" I'm telling you that the vision you have of what you want, is someone else's vision to help you make it happen! Yes, it is just that easy! Every person you meet is alive and trying to make it in their life too. Once you quit hurting yourself with destructive behaviors and begin looking at others as tools who want to help you succeed, you don't feel the need to steal from them. You no longer will want to cheat on, wound, or destroy everyone you come in contact with. You will find that the people around you haven't changed, you have!

In reality, this isn't anything new. This is just something you may not be aware of and if you're not aware of it, is there any wonder you have not made any lasting changes? Do you want to change? If you do, you must look at things with a new perspective. Go back to your childhood dreams. What did you want to become back when you thought you could do anything you wanted? Every dream has a wealth of motivation hidden in it. Every failure has within it the power to sharpen that dream. What stirs your soul, makes your heart beat faster and fuels you with indescribable energy? Don't lose sight of that! Not every day will suddenly become perfect, but you should be able to see a pattern developing that is taking you away from bad habits and bringing you towards what you know you were created for. The essence of your life will flow with a new peace and there will be purpose to your days.

I cannot convince you. You have to choose this. You can continue on with the path you are taking, or you can make a choice to change it. I am walking you through my journey so that you can see that lasting change is possible!

Testing the Theory

There are man-made laws, that can be changed and adjusted at will and then there's the laws of the universe that no one can change, adjust or escape. You don't have to be a "believer" to be affected by it any more than you have to believe in gravity in order to be affected by the laws of gravity. If a brick falls on your head, it's going to hurt! It is the same with the laws of cause and effect.

I really didn't understand this concept, or for that matter, even know that it existed when I began my new adventures with my newly discovered knowledge. I made lots of mistakes as I tested theory after theory at different stages in the next four years. I wasn't really sure about this new awareness that I seemed to be experiencing or even why this was happening to me.

I suppose my first real enlightening experience came when I decided to test my new concept of thought equals reality. I had always thought of myself as illiterate, or at least very slow. I really wanted to be regarded as intelligent and I wanted to be a good con. So while my initial motivation wasn't truly honorable, it was a place to start. I immediately started to see myself as this person I wanted to be and the people around me begin to react to me differently. How could anyone think I was intelligent when I acted like I wasn't? If I wanted others to think I was intelligent, I realized I would have to believe that I was. I was shocked at the results. Where once I asked questions, people were now asking me for answers. Unbelievable.

I was now looking for truth and my fellow inmates were a great source of knowledge. While some inmates were examples of how *not* to live, some were positive influences on me that helped change my life forever.

Owen

One such guy was Owen Hughes. He was a pseudo-hippie/artist who could have easily been the reincarnation of Michelangelo himself. Owen was serving time for aggravated armed robbery just like I was, only he received an eight-year sentence even though he actually shot someone in the robbery. Owen really wasn't the type of person that would do something like a robbery unless he was stinking drunk. Which, of course, he was. Owen was very skillful with all forms of painting, drawing, and sculpturing. I don't know if you are familiar with the famous painting *The Man in the Golden Helmet* by Rembrandt. If you are, I'm sure that you will appreciate that Owen once painted that in perfect likeness in oils, on a 1" x 1.5" canvas. And he accomplished that feat using a single hair of a brush.

In addition to being a fantastic artist, Owen was very knowledgeable. Some of the bizarre things that he told me might have caused someone else to doubt his sanity. Yet, even though I had never heard of these things before, it was clear in my mind that they were true and correct and it felt like he was reminding me of something I already knew. Most of the information that Owen was in possession of was philosophical, or at least he had not yet arrived at a level of consciousness where he could substantiate some of the things that he really could only talk about. He talked truth, but didn't apply it to his own life.

You'll find this a lot in life. People talk it but don't walk it. Owen was brilliant and could talk about things that took me a long time to understand. There's a lesson in Owen's life that may help you better understand your own personal abilities.

Talent, Knowledge and Failure

Wouldn't you think that someone with Owens talents and wisdom would be a shoe-in for success? But the truth is, Owen was a drug addicted alcoholic and just as messed up as they come. Owen was definitely a lesson in the fact that talent and knowledge are not all that is needed in order to succeed in life. Owen, like all of us, had outstanding marketable talents and knowledge. He took it all for granted, trading his skills and knowledge for drugs and alcohol to alter his present state of mind.

I lost contact with Owen many years ago, so I can't tell you what became of him. I don't know if he continued the life he was living when I last saw him. My guess is that he is no longer among the living. It kind of makes you wonder how someone can clearly have superior talents, skills and intelligence, yet still be screwed up beyond all recognition. Let's get another misconception out in the open. Just because you are smart, skilled, gifted, educated, or walking on a sure path, does not mean that you will skip through life and all will be easy. Judging by the books they write and the words they preach, you can pick up almost any book written by motivational writers and get the impression that they really have it together. They no doubt are in possession of certain assets that make their lives more manageable than the average person, but don't think for one minute that they don't have shortcomings or problems. They are challenged every day of their lives just like you and me. Just because I am aware of all of these things and I have managed to overcome many things that controlled and manipulated my life, don't make the mistake of thinking that I am any different than you. Sure, when I am writing this or counseling someone, I am very sure of myself! I have no doubt about where I'm coming from or where I'm going. I am not always in this frame of mind. Every once in a while, I am blindsided by something I had not anticipated. I can't predict what other people might do or how I will personally react to them.

The Mind
Sometimes I have less than perfect control of myself. It's as if I have two separate personalities; a positive side and a negative side. The positive side is the side that is always in control and never in doubt. It is confident and firm. I guess that is why it is "positive", huh? These are the best of days and I would love if that was the way it was without fail. Is this the reality of living? There is a negative side that we all must face. This is the side that questions and wonders, reacting impulsively without reason at times.

Common sense tells me that peace of mind is found within equal balance of the two separate sides. Common sense also tells me that there really are not two separate sides. The illusion is caused by the subconscious mind which takes orders from the conscious mind. The subconscious mind doesn't know right from wrong and doesn't always do what's necessarily right or what is in your best interest. It just reacts. Those reactions are programmed. Your subconscious does everything that you program it to do. Another concept that describes the subconscious mind and makes it easily understood, is that it is the part of you that automatically reacts to whatever it's told without question or regard of consequences, good or bad. It's like your conscious mind is the teacher and your subconscious mind is the student. Or depending on what fries your chicken, you are the captain and your subconscious is the crew. Yet again, you are the ruler and your subconscious is the loyal subject.

The point is, whatever commands you feed your subconscious, intentionally or unintentionally, it will then react by carrying out those orders. While it all began with a conscious thought, when that thought gets transferred to your subconscious, it soon takes on a life of its own and you wonder how or why you are reacting without thinking. The way your subconscious is programmed is by repetitive affirmations. Long after you have consciously thought something, your programmed subconscious is still following your last order on the subject.

We need to have better communication between our conscious and subconscious minds! So with this understanding, we can retrain our subconscious to react in healthy patterns.

Juggling

How do we accomplish this? I am not joking when I say that it will take a conscious effort! Going back to my learning how to juggle three balls, in the beginning, I had to learn how to consistently throw one ball at about eye level from one hand to the other. Then I had to learn the same maneuver with two balls; one in each hand. First, I'd throw the ball in the right hand in an arc over to the left hand, then, release the ball in the left hand just as the ball from the right hand reached its highest point and began to fall into the left hand. I did this until I became consistent. At that point the third ball was added to my right hand. The procedure was exactly the same as with two balls, only the third ball was released to the left hand when the ball from the left hand reached its highest point. Confused? Yes, it is difficult without the use of the unconscious mind. Consciously, I could not do it. So I had to teach my subconscious mind to drop that third ball before I could actually juggle it. The way I accomplished that, was by dropping the third ball on the floor without even trying to catch it until my subconscious mind was used to letting it go, at which point I could consciously maneuver the ball where I wanted it to go.

I suppose at this point it would be helpful to mention that before I ever picked up a set of juggling balls and tried to juggle them, I first visualized myself juggling. I actually practiced every day in my mind for a couple of weeks until I could see how it was done. Then I actually picked up the balls and started juggling in reality. It took me less time in reality than it did in my imagination, but I can assure you that if I hadn't imagined it first, it would have never happened in reality.

What I've just explained is the key to obtaining anything and everything that you ever wanted. The way to maintain this simple path to success is to train your subconscious mind to accept better values which will raise your self-esteem and provide outstanding motivation for change. I mean, who doesn't want to be successful? And the way to train your subconscious mind is by feeding it positive affirmations day in and day out. You will be amazed at how fast things turn around for you once you start this process. I find it necessary to remember that any kind of positive input needs to be replenished often and consistently. What I want to experience becomes a way of life. It will wear off like the food I feed my body if I don't continue to feed my mind a good steady diet of positive input.

Old Habits

To go on with my story, Owen and I became good friends and occasionally did drugs together. Sure, we were in prison, but we could get speed, pot, LSD, and sometimes liquor. Basically, whatever was available outside was also available, in small quantities, in prison.

I don't know how it is now, but in the 70's, Stillwater prison was like a miniature society with segregated neighborhoods like on the outside. There was an Indian reservation, a black ghetto, a white trash neighborhood and a higher echelon where the more level headed white-collar prisoners lived.

I began to realize how much power was available to whoever could provide inmates with money, drugs, and cigarettes. I began to imagine a way to gain control of all these things.

You are now thinking, "I thought you were free from your addictions!" Yes, I told you that I was on the road to healthy behavior, but by no means was this transition a smooth one. I had a lot of negative behaviors and habits to deal with. Most dangerous of all, I was planning to use my new found mental edge to selfishly benefit myself and perform illegal activity inside the Stillwater State Prison. Go figure.

Gaining Control

I had my own method of protection. My idea was to see if my newly acquired knowledge actually worked the way I thought it would, and to see if it could offer me protection. I decided to put my new skills to the test.

Gaining control of the drugs was the first step that would put me in control of the money and the means to stock pile cigarettes. With those three commodities I could buy anything including guards which enabled me to get anyone to do anything I needed done. It wasn't like you see on TV were some wimp with a wimp attitude has people killed for selfish reasons and it wasn't a time when known snitches were killed just because they knew things and couldn't keep their mouth shut. Most snitches snitched in exchange for favors. I needed snitches to work for me.

I took good care of them and they in turn took care of me. Back in the mob days snitches were considered the lowest life form ranking right next to child molesters. Neither survived for long in prison population. Most served their time in isolation back in those days. This kind of honor among thugs and gangsters is a thing of the past.

I partnered up with a guy by the name of Donnie who was soon to be released. I talked him into putting his girlfriend on my visiting list so that she could bring drugs to me, that I would in turn sell, and send the money back out to Donnie on the outside. The plan was based on the drug situation and how it unfolded. It was almost exactly the same way every two weeks. For one week, the prison was flooded with drugs, but no one had any money to buy them, because the money had been sent out to acquire more drugs. By the second week, the drugs had depleted and money was abundant. The idea was to stockpile drugs until no one had any drugs left and then bring my drugs out and take all the money. The plan worked better than expected as there was a big drug bust on the outside right about the time that the drugs dried up on the inside. This meant that all drugs would be dried up for possibly an additional week and inmates would be frantic. Usually there was a little bit of pot floating around but even that was dried up. That's when I made my move.

In the penitentiary, no matter who you are, you need protection if you are involved in drug deals. Bill and Chuck, along with the entire Indian Reservation were my protection. But unfortunately, there is a price for that protection. My protectors consumed most of the profits until my suppliers started to become discouraged. I knew that I had the right idea but I needed to get away from the reservation and find a new supplier in order to complete my plan.

So, I got myself moved from A-Hall. I moved away from what could be considered the "den of iniquity." A- Hall was where the majority of the rapes, muggings, stabbings, beatings, murders, and suicides took place and all riots began. I went to B-Hall where mostly long-term model prisoners lived (the higher echelon).

Chaos

The year was 1974. This was the year that a new commissioner of corrections took over and tried a concept that had been somewhat successful in California. The commissioner's idea was to open the prison to the public with the idea of each getting a good understanding of the other. This was supposed to reduce criminal activity on the outside and minimize repeat offenders. What it actually did is create chaos. With all this contact with the outside, drugs became so plentiful that most were shared rather than sold. I don't recall just how many murders, stabbings and rapes there were that year, but there were 21 suicides. All 21 were drug related. The inmates had literally taken over the penitentiary and there was very little, if any, order. Normally at count time, we were all locked in our cells and were required to stand with our hand on the bars; this took no more than 10 minutes to count over 900 inmates before we were released one tier at a time for chow.

The new system didn't even require us to be in our own cell. Guards would come by taking count while four or five people would be in one cell smoking pot. Often the guard taking count would step in a cell for a moment to take a couple of hits on a joint, pass it on and continue counting. It wasn't uncommon for count to last over an hour because the guards would lose count and inmates would move around and be counted twice or not at all. I remember one time there was a guard standing on flag (the main floor) when an inmate on the first tier leaned over the rails causing a 10" shank to fall from his waistband and clatter to the floor at the feet of the guard. The guard calmly looked down at his feet than up at the inmate. He bent, picked the shank up from the floor, and handed it back to the inmate.

After a few escapes, because of the lack of control, officials slowly began to regain control and the doors that had once been open to the public were slowly being closed. This restored my opportunity to run drugs for money inside the prison. Donnie had just sent me a couple grams of cocaine and some LSD. Donnie's weakness was cocaine so by the time the cocaine got to me, it had been stepped on so many times that it was worthless.

For obvious reasons, not very many people were into LSD in prison, so it was a difficult sell. Amphetamines were by far the most popular and profitable of all the drugs but methamphetamine had just recently become a controlled substance and almost impossible to obtain. Since all the programs that brought people from the outside in were being discontinued, I moved Donnie's girlfriend to an art class which was one of the only programs left that no one else had even thought of for a drug inlet. When some cocaine came in, a friend and I shot up all of it trying to get a buzz, but got nothing but new holes in our arms. The LSD that I got, I gave to my dealers to be sold.

The next day we were locked down, as that's what administration always did when they wanted to take something away from us or make some changes in the system. By the time we were off of lock down, all my drugs were gone and I had no money to send out. Donnie's girlfriend came one last time. I explained what had happened but it was the last time I ever saw her.

New Ventures

I put everything on the back burner for the time being and started using other skills to make money and keep myself in drugs. I became a prison plumber. "A-House" and most of "B-House" did not have hot running water in the cells, so for $10 a pop, I would plumb hot water into a cell. The first cell to get hot water was mine. Being a plumber also gave me access to the entire penitentiary, as well as areas that guards were not even admitted to. This allowed me to transport things from the industry back to the cellblocks and from cellblock to cellblock. This turned out to be nicely profitable.

After about a year, I became bored, and decided to become a prison electrician. This still allowed me the freedom of the penitentiary. I turned my cell into a light show with a panel of switches that controlled everything in my cell while lying in bed. After a year of being a prison electrician, I decided to become a prison electronic technician because almost everyone had a personal television set in their cell and some had stereos. Every television set that came into the penitentiary had a resistor added to the circuitry that prevented the volume from being turned beyond a certain point. Inmates paid me to find the resistor and remove it from their televisions. I was enjoying the money and the challenge was a welcomed break from the monotony of the days. At that time, electronic circuitry was evolving and computers were just beginning to find their place in business. Even though I was in prison, I was staying on the front edge of technology.

There certainly were a lot of different characters in Stillwater. There were those in prison for some of the stupidest things and also some of the most disturbing things. Serial killers were the most interesting inmates. They always look like they could pass for anything other than what they really are. All of the ones I've known were good-looking, very intelligent, responsible, even highly successful in the free world, and model prisoners.

Obsession

For example, the head electrician, Harold, was a serial killer wanted for murder in several states. There was absolutely nothing that would suggest that Harold would even be capable of taking someone's life. Harold told me that he had eluded the police by hanging around them, all the time listening to almost every plan they came up with to catch him. I studied Harold. I could probably write a book about him, but Harold and others like him, were just another lesson to be learned. When Harold committed the murders, he was "in the zone" as I call it. You know, that place that we all experience from time to time that is fueled by obsession.

I have no idea what might have triggered Harold's obsession to rape and murder innocent women, but I'll bet you that he wasn't born with the destiny to rape and murder. The professionals (meaning doctors and psychiatrists) all have theories, but I don't think they really know any more than you or I do. If they did, they would have already discovered a cure more humane than a lobotomy. Talking to Harold, I could never detect a shred of remorse for his unconscionable acts. What I did detect, was a sense of pride for being able to elude the police for so long and now, he seemed to be content to spend the rest of his life fantasizing as he relived the murders he committed over and over again.

What "zone" do you think those third-world people are in who were born innocent, then raised to hate everything that the American people stand for and sworn to eradicate all of us by becoming human bombs? Think about it. Anyone can be brainwashed into believing anything and to some degree, we all are brainwashed into believing all sorts of things that are detrimental to our personal cause and or our existence. I'm not saying that Harold was brainwashed into becoming a serial killer, but I am saying that he no doubt experienced some sort of trauma that triggered his impulsive obsession that caused him to rape and murder. This may very well have been the only way Harold could find a way to maintain the character that everyone thought was a peaceful, intelligent, trustworthy individual that could be trusted with life.

How many times, at another level, have you witnessed an insecure bully picking on the weak so that they can feed their insecurities and still deny that their insecurities exist? Or, even at a lesser level, when one puts another down in order to feel superior. Haven't we all been a part of that childish behavior at some time in our adult lives? Point is, insecurities can turn you, me, or anyone into a monster if we don't take the time to discover who we really are. It's by understanding ourselves that we can begin to have compassion for others.

Normal Criminals

One of the most disturbing facts I discovered while at Stillwater State Penitentiary, is that we are all closer to being the worst version of ourselves than we think. We are all a hair's breadth away from making a serious, life altering mistake. Once the downward spiral has begun, it is very difficult to stop it. Who hasn't struggled to keep their temper or control their tongue? Who hasn't had opportunity to cheat on a spouse, or lie to their kids? Do we know better? Yes, we do. But when I realized how "normal" some of these "hardened criminals" really were, I also came to the realization that I was not odd, weird, or in any way worse off than most of these fellows. What separated us from each other, and the outside world, was our own individual choices.

Hold that thought. My whole life I lived under the lie that my life was just happening around me. But I was beginning to understand. I began to realize, that at a very deep level, despite all circumstances, good and bad, I had a free will, a brain, and the ability to choose. I was no different than anyone else in this matter. Yes, even the abandoned, discarded, lonely, illiterate Randy Miller. He had made choices that landed him in several state prisons. But what if? What if he armed himself with a new truth, discarded the lies, and diligently worked hard to change his life? Could he? I was in the trenches of some very new thinking for me. I was peering out from my personal trench watching everyone and studying the men I was serving time with.

Fast Jack

Another interesting character I met in Stillwater was a fellow by the name of Jack who I called "Fast Jack the Ripper." Jack reminded me of Poindexter, a proper gentleman. But as I have been pointing out, looks can be very deceiving.

In the outside world, Jack had run a good number of confidence scams and graduated from boosting merchandise from stores (where someone would place an order for a certain product and Jack would shoplift it for a percentage of the original price.) He would normally go into stores with a shopping list that represented several orders from several different people. Jack graduated from this program, which wasn't making him enough money, to stealing truckloads of goods in broad daylight. Jack simply put on a uniform, rented a truck, backed it up to the dock, and walked right up to the shipping supervisor with his clipboard that contained all of the merchandise and item numbers he wanted. The shipping department pulled the orders and loaded them unto the truck. Fast Jack drove off with thousands of dollars in merchandise. Montgomery Wards was one of his favorite places to run this scam. (Geez maybe that's why they are out of business now.)

One day, Jack and I were standing down on flag having a conversation about cons. Just teasing, I told Jackie he wouldn't make a pimple on a con man's posterior. Jack looked almost as if I'd bitch slapped him as he began to get all indignant with me. I said, "Well Jack, there is a way to settle this."

There were several good cons that I knew in Stillwater, and Jack probably was the best. But there was one other that was running a very close second place. I can't remember what his name was, but he was the kind of person that if his lips were moving and you were listening, you were getting ripped off. This guy ran the galleys from the time the cell doors opened until the time they closed. He roamed around every day trading and selling things that were mostly prison issue, and free to anyone for the asking, but this guy could convince you that whatever he was selling was better than anything else you could get anywhere in the joint. And you would believe him if you listened to him.

Normally, commissary was once a week, but every month, the last week is skipped. While we all knew the routine, no one ever planned ahead for this missing week, including myself at that time. The result of our poor planning, was that the smokers ran out of cigarettes a few days into that last week. Cigarettes would become more valuable than drugs, money, food or any other commodity. This particular day that Jack and I were talking, was close to the end of that period when very few were in possession of cigarettes and not letting them go for anything.

As I looked up to the third tier from flag where Jack and I were standing, I could see the person in question going from cell to cell peddling his junk as usual. I told Jack that I would give him one hour to con that guy into conning someone else out of one pack of Camel cigarettes. I told Jack, "Bring me that pack of Camels and I will never doubt you again." Within 30 minutes, Jack came strolling back, pulled a pack of Camels out of his pocket and handed them to me with a big smile on his face. I tucked the cigarettes into my pocket as I walked away. Over my shoulder I said, "I'm convinced Jack. You are the best."

I was almost out of hearing distance when I heard him yelling, "Hey! Wait a minute." The fact is, before I even began a conversation with Jack, I had planned on him getting me a pack of cigarettes. I never doubted for a moment that he wouldn't succeed, because I was going to use a version of his own con game and manipulate him by putting his reputation on the line. Cons rarely ever recognize their own game when it's used on them. There are a multitude of reasons for that, but for the most part, it's what we don't anticipate that renders us helpless and takes us by surprise.

Just like everyone else I spent time with, there was a lesson to be learned from Jack. That is, cons are not necessarily bad people. We are all manipulative to some unconscious degree. "Good" cons are consciously aware of this ability, and use it for their own personal gain, with little or no concern for others. But the universal laws of cause and effect will surely come around in due time. These cons end up in trouble and while they are gifted, they are not respected, and usually viewed as "scoundrels."

But there are "Masters of Con" and they are to be studied and emulated. The Masters understand human nature at a very deep level, and then quickly study and assess everyone they deal with. They use their knowledge for the benefit of everyone concerned. In other words, if I can manipulate you into doing something that benefits me personally, I will only do so if that "manipulation" also benefits you. That leaves both of us satisfied, and we have mutual respect for ourselves and each other. Such as, you reading this book is a personal benefit to me because you may have paid to buy this book. However, I know that every cent you spent will be beneficial to you. As important as it is to me that you know everything that I know, let's not pretend that material gain has no part in my personal motivation. It is most definitely a selfish act on my part because I get satisfaction in sharing my personal knowledge with you. And yet, while I see how all of this benefits me, I also believe that I do truly want a better life for you too. That is the goal of the Master Con; mutual benefit for all concerned. I no longer want to use my skills to intentionally hurt anyone, but rather, I am motivated for doing the most good. I am fulfilled only when there is goodness coming out of my heart and the promise of a better life for more than just myself. That is what I learned from Jack. I assure you that there are better, more positive sounding words to describe what I just said but my intentions were that you connect with where the idea came from. I truly believe that all vices can become positive assets with the perspective to use them for the good of all concerned.

Strangely Intelligent

It was right about this time that my awareness intensified. My understanding seemed to be doubled and tripled within, what seemed to me, an instant. It seemed as though I was hearing people for the first time. I mean really hearing what they were saying! Everyone seemed to be filled with knowledge and wisdom speaking on a level I never knew existed until that very moment when everything became clear.

I thought, Wow! At last I am like everyone else." I understood everyone and what they were saying. I no longer felt illiterate and alone. I could see the inner workings of people's minds. But to my disappointment, I once again found myself alone when I realized that no one was aware of the knowledge they possessed. They began to see me as intelligent. But they didn't fully understand what I was talking about. They just agreed with everything I said rather than appear ignorant. The word finally got back to me that I was not only intelligent, but very strange. I thought, "Somewhere within these four walls there is someone I can relate too."

At this point, I believe, I had surpassed the awareness of Owen. Although we could speak on multi levels, he seemed to be confined within those levels. It was as though he was repeating something he had read in a book rather than expounding on what he truly experienced within himself. He was bound to basic concepts rather than open to the freedom I began to experience. I wanted to go beyond, to wander through and explore actual experience. After all, what good are clever ideas, if they don't impact our daily life?

Knowledge

I think now, 35 years later, that people still find conversations such as this, strange. But I also think that more people have awakened to where they are beginning to understand and accept the responsibilities for the knowledge that we all possess.

A couple of hundred years ago, this type of conversation would have caused my incarceration in an asylum. If a woman were to have this type of conversation, she would most likely be burned at the stake. Yes, I firmly believe that we now have more knowledge available to the general public. We also have the ability to get our hands on any topic that we want to wrap our heads around. I am living proof that once we convince the most hopeless man that he has a greater purpose and a higher calling than mere selfish existence, we have the ability to change the face of modern civilization.

May I be so bold as to suggest that while we have had fantastic knowledge and truth available to us for a long time, it is now time to purposely apply all that we know. It is no longer enough to hear truth and recognize it; it is our responsibility, not to mention our duty and great privilege, to use these tools.

I had been studying my fellow inmates, but I wanted to learn more. I had a thirst for knowledge. So I began looking for chances to learn. Augsburg College was offering some courses in group leadership and discussion through the third-floor education department at the penitentiary. I signed up. Every Friday night, a teacher and some college students from Augsburg would come to the penitentiary for this class. One of the students, a pretty little girl by the name of Debbie, who could've passed for Snow White, was my next challenge. As it turned out she was very easy to manipulate, and in no time at all, I had her on my visiting list.

The next people I became involved with were two transfers from a federal penitentiary. "Bubba" and "Chief." Bubba was doing life for the murder of some groundskeeper in a cemetery. Chief was doing forty years for the same crime. My interest was mainly in Bubba, as he seemed to be very knowledgeable and someone that I could relate too. But I quickly realized that any knowledge that Bubba had, was definitely from the dark side. But it was knowledge and I figured it was going to be useful.

At this point, I wasn't sure at all where I fit in. Being "different" makes you feel all alone and insecure. The loneliness can cause you to do many foolish things that are not good for you or anyone else as I have already demonstrated throughout this book. Regardless of my intelligence at this point (intelligence doesn't mean you're smart), I was still ignorant enough to forget what enabled me to be given 20 years in prison. As in the past, the opportunity to belong somewhere, anywhere, were more important to me than any consequences I might suffer for my poor decisions.

I fell back into the zone where I placed no value on my life or anyone else's. The concept was, "Get in my way, and you're going down." I took to packing a shank. Meanwhile, Bubba, Chief, myself and five other inmates put our pathetic heads together and began to plan our escape from the penitentiary.

Busting Out

In the early stages of our plan, we were trying to keep the operation simple and small. But Bubba got into some trouble and was thrown in the hole. We needed more resources, so we brought in some other guys. Duane and Benny were both doing twenty for armed robbery. Tank was doing life for murder, while Sam was doing forty for murder. There was another inmate whose name I can't remember. He was doing ten for forgery.

I did not know it at the time but the only reason Benny was invited was to enable Sam and Tank to kill him once we were free of the penitentiary as a favor to someone that Benny had wronged. I didn't necessarily like the new plan, but it did increase our resources to get out and to get away once we were out.

The plan involved several phases. First, we would need to gain access to the third floor education area where we must somehow open a locked gate. Once we were through the locked gate, and had access to the stairway, we knew we would find at the top of the steps, a trap door 10 feet off the floor. The trap door was secured by a padlock; beyond the trap door was a compartment that led to the air shafts. On each end of the building, where the peaks were, there was a 3-foot high by 18-inch wide window with bars. The bars would need to be hack sawed out enough to get the biggest guy through. From here, thirty feet below was the rotunda roof. We planned to rappel that thirty feet on rope, and from the rotunda roof to the ground was an 8-foot jump. Our final hurdle was the 10-foot fence that was made to keep people out rather than in. Beyond that? Freedom.

We had our plan and we knew it was a good one. The most difficult part was getting all of the tools needed to cut and saw our way out. We made a master list of needed supplies. We would need a key to unlock that door that separated us from the third floor education department, something to cut the padlock off of the trap door, a hacksaw blade with a holder to cut the bars from the vent window, about thirty feet of rope to get from the window to the rotunda roof and a getaway car waiting just beyond the fence. Piece of cake.

The hacksaw blades were provided by the one guy I can't remember. He worked in the machine shop cutting metal angle iron with a band saw. He purposely broke a blade, knowing the blades were still sharp. Under prison regulations, when band saw blades broke, they were broken into 10-inch pieces, measured, and disposed of by a guard. Two sections of saw were replaced with two sections of metal banding material that was carefully cut and bent to resemble a saw blade. Once he got the blades, he got them to me. I walked past the guard in the metal detectors several times a day with my tool belt full of metal tools and I was never scanned. So, bringing the blades in was the first piece of the cake.

Next we needed 30 feet of rope. There was a poetry group that was available to all inmates and they met once a week on the stage of the auditorium. The stage curtains were controlled by ropes. As long as the ropes were not used to raise and lower the curtains, I could take 30 or 40 feet that wouldn't be noticed until someone tried to operate the curtains. That was next to never. We had our rope.

Tank and Sam secured a 36-inch set of bolt cutters when an outside crew of workers were doing some work in the prison yard. The bolt cutters were left unattended long enough for Sam and Tank to bury them under some sod in the yard. Normally, they would have been found, in no time, using a metal detector. But, it is our guess that they were never reported as missing because of the consequences involved if prison officials found out some idiot was careless enough to lose something as large as a bolt cutter in a prison. The tool remained undetected for several months. We had another piece of our cake.

We managed to get an impression of the key we needed to gain access to the stairway to the third floor education department. But, we were missing something. The key turned only half way rotating only half of the tumblers. After several weeks of sneaking around, trying and failing to open the gate, we scrapped the key idea.

The new plan wouldn't require a key at all.

The plan unfolded on a Monday night when everyone was coming and going to commissary. Guys were carrying packages containing their commissary items to almost every part of the penitentiary, including third-floor education. There was a class being conducted on that particular night, so the door to the stairway was left open. Anyone could come and go as they pleased. There wasn't a guard posted because there never was a problem.

The rope was put into a commissary sack with the hacksaw blades. I carried them. The bolt cutters were separated into three pieces. One piece was the cutter head. Duane hid it in the front of his pants. One handle was strapped to Sam's leg and the other was strapped to Tank's leg. The guy whose name I can't remember was very tall and Benny was light weight, yet taller than the rest of us. These two would be the two responsible for cutting the padlock and Benny would be the first to enter the compartment inside the trapdoor. At the last minute, the guy whose name I can't remember, decided not to go, but still helped us get to this point. I guess that's why I can't remember his name.

Everything happened like clockwork. Our beds were made up to look like we were in them and all of us were crammed in the compartment. The only obstacle that we had not anticipated was a large metal vent that blocked our way. We weren't heating and air conditioning people so how would we know that was there? With a little ingenuity and the use of the bolt cutters, we were able to cut a hole in the vent and enter. The two window bars were cut and removed quickly. We were ahead of time and needed to wait until our ride was available.

As we sat there in the dark, we could see the little beady eyes of bats around us. And where there are bats, there is bat crap. We sat in four or five inches of it. But it didn't bother us much. All was good.

Count came and passed and no sirens sounded announcing our escape. Finally it was time to leave the vent system. I don't know if you've ever tried this, but imagine if you will, trying to slow your descent from a 30 foot drop holding onto a half-inch rope. Unless you've had commando training, it's not easy. We all hit the roof very hard. I got a slight sprain in my foot but wasn't going to let it slow me down. We all jumped from the rotunda roof onto the ground and made our way to the fence, when suddenly the lights came on and guns were pointing at us from everywhere. By this time, McManus, the warden, was pretty much fed up and ordered us to be shot if we moved an inch. We all knew that he preferred that we resist just a little bit so that he could justify killing all of us and making us an example. We were stupid enough to try to escape, but we weren't stupid enough to move when surrounded by armed guards.

Back To Square One, Again

We each got 90 days in segregation for our efforts. We were back to square one after practically tasting freedom.

I had a lot of time to think, as there were very few visitors for me. My girlfriend, Debbie, came up to see me almost every visiting day. Remember Bill? He had been one of my partners in crime back in the day. Although serving a sentence himself, Bill had been appointed as a prison counselor for Indians, and was allowed back in segregation to console me.

We talked a little bit about why I didn't invite him along on the breakout. He told me that he had some plans himself that hinged on someone on the outside. But he never gave me the name of that person, or any idea of how they were involved. That visit was the last time I ever saw Bill. Right after I got out of segregation, I received word from the reservation in A Hall that he had committed suicide by hanging himself. I wish I had realized that he was that screwed up. I liked him a lot in spite of the fact that he had messed around with Chick when she and I were still married.

To top it all off, just before we were released from segregation, Chief attempted to kill himself by slashing both of his wrists with a razor blade. I never did find out why, but I think it had something to do with paranoia, Bubba, and Chief's loyalty to him.

Debbie would occasionally bring me things when she came to visit me. One day I talked her into purchasing a pound of reefer for me. She gave it to someone else on the outside, who was connected to someone on the inside, who was willing to bring it in to the prison for a very small price.

The phase I was going through at this time was enabling me to become an effective con. Old habits are hard to break and I was frustrated. That brought me back to drugs and other destructive behaviors. I still wasn't able to choose wisely when I was under pressure.

Anyway, the kid that brought the reefer in for me was a Vietnam War veteran about 22 years old. Since he could only get it in an ounce or two at a time (this was achieved by sticking it up his posterior), it took a number of visits to accomplish receiving the whole pound. I would sell half of what was brought in and smoked the rest with friends. One of the friends was Benny and the other one was the kid who brought it in. I was beginning to enter another phase in addition to being a con. I was becoming much more compassionate. The only thing I had to share was drugs, but I had never cared about others enough to share my drugs without receiving financial gain. Something was different inside of me. I attempted to provoke friendship by sharing drugs.

At about that time, I began to think hard about the purpose of having material possessions. For a while I actually abandoned my possessions and began to visualize myself living somewhere in the woods away from civilization and modern conveniences. Coming from the guy who had all the bells and whistles in his cell attached to switches, this was radical. I realized that I had come to this existence for the experience of life and all it encompassed. So, with that thought, I began to regain possessions, but with a different perspective. My new found knowledge allowed me to place less value on possessions themselves and more on the experience of having them. In other words, my spirit could no longer be broken by taking my possessions away because my only link to them is the experience; once you have the experience, no one can ever take it away. A wealth of money and material things is simple to acquire once you know how. But all too often, we have great material possessions without the slightest satisfaction that should come with them.

Objectively Reviewing The Past

This concept compliments the words of Maxwell Maltz and his statement that the human nervous system cannot tell the difference between a real or imagined experience. Whatever you think or believe to be true, your nervous system will always react accordingly. A simple example is misunderstanding a situation, which then causes you to react to something that doesn't exist in reality. Have you felt a deep fear that causes your imagination to conjure up something so seemingly real that you become sick to your stomach? This is what I am talking about when I say that your nervous system follows what you put in it, not necessarily truth and all that is real.

Reflecting on my younger years, I find it easy to analyze everything that happened. However, the circumstances before me at that time, had complete power over me through those years. When I was finally able to understand those circumstances well enough to make a healthy decision, it was rather simple. I just needed to let go of the things that continued to harm me.

But, as I get closer to my present age and analyze current problems, things become more personal, emotional and complex. Reflecting back so many years, it is as if I were looking at some one's life other than my own. Then, as an observer, I am able to see without emotional boundaries that which often hinders my abilities to determine, assess, and cope with my circumstances. Being so far removed from those circumstances so long ago, without the influence of emotions to affect me, makes it unmistakably clear what the circumstances really were and how I could have effectively dealt with them for the best possible outcome. Yet, as I get closer to my actual age, in "real life time", my emotions tend to take over. They blur the lines between rational and radical behavior. In other words, emotions make lousy life choices and are not to be trusted.

If you can't see the connection in your life, then you can look at my own poor decisions brought on by emotions, caused by circumstances. It is at this time that I can give you another gem of wisdom to help you in your life. When you or I are able to remove ourselves emotionally from the circle of circumstances in which we are involved and regard ourselves as a stranger peering through a window without emotional connections of any kind at any level, it is then that we are able to make very clear decisions that can be trusted. As I objectively review my own life and the circumstances that surround me, it is in this moment that I am able, once again, to determine, assess and cope with any set of circumstances before me for the best possible outcome.

The first few times you do this it is necessary to actually stop and think about putting yourself into this state of mind before making any permanent decisions. But just like all things that we learn, with practice and consistency, we will no longer have to stop and think about what our minds have learned to analyze in the blink of an eye. People who seem to have all the right answers and make all the right moves have actually learned the art of processing information at lightning speed through repetitive practice.

If you think about it for a moment, I am sure that you can relate. You must have abilities within yourself that are very similar; something that has always been outstanding in you, or you have practiced until you can perform without stopping to think. Don't fool yourself into thinking that others are born with extraordinary talents that you can't master. It's just not true. With practice we can accomplish great things too! There isn't one of us on this planet that wasn't born with an outstanding quality that others admire. But we sell ourselves short. We take for granted what comes natural to us, thinking that it is of no value. Just because the gifts you have will take little effort on your part, it may, in all actuality, be the most valuable thing you possess. Be open minded enough to honestly evaluate what is naturally in you that others may have to work hard at. On the other hand, you can be sure that your admirer possesses something just as outstanding as you; something that comes natural to them. I believe that if we all realized our special talents and became the best that we can be at those things that come natural to us, accepting the challenge of things that appear difficult to us, we may find ourselves properly balanced and at peace with ourselves.

Institutionalization

It was a Monday morning in 1975. I hadn't slept well because I was deeply bothered by what I had watched the previous day.

On Sunday afternoons, everyone's cell was left open so that we could go to the chow hall for Sunday dinner. This particular day, the dinner bell did not ring. I looked at my watch and looked at the clock on the wall. It was time for Sunday dinner, so I then headed for the chow hall. When I got there, instead of joining the usual long line, I found that there wasn't another soul in the room except the servers and the kitchen help. Not another man had come to dinner out of the hundreds in the building. This struck me as not only strange, but disturbing. Just because a bell didn't ring to signal it was time to eat, no one came. If that's not institutionalization in its purest form, I don't know what is.

I pondered this situation through the night. The next morning I reported to sick call. When it came to my turn with the doctor, he asked me what the problem was. I said, "I am sick of doing time. If I continue to allow myself to be institutionalized I will be back again and again just like a lot of other people you see coming and going." He asked me how he could possibly help me and I replied, "Give me a Permanent Idle." (That is a special privilege reserved for inmates who are unable to work for physical or mental reasons.) He said, "But there is nothing wrong with you." I said, "Oh yes there is! Like I said, I'm being programmed! Programmed to come back to this living hell and I am sick of it. I need to find a way to stay out of here." For the next two years I was on Permanent Idle.

Two of the three most influential people I met in the seven years I spent in Stillwater were about to enter my life. Owen was the first, Ellsworth was the second, and Roger was the third. Ellsworth and Roger were like Ying and Yang, positive and negative.

Ellsworth

Ellsworth was doing a life sentence for a murder he didn't commit. Really. He was actually framed. After five years full of hardships and obstacles set before him by the prosecution, his case was overturned and he was set free. Many people lost their jobs when the truth was exposed involving them in the framing of Ellsworth. He had employed several lawyers to work on his case. But they all bailed out when they were threatened by the people who had framed him. Once it was evident that he was all alone in his fight for freedom, he went to work for the prison education system. He spent much of his time in the library pouring through law books teaching himself the law.

Ellsworth always told me that it was a lie that found him guilty and no matter what anyone said or did, it would always be a lie, and that it would be exposed in the end. He told me his story and I couldn't believe this man was in prison with all of us that completely deserved our sentences.

Ellsworth told me that the whole thing started when a frantic woman called the police department and reported that her husband had just been shot and killed on the front porch by so-and-so. It became a matter of record, as did the radio conversations between law officers after that call was received. One of the law officers was related to the real killer. Ellsworth worked for a very large well-known corporation at the time, as did the killer and the man who was murdered. Ellsworth was close friends with the killer. Ellsworth was also right in the middle of a discrimination suit that he had filed on the corporation when they promoted someone with less qualifications and seniority into a position that he had applied for within the company.

As the story goes, almost everyone who liked to unwind at the end of the day went to a nearby bar. On this particular day, Ellsworth and the deceased victim got into an argument that turned into a pushing match and nothing more. When the actual killer found out that Ellsworth (his close friend) had gotten into a fight, the word was that Ellsworth had gotten beat up. You know how stories change, especially when they're handed down from one drunk to another.

Ellsworth's friend then went to the victim's home and shot him dead in front of his wife to avenge Ellsworth's honor.

If Ellsworth had any weaknesses, it would have to be his bond to loyalty. Because of his loyalty to his friend, he let himself be arrested, tried and convicted without saying a word that would implicate the real killer, who actually became the state's star witness after being offered immunity for his testimony against Ellsworth. Ellsworth always thought that the truth would be discovered before he was ever sentenced and that he would be set free. He thought that his friend would never be prosecuted because he had been granted immunity. What Ellsworth didn't know, was what the prosecution was willing to do to cover up the facts that would expose the lie. Ellsworth told me that the real reason his friend had snapped was because he was depressed. He was going through a divorce, he had lost his home and was just looking for trouble.

All of this happened to Ellsworth, yet he remained positive and determined to advocate for the truth all by himself. Here again, is the beginning of what could be another book about an extraordinary man whom I never will forget. How Ellsworth played a part in my life had to do with his high intelligence and insight. His answer to every question was like a finger pointing to the direction in which the answer could be found. He didn't give an absolute answer of his personal choice. He often questioned my concepts. Concepts such as, "Good things don't come easy." His answer was a question. "Why not?"

I answered, "Isn't that what we are told all of our lives?"

"Yes. But that doesn't make it true. Would you rather things come with much difficulty, or easy? The real answer to this question, of course, lies within each of us and what we believe to be easy and what we believe to be difficult." But we mostly go by what we have been told all of our lives.

Ellsworth determined early on in our relationship that I wasn't very skilled in the art of thinking. So, after all of his questions, he taught me how to think in a positive way and never to accept something at face value without careful thought.

Setting Goals

I took a mail-order course in electronics because that seemed to be the wave of the future. I stopped all my drug activity (with the exception of reefer) and began to get serious about finding a way to stay out a prison rather than just get out.

I started to spend some time analyzing inmates that were getting out of prison and who then returned within a short period of time. I wanted to know why they couldn't seem to stay out so that I wouldn't make the same mistakes. I knew most of them really wanted to stay out. So what actually was the problem that caused so many to forfeit their freedom over and over doing life on the installment plan in this living hell?

One person I spoke with just before he was released, made it obvious to me why he was bound to return. Prior to leaving, he spoke at length about his plans when he got out. He was going to work hard at making good drug connections on the outside, so that he would have a reliable drug source when he returned. He was visualizing his return, even before he was released! The outcome was inevitable.

We often think of setting goals as a good thing. If the goal is a healthy one, then I would agree. What we fail to process, however, is that we all too often set goals that will bring dysfunction. The success of reaching any goal is not determined by what is positive and what is negative, or what is good and what is bad. It is determined by our determination to reach the goal that is set, whatever that goal might be. In this young man's case, the goal was to return to prison with good drug connections. In some realm, his actions may be considered positive. He had set a goal and he was willing to work for it. He would be achieving what he wanted, right? But the question needs to be asked; why didn't he set up healthy goals outside of prison? Why was his aim to make prison more comfortable for himself, instead of the pursuit of complete freedom? Do you see what I am saying about goals?

Why They Return

Some of the other inmates I interviewed before their release and after their return were not so obvious. But all of them seem to have one common denominator. They were all institutionalized prior to release and not at all prepared to deal with the responsibilities that had been restored to them. The ones that were successful at adjusting, were the people doing time for crimes of passion or white collar crime. They had been, at one time, upstanding responsible citizens, before committing some stupid crime brought on by emotional stress or greed. Why did these guys do well once released? Because they already knew how to be responsible and it was just a matter of readjusting.

For those of us who had never been responsible, like myself, it was necessary to be surrounded by solid people and learn from them. The guys who were released and went back to rubbing shoulders with troublemakers, looking for the easy way (which covers roughly 90% of the prison population) eventually found their way back to the penitentiary.

Inmates hated the dysfunctional life that led them to the penitentiary. Yet it was the only life they understood. When they became cold, tired, hungry and confused, prison life represented the security of essential things, like food, shelter, and the warm bed that they needed for survival. Prison life brought them security without the complexities of unfamiliar responsibilities.

The institutions across the nation are filled with people just like you and me that only dream of being free, because they have never found a better way. They are regarded, for the most part, as the scum of the earth. They are treated as though they are people without feelings or regard for human life, not even their own. The truth is, that not one of them was born criminally insane. Criminal insanity is something they learned. Anything we learn, can be unlearned.

If it was my experience why can't it be yours? It was only the want, need, and desire to be free that caused me to accept all responsibilities for myself without blaming another living soul for any of my misfortunes or shortcomings. In fact, when someone tries to take the blame for something that happens to me, I gladly shoulder the blame, because that gives me the right to learn from my mistakes rather than forfeit that freedom to someone else. Freedom was my only reason for stopping the abuse of drugs, alcohol, and tobacco. All these things caused me to do things that I really didn't want to do in order to obtain them. Once I had obtained them, they ruled my life almost completely without mercy or consideration for another living soul.

Making Your Dream a Reality

If it were not for all the things that hold you down, what would you make of your life? If you have the answer to that question, then set yourself free and make it happen. It's easier than you think. It would have been good if I had been more than just aware of this knowledge at this point in my life but I had a long way to go. Being aware isn't enough. I knew the truth but I had not been able to put it to practical use. I'm sure you have heard the term "knowledge is power," but knowledge is nothing unless you are aware of that knowledge and know how to use it. Awareness holds no more value than a dream until you incorporate your awareness into your daily life where it becomes a vision. The vision needs to have a large dose of action, if you are to have lasting change. Each step is vital, but the final action step is where most people never put it all together. The knowledge, the awareness, the dream, and the vision all need to come together under the action heading. You need to visualize this plan, then act on it if you are going to make your dreams a reality.

Good People, Bad People

There was a constant pull of good and bad influences in my life, as I am sure there is in your life. Ellsworth was good. He was an inspiration to me. But eventually I teamed up with another inmate, Roger. He was a positive influence in a negative way by reminding me of a life I no longer wanted. If you're going to deal drugs in prison, then you need plenty of protection. I don't care who you are or how tough you are, drug addicts will take you down anyway they can to get a fix. Roger was black and well-established with the brothers in the penitentiary.

One evening, I had a problem with some black inmates over in A Hall who didn't know me. (A Hall is where all the new prisoners live along with the radicals who have not yet adjusted to prison life.) I had traded some reefer that Roy had received in payment from another inmate in that hall. It turned out that every other joint was nothing more than Bull Durham.

I was called on the loudspeaker to the rotunda, which was the tier between A House and B House. Previously such a call was someone wanting to borrow money. When I got to the tier, there were about 10 or 12 black inmates trying to talk me into going down the tier with them to do business. I knew they wanted me down that hallway because there weren't any camera's down there. I asked them to wait for a few minutes and went back inside and told Roger what was happening. Within five minutes, I was back in the rotunda with about 30 brothers behind me.

"Let's go do business," I said, but they declined. Instead, they began telling me what had happened.

I said, "That's not a problem", refunded them money to replace their drugs and told them who was responsible for the bad reefer. The last word I heard was that the inmate responsible for the bad reefer was back in protective custody nursing cuts, bruises and torn rectum tissue.

If you think prison is cool in any way, let me remind you again, that I could fill an entire book with all the sick, perverted, unfair, crass, and disgusting behaviors I witnessed in prison. There isn't any reason to dwell in hell. Very few people leave prison without some new emotional baggage from their experiences there. Don't allow yourself to think that you would be the exception. Just steer clear.

Together Roger and I became the drug lords and loan sharks of the penitentiary. My justification at this point was "What can I do that's 'wrong' when this whole institution and everyone in it is wrong?" We had guards on our payroll as well as inmates. We even had all known snitches on the payroll so they snitched to us, rather than on us.

A Bizarre Business

It was kind of a bizarre business. Being in control of the drugs, the money, and the cigarettes enabled us to buy drugs from other inmates as they brought them in, in small quantities at less than half the going price. Then often, we'd sell them right back to them at full price, using money they borrowed from us to purchase the same drugs they sold us for less than half price. Did they know it was their drugs? No, not that it would have made any difference, but the less people know the better. The fact is, we rarely ever had drugs in our possession. We paid inmates to hold them and we paid inmates to deal them. The dealers never knew who they were really selling for and the people that held the drugs would die before they would gave up our names. Everyone knew that we were loan sharks, but almost no one knew that we were drug dealers.

Roger didn't use drugs. Period. The people I partied with, just thought I bought my drugs like everyone else did. They had no idea what I was really into.

Here's an example of one of our money scams.

Someone was always asking me to front them some money with a promise that I would be paid based on someone on the outside's ability to come through for them. It had been my experience that rarely, if ever, do those people on the outside come through on time, because they are usually relying on someone else. And so on and so on. Welcome to the drug world. I usually would stop this short and say, "I don't care about your connections on the outside. I'm not dealing with them, I'm dealing with you. You give me some collateral that I can hold until you bring me my money, whenever that might be, and we're in business". No one would ever come back when they say they're going to. But they did eventually come around to retrieve their collateral or sell it to us, as we never imposed deadlines. Deadlines caused resentments and were bad for business.

The most popular form of collateral was a television set. Every inmate wasn't fortunate enough to have their own private television set, unless they had the money to buy one, or someone on the outside to purchase one for them. Televisions are pawned in 30-day increments for $10. At the end of 30 days, their television could be retrieved for $15. Why 30 days? Because we couldn't hold the television sets that were in pawn at any given time in our cell. So, we rented them out for $10 a month to other inmates who couldn't afford a television set of their own but could afford a rental from time to time.

If you didn't have money on the books when you come in, or someone to send you money from the outside, or a way to make money on the inside, you had to rely on the $.50 a day the state paid you for welding manure spreaders, grain wagons, machining, metal fabricating, cooking, cleaning, and other basic skills. As an electronic technician, plumber, and as an electrician, I was considered skilled labor. They paid me $1.50 a day. I suppose that's changed in the past 30 years, but I bet not much.

I had requested to be placed on "permanent idle" from the doctor, but in 1976 I returned to work in order to keep a low profile. One of the positive things I learned from Roger that would help me on the outside, was to get up early and go to work and give my employers 100 percent, regardless of the pay. He also taught me basic business maneuvers. How to read people. How to find their weaknesses, as well as their strengths.

Drugs, Money and Power

At Roger's insistence I took a job in the industrial shop as a welder again. While I was learning some basic business skills there, I was never far away from the life I knew best. I had several good Class-A drug connections, with emphasis on pharmaceuticals. I could get synthetic morphine, cocaine, barbiturates and amphetamines. But I didn't have a good reefer connection.

That changed when a fellow inmate introduced me to his wife's friend, Loren. She was a hair stylist. We hit it off pretty well and before long, I had introduced her to a new source of income. The first time she brought me reefer was when I had her put on a visiting list for an Indian powwow in the prison auditorium. She began to enjoy the visits, especially when she went out with a pocket full of cash! Every time she came up for a visit, or to bring me drugs, she left with a wad of bills. Soon, she no longer needed to personally carry in the drugs. Roger had hooked up a guard to do the job for us. We could buy a pound of reefer for as little as $110 a pound. After we paid the guard to bring it in, someone to hold it for us, another to roll it up into toothpick sized joints and finally someone to sell it for us, we still cleared a profit of $1600 within the month it took to sell it. Every month we repeated this process.

Loren kept coming to visit.

Every once in while one of the dealers would take more than their cut. We knew when this happened, because they would then check into the protective custody unit which is segregated from the rest of the population. They were "hiding" from us and we knew why. It never presented much of a problem to us because we would send in a few joints with a messenger (usually an inmate counselor), who would give the joints to someone who would in turn, beat the living crap out of the "thief" and convince them to come out and face the music. All we did at that point, was tell the persons holding our drugs to make them work off what they owed us.

It was humorous, really. Inmates would often tell me stories about dealers in the prison who had gotten badly hurt because they had cheated someone. Even the dealers themselves told me about what had happened to them when they tried to rip off an unknown, top dealer. They never once suspected that I was one of the people responsible for their beatings. I had drugs, money and power. Using the drugs and money, I had power over these people and they didn't even know it.

Nightclub in Prison

Thirty years ago in Stillwater Prison, the rule was if you could get something into your cell, you could keep it. My cell resembled a nightclub.

I had a drop ceiling with Plexiglas panels dropped into wood frames. Each panel was covered with black light posters and lights behind them. I had a huge black light that hung over a full-size roll top desk. There was a cushioned seat on my toilet. I had my bed removed from the wall where it was chained and hired the best carpenter in the penitentiary to build me a Hollywood bed and a cabinet at the foot of the bed. On that cabinet I placed a 17-inch color TV. There was a stereo system at the head of my bed and I personally built a control panel that allowed me to control everything while lying on my back. Lights, fans, TV, stereo and anything that had a switch could be controlled from my bed. The same carpenter who created the ceiling panels and Hollywood bed, also built a set of cabinets that extended across the entire back wall. The cabinets were about 2 feet high with glazed Plexiglas doors with colored lights behind them. It was a sight to behold. Inmates would often come by just to look at it. It was the only one of its kind and I've heard it was never repeated after I left.

There are many stories I could tell you about my prison life but I think that would constitute yet another book.

I Had a Plan

Every day towards the end of my time in Stillwater, I would get up with the vision of what I would do once I left that place. I had a plan.

I would immediately stop all drug activity and concentrate on making a new life. Everything I wanted was as clear to me as if it had already happened. Any thought of failure never even crossed my mind. I was absolutely sure of myself. More so than I ever have been in my entire life. I would misplace a lot of that confidence over the next thirty years, as the noise of the world became louder than the voice within me. Yet today, I am getting close to total recall with a lot of added clarity and wisdom. I had the vision back then, but lacked the discipline and wisdom to put that vision into practical use. Still, it was a start and much more positive then I had ever been before.

It's probably pretty hard for you to understand how I could physically do one thing and imagine myself doing something totally different. Actually, the reality of prison constantly reminded me of everything negative that I wanted to be free of. So it became rather easy to fill my thoughts with visions of the good things which would replace the bad. This must have been where the concept of Dr. Jekyll and Mr. Hyde originated, because the things I was doing in reality were totally opposite of the things I created in my mind and envisioned as real.

Prior to release, after doing a long stretch of prison time, everyone I've ever witnessed has gone through separation anxieties which I call "pre-release blues." Almost everyone does something to screw up just before they get released as if to be saying, "don't let me out." Being very well aware of this, I still managed to screw up. To make a long story short, I got caught with a needle in my arm and was put in the hole just one week before I was to be released. I was, in fact, still doing hole time the day I was released. On the big day, they let me go back to my cell to gather up my personal belongings before they sent me out front to the holding cell.

On The Outside

Released

The date was February 7, 1977. I was finally out of Stillwater State Penitentiary. I was paroled to a halfway house called 180 Degrees, which was run by a bunch of surly people who seemed to get off on tormenting newly released prisoners. Maybe their program started out as a good thing but it had turned into something not so good.

Loren had stuck with me and now we were engaged. While I was in prison, she had been staying with Roger's wife and three kids. The drug money had been helping pay the house payments, so Loren was living in an upstairs apartment.

While I was technically living in the halfway house, as long as I kept my nose clean, I was permitted to go wherever I pleased. I could spend the weekend at Loren's or she could come for the weekend at my place.

I got a job pulling air conditioning units out of apartment buildings. My job was to clean or replace them. I worked hard and got promoted to supervisor, which only meant I got to tell people what to do by showing them.

About the second week Loren and I were together, we went up north to visit my mother and father. From there, we went on to Fargo and picked up my oldest son Tyron, and daughter Charmane, along with their sister Crystal. We then headed for South Dakota in our 1972 Olds dynamic 88, where I made 19-year-old Loren Kay my third wife in the presence of Tyron, Charmane, and Crystal. The halfway house wasn't happy when I told them I had gotten married over the weekend. Luckily, they got over it.

We kept our marriage a secret from her mother, father, sisters and brothers until I was able to formally ask her father for her hand in marriage. A few months after our South Dakota "wedding," we exchanged vows again at her mother and father's home with my old friend from Stillwater, Owen, as best man. Owen was barely holding his own when our paths crossed again just before Loren and I got married for the second time. In spite of all his artistic talents, he had chosen to continue throwing his life away as he quickly became a hopeless drunk. He didn't remain in my life much longer. We moved and I never saw him again.

The next one of my Stillwater buddies to re-enter my life was Ellsworth. We met again just after Loren and I bought our three year old, five bedroom home in a quiet old neighborhood in north Minneapolis. One day I just happened to be thinking about him and wondered if he was out of prison. I looked him up in the phone book, called him and sure enough, he was free! He, his wife and daughter and new son were living in the projects in St. Paul. He didn't own a car and rode a bicycle everywhere, keeping him in top shape.

Ellsworth was always an asset to me. I just wish I had listened to him a little closer at times. He was not the kind of person who would tell you what to do, but he would give you enough information that would help you determine what to do.

I would be willing to bet that if I looked him up today he would be a millionaire. The people responsible for his incarceration were offering him a lot of money, but he kept refusing it. What he really wanted was all of their jobs. It wasn't about money for him. He didn't feel that they should be in a position of public trust after what they did to him.

If I had been aware then, of what I am aware of now, I would have offered him some advice concerning his bitterness toward those people he was out to get. What he was trying to do to them, wasn't nearly as bad as what he was doing to himself by holding onto something that was weighing him down. Ellsworth was an extraordinary person and though I will most likely never see him again, I would like to believe that he and his family are doing well.

Back Pain

I was making just a little bit over minimum wage pulling those air conditioning units from apartment buildings and cleaning them. I needed more money. I applied for a job at a cement plant and got it. I actually had experience in that area from my days in Fargo, North Dakota where I worked for a concrete company just after Gloria and I got married in 1965. This job was union scale and paid $2.50 more per hour than I was making, so I gave my notice, and started my new job.

Two weeks into the job I ruptured a disc in my back. Ninety-eight pound bags of ready mix cement were coming back to back on a conveyor belt and it was my job to stack them neatly on pallets. My back started to hurt. At first it was just uncomfortable. When we broke for lunch one day it turned into serious pain. I mentioned it to a few people at work. I told them that I had messed something up in my back.

By the next morning, I was bent over and unable to get out of bed. I needed a ride to the hospital. The heads of the halfway house thought I was pretending, so that I could scam some drugs. They actually called General Hospital and warned them that I might be pretending so the doctors didn't take me very seriously. I was experiencing constant, radiating waves of pain. I waited six weeks to be admitted and during that time I dropped from 150 pounds to 115. Several doctors attempted to diagnose my problem. At one point, they tried to inject ink into my spine, which required me to lay flat on my stomach. But the pain was too bad. I couldn't lay face down. So, they had to abort their efforts. Eight days later I was released with more pain than when I arrived.

Finally, one night on a weekend with Loren, I sat in a chair and watched her sleep. She got up to go to work, came home and went to sleep again, while I sat in that chair trying everything I could to escape the pain. The only sleep I got was to occasionally pass out from exhaustion for a few minutes at a time. I was full of drugs and alcohol, and still there was no escape from the pain. I began to pray. I asked my higher power, "Why? Wasn't I doing the right things? Wasn't I going in the right direction? Didn't I already pay for the wrong I had done? There must be a reason for this pain. Whatever that reason is, I accept it."

Perhaps it was final payment for all the pain I had caused so many innocent people over the years.

Just before daybreak, I decided that I couldn't stand the pain any longer. Instead of calling General Hospital, I called the University of Minnesota. I explained the past six weeks and was told to get to the hospital immediately. I didn't wake Loren. I just got in the car and started to drive myself to the hospital. I was drunk and full of drugs. My driving skills sucked. I had no feeling in my right leg and couldn't determine pressures on the foot feed or the brake. I was bumping into the bumpers of other cars. I was slamming on my brakes where there was no need. I have no idea how I managed to make it to the hospital without hurting anyone, but I did.

I look back on that day now and think what a fool I was to make that drive alone in my condition.

After a short check-in process, I was put on a gurney. Shortly after that a big black lady neurosurgeon came in asked me to stand as best as I could, which was bent over about 45°. She put one hand on the small of my back and the other on my chest and pushed the small of my back in. As she pushed my chest back, I thought, "This must be what childbirth feels like."

The pain was excruciating. She told me, "Honey, you have a herniated disk."

She could feel it with her hand. It needed to be surgically removed. She ordered me a shot of Demerol and for the first time in six weeks, there was relief. Four days later, I walked out of the hospital standing straight. I hadn't done that for six weeks. Before that surgery, I was beginning to believe there was no escape for me. I was going to be a cripple.

The halfway house cut me loose while I was still in the hospital. I don't think they wanted me around to remind them of what they had done to me. Besides, I could've made a lot of trouble for them.

Things Going Well
Sometimes it's really strange how things work out.

I mean, one minute you're doing everything within your power to make your visions a reality and in the next you're on your knees. My faith still wasn't shaken. My dream was to own a home with Loren. I could still see us owning that house within five years. After all, I still had my job that paid a little bit above average. Then one day, a check came in the mail from Worker's Compensation. It was a big one that covered the last few weeks that I was out of work. When I did return to work at the concrete plant, it was short lived. I slowly began to experience pain and became bent over again. I talked to my doctor and he told me to see a lawyer, which I did.

I attended school for a while to learn business and sales. Then, two years later, I received a settlement. It was enough money in one lump sum to buy that first house.

So, there I was in 1979, with a brand-new Pontiac Grand Prix company car, an almost new five bedroom home in a good part of town, an almost new Ford Thunderbird of my own and an almost new Mustang for Loren. We had money to burn and life was good.

Oh, did I mention a baby on the way? My parole officer decided I was doing better than he was and recommended me to the board for a full pardon, which I was granted with all rights restored to me.

I still had my vision for the future and things were going well. My back injury was rated at 15% permanent disability of the spine. Actually, I don't believe I have any disability of the spine. I don't experience anymore backaches than anyone else does and probably a lot less than most people my age. The most debilitating thing that came from my back injury was that I began to drink and do drugs again which caused my focus to fade over the next few years.

While attending school for business and sales, I did my summer internship working for a company that sold home improvements, mostly insulation. I caught on fast and did so well that I received a company car. (That's how I got the Pontiac.)

After business school I landed a job working for a large food chain as a manager. Now you would think that a person with my background as an ex-con, four-time loser, convicted car thief, burglar, armed robber, and free for only two years wouldn't even be considered a prospect. What are the chances of being given the combinations to safes containing large sums of money and the keys to the front door of their largest restaurant? This might seem impossible, but I never gave a second thought about any possibilities of not getting the job. When I was asked if I had ever been arrested I said yes and told them why, adding that it wouldn't be a problem. They believed me.

The Unraveling

I worked as a manager for two years, but I was still drinking and occasionally doing drugs.

Loren and I invited Tyrone, Charmane and Crystal to come and stay with us for the summer. Tyrone came first and then later on the girls came. I think it was a very special time for Tyrone, as it certainly was for me. There was some friction between Loren and the kids, but then, Loren was pretty much a kid herself at the time.

Sadly, the relationship between Loren and I eventually began to go bad. Ellsworth warned me that some of my behavior was not doing the marriage any good. But I didn't listen. I continued to drink and do drugs. I constantly cheated on her and treated her with very little respect. Shortly after our daughter Jenna was born, we separated and shortly after that, divorced. She got the house, our daughter, and everything else except for the clothes on my back, a mattress and box spring, and a chest of drawers. I probably got more than I deserved under the circumstances.

She really never presented a problem for me that I couldn't handle, because I knew the best of her. I accept the responsibility for that broken relationship.

I can't remember any time that she deserved the crap that I put her through. She had every right in the world to leave me. Although we didn't meet under the best of circumstances, she was a positive influence in my life and she was there when I really needed someone. She showed me what she knew about society and how to deal with it. She did point me in the right direction. I am ashamed of the way I acted and the way I treated her and I would like to take this time to apologize for my inconsiderate behavior, as well as all the mean things I said and did in a fit of anger or while intoxicated, or high. I have no excuses and I offer only my sincere apology. Loren was truly a good person and it is my wish that she finds what she really wants in life and makes it hers.

More than just my marriage was in trouble. Things began to go bad at work as well because of my drinking. Once I quit denying my addiction, I checked myself into treatment. The company I worked for was kind enough to pay for the treatment. So for 30 days, I was an inpatient at a drug treatment facility in Minneapolis.

While in treatment, I met my fourth wife, Sybil.

After 30 days my treatment was completed or, shall I say, mostly completed. I say this because there was a part of the program where we were to confess our wrongs to a priest and ask for forgiveness. I couldn't understand why I should beat myself up all over again when I felt that I had already confessed everything to a power greater than the man standing before me and felt that I had been forgiven. Because I would not confess to a priest, I was never given my thirty-day medallion like the rest of the group.

From there, I was accepted into an after-care program where we continued to have regular group meetings while we adjusted to our lives without the aid of alcohol and drugs to screw it up. Sybil got out a couple weeks after I did and was accepted into the same program. We were free to do whatever we wanted to off the premises, but on the premises, we could visit girlfriends and spend the whole evening together as long as we were in our own rooms by curfew. Sexual intercourse was forbidden and punishable by immediate dismissal from the program.

When I say immediate I don't mean as soon as you find another place to live. Or even the next day. I mean right now! Gather your things and leave at once.

One night, Sybil and I spent the night together and she made the mistake of telling her roommate why she hadn't come home that night. Her roommate told one of the counselors. Within minutes, we were ordered to leave. Sybil found a run-down, one-room apartment somewhere. I was invited back home to live in the basement of my home with Loren and Jenna.

While I was managing the drugs and alcohol issues in my life, I was still strung out on this pretty little 21-year-old redhead that I just couldn't resist. Sybil and I hadn't seen each other for about a month when, one day, she walked into the restaurant that I was managing looking hot and sexy. I moved out of the basement and into an apartment with a guy I met at an AA meeting. Sybil was spending so much time over at my place that she finally just moved in with me.

The apartment was located in one of the worst known parts of town, where shootings, stabbings, rapes, muggings, theft and robberies were a way of life. Seems like I was going backwards, doesn't it? My dreams of owning a home and having financial freedom were gone as I looked around my crappy apartment. While I didn't see it then, I was going to have to manage drugs, alcohol and my sex life before I would be able to fully realize my dreams. I don't believe there is any way for an addict to manage drugs and alcohol other than to leave it alone. Period. The next step is to stop going to places and events and discontinue associating with people that are a temptation that will take you by surprise and dump you into the same hole you just crawled out of. I tried everything imaginable with no good results until I stopped and removed myself from all temptations.

Toilet Bowl Man

My job as a restaurant manager ended shortly after the company was sold and then downsized. I was laid off but still received unemployment checks. My roommate was good at buying cars out of the daily newspaper at bargain prices and then reselling them in the same paper at a substantial profit. He taught me the tricks of the trade and soon I began to enjoy some of the same profits. Then Roy and I crossed paths again.

There seemed to be a pattern to how people influenced my life. In Stillwater I started out with Owen at a time when I was just beginning a new 15-year sentence. He helped me to become aware of the knowledge I never knew existed. Then Ellsworth substantiated what I had discovered and helped me put it into practical use. And now Roy showed up to remind me of the life I didn't want.

Soon we were in the business of buying and selling so many cars we ran out of room to park them. Roger and I decided to try our hand at a legitimate business, which eventually turned into an auto body repair shop. But his agenda and mine where total opposites. His idea was to lie, cheat, steal and do whatever was necessary to raise money. That didn't sit well with me, but I found myself slipping back to where I had come from. I was surrounded by drug addicts, thieves, killers and whatever type you might find in the penitentiary.

It wasn't long before I gave in to one of my many weaknesses and started to shoot speed again. I was losing ground fast. I became irrational, impulsive and irresponsible. I stopped paying my bills so that I could afford drugs. When I ran out of money, I began to trade the things I valued most to the drug pusher. Bills would come in and I wouldn't even bother to open them. Almost every day a bill collector would call and threaten to take things that I no longer had. Problem solved, telephone was disconnected. Then there were knocks on the door.

I began to feel like the tidy bowl man, swirling around in a flushed toilet of that blue stuff that hides the stench of what is really on its way to the sewer. I retained just barely enough intelligence to realize that I had to get away fast, before it was too late, and find a way to start all over again.

Escape To Waco
Roger got busted for shoplifting, and was doing weekends in the workhouse. I needed to get far away. I took the opportunity one weekend, packed my belongings, and headed for Texas with a speed freak I knew from Stillwater leaving behind a business, all the tools and equipment and all the supplies and inventory that I had worked so hard to accumulate. I left the house full of furniture, clothing, and other personal items. I was taking only what I needed to get by.

My speed buddy made his way through life shooting speed and stealing for a living, but he was the only person desperate enough to hit the road with me. I was very insecure and it never occurred to me that I could leave on my own. Somehow I needed the security of a speed addict.

By this time Sybil had moved out and was living close to where she was working .We were still seeing each other but it wasn't anything very serious. I stopped by and told her goodbye and left her a car full of household things and the title to the car. Then I was on my way to Texas with enough pharmaceutical speed to keep us up for days.

We headed down I35 to Waco since I had brothers and sisters there who might be able to help me get set up in business. I had no intentions of ever returning to Minnesota.

Somewhere in Oklahoma we pulled into a large parking lot where a lot of cowboys and girls were attending something that was equivalent to the grand old Opry. We spotted a nice, unlocked pickup truck. My buddy slid out with a dent puller/slide hammer and jumped into the pick-up. He screwed the puller into the ignition and ripped it out in one quick motion. The pickup truck was loaded with tools and must have belonged to a contractor. I drove it all the way to Waco with my buddy following closely behind.

It seemed as though I was well on my way back to where I had come from and that everything I had learned was almost all forgotten.

Slipping Back

Was leaving Minnesota the answer to my problems at the time? Having the strength to resist temptation would have been much better, but I couldn't find that strength within my circumstances. Without much of a fight, I gave in to all the crap that I had struggled to be free of. I only remembered enough of what I had learned from all my mistakes to know that I desperately needed to change, and change fast before it was too late. Right or wrong, I tried to make that change by heading to Texas. It allowed me just enough time to slow down and remember the lessons that I had paid such a high price to learn.

When I was around Roger, my soul was slowly slipping into a pit that was so dark I couldn't do any more than survive. All of my addictions and habits came back into my life.

My brother Ray had just gotten out of Huntsville Prison and was living with a woman who had been a friend of the family for years. I moved in with them, thinking that Ray and I might be able to relate to each other. My speed addicted co-pilot turned out to be too weird and scary for Ray's girlfriend, so we sent him back to Minnesota.

It wasn't long before I discovered that living around my sisters and brothers in Texas was not much better than where I had just come from. Everyone in the family smoked dope and drank beer and really had no definite aim in life. I began to drink and smoke dope with them. My youngest brother, Davey, thought it was cute to get his two-year-old son stoned on marijuana. It was another toxic environment.

I decided that my brothers, sisters and I had nothing in common that would enable any of us, under the circumstances, to make any progress toward anything positive.

Heading Back North

Sybil decided to come down to visit me for a weekend. When she left, I went back to Minnesota with her.

The first thing I did was reunite with my daughter Jenna who was about two. Her mother, Loren, allowed me visiting rights on the weekends where I occasionally took her home with me.

After a few months back in Minnesota living with Sybil, we decided to marry. In case you've lost count, this was my fourth marriage. And, as had happened before, our relationship began to deteriorate and the pressure began to build. It was not easy for me to be around her. PMS attacks made her crazy. She would lay in bed for days and complain about the slightest little noise.

One day I had brought her a gift, a red rose in a little glass vase. I don't recall what the occasion was, perhaps it was just too make her feel a little better. I went outside with little Jenna and was visiting with Sybil's brother when Jenna needed to go to the bathroom. I asked her to go quietly into the house and go. When she came out of the bathroom she asked me a question and when Sybil heard her voice, she came storming out of the bedroom in a rage, cursing.

"What is she doing here?" she screamed.

I answered, "She's my daughter. Why shouldn't she be here?" There was a barrage of cursing and yelling. I told her, "Just shut up and go back to sleep."

That's when she picked up the little glass vase with the rose in it and smashed it on the floor. Then she picked up a piece of the broken glass and slit her arm open, making a bloody mess. Jenna began to scream. I picked her up to comfort her as I looked at Sybil with disgust. Then I turned with Jenna in my arms and walked out the door.

"You might want to look in on your sister, she just slit her wrists," I told her brother.

That was the worst of many such episodes. It involved a two year old child who couldn't possibly understand what was going on.

Sybil recovered from her superficial wounds and within days acted as though the incident had never taken place. It was a bizarre relationship to say the least. It was all inflamed by drugs and alcohol.

Tyrone

My oldest son, Tyrone, came to live with us for a short while. I was working as an employment counselor at the time. Can you imagine that? Because of my position, I was able to find him a job in a warehouse. But it was a long way to drive for not much money and he soon became frustrated with the job. I pointed out that it was better than nothing and that he should keep at it because it might be the start towards something better. But he wanted to go back to Fargo. So we sat down and had a talk.

My mind was beginning to clear a bit. I could see how I had nearly slipped back into the sewer of no escape and I was beginning to remember some of the positive things I had learned in Stillwater. I had a long way to go. But there were times when I could think straight and communicate clearly. This little talk with Tyrone was a chance to convey some wisdom to my son. He wanted something from me. But I wasn't sure just what it was or how to talk to him about it.

One day I just came right out and asked him, "What is it that you want, Tyrone?"

He looked at me, then looked away, thinking. "Peace of mind," he said.

"What do you think would give you peace of mind?" I asked. This was something. We were actually talking about important things.

He shrugged his shoulders. "I don't know."

I thought about this a moment and asked him, "How about if I gave you a thousand dollars. Would that give you peace of mind?"

He turned to me and smiled. His eyes got real wide for a couple of seconds until I informed him that that wouldn't be happening. His expression changed to disappointment. Then I said, "You can't find peace of mind in any amount of money, because once the money runs out, so does your peace of mind. Peace of mind exists within you and if you can't find it at any given moment on the spot in which you stand, then you will never find it anywhere else on earth." I knew the truth when I spoke it.

The next day Tyrone headed back to Fargo.

Looking back, I think what my son wanted from me was something that he had never had. He had a father. But what he really needed was a dad. There's a big difference. Any idiot can be a father. But it takes something special to be a dad to a child. I think that's all he ever wanted from me. But I didn't know much about being a dad and failed to be one to him.

Living with regrets can become overwhelming, so when I say that one of the biggest regrets of my life is that I failed to give Tyrone the relationship he so desperately wanted with me. You need to know that I have had to forgive myself for missing that opportunity. We will get into it more a little later, but my son died before I ever gave him what he needed from me. Even in the end, just before his death, I was pointing out the flaws in him rather than his many assets. Now I can't go back and tell him all the good things that I've seen in him and how they far outweighed the little flaws. I hope he knew that I wasn't purposely withholding love and acceptance from him. I just couldn't give away something that I didn't have.

Bad Decisions

After Tyrone left, Sybil and I went back to coping with our pathetic marriage by avoiding each other whenever possible. I continued to drink and to make bad decisions.

Sometimes I would go out drinking and not even bother to come home. I would simply pass out in my car where I would stay all night. One night, I had been out drinking, when I came home around 2am. For some reason, that I can't for the life of me recall why, I decided to take my life. Sybil and I lived in an apartment building that had those little one car garages connected to each other in a long line that were numbered to indicate the apartment number it belonged to. These garages were located across the parking lot from the apartments. I pulled my big, old, ugly 75 Coupe Deville into the garage, shut the door and got in the front seat behind the wheel. I started the car, lowered the windows and passed out. The next thing I recall is Sybil waking me up. To this day I am baffled as to how she showed up at the garage at 2 in the morning when she had been in bed sleeping when I arrived. What in the world was at work in my life preventing me from killing myself? Could it be the same power that saved me so many times before? She did ask me why, but I couldn't tell her because I really didn't know. Does anything drunks do make sense? She just said "do you realize that if you had succeeded I would have never known why you decided to take your life? We never talked about that incident after that.

Another time was New Year's when I was drinking in a bar that was notorious for gangs and fights. In a drunken state I said the wrong thing to someone and ended up with three broken ribs.

In another drunken state, I decided to try my hand at shop lifting since I had watched both Sybil and Roger do it. I stole a boom box from Montgomery Wards and a couple of telephone systems from AT&T at one of the malls. I shoplifted a miniature television set from another store.

Another time, I got caught stealing a leather jacket from Montgomery Wards. I had enough money on me to buy 10 leather jackets and to this day I couldn't really tell you why I found it necessary to steal that jacket. But let's not forget that there is a reason for everything and that our calls for help may not always make good sense. There I was again right back where I started from. Locked up in the Dakota County jail with nothing but time on my hands to make some serious decisions about my life. My decision was to stop drinking and straighten out my life again, what was different this time? Had I not made a decision to reconstruct my life before? The problem was that I had lost sight of my dream and the desire to make it real. What I had not done yet is to make a firm commitment to myself that I would, without fail, no matter how many wrong turns I took, find my way back and make my dream real. Let me explain this another way.

Picture a home with all that you hold dear in it. The people you love, your hopes and dreams, everything. Now let's say that you have made sure that a flood could never hurt you because you have a sump pump and even a backup pump. You are certain you would be warm, as you installed a brand new furnace. You have a fridge and freezer full of fantastic food and a state of the art chef's kitchen. You are feeling pretty good about the situation you have set up. But then everything begins to unravel. The house is cold, the basement is flooded and the food is rotten. You just don't understand how this could be happening after all of your hard work. You now have a choice. You could leave this place that you have worked so hard for and go back to your world of having nothing. Or, you could take a clear inventory of why all that you have worked for is unraveling? Upon honest evaluation, you will discover that you prepared very well for all that you wanted, but you forgot one key ingredient to your plan. You never ran the electricity to your dream home! That is why the food rotted, the pump never ran and your perfect furnace did nothing to keep you warm.

Overcoming old habits are not a lot different than drug and alcohol addiction. We can't change the past but we can overcome it minute by minute, day by day and step by step by acknowledging our addictions and bad habits by consciously choosing to be true to our self and our dreams. Once an addict, we will always be an addict recovering every single day of our life. It is no different with bad habits that are now a part of us. We will always be recovering from those old habits for our entire life. We need to make a firm commitment to ourselves to stay focused on what we want instead of what we don't want. It's a way of life. We are always free to choose our own path.

That was the commitment I made back in 1985 and I honor it today. I haven't touched a drop of liquor, stolen anything, or done any type of drug since.

Sybil bailed me out and it wasn't long before she started cheating on me with a guy she met at her new job as an aerobics instructor. He was a weightlifting instructor about the same age as her. I took this hard and became very depressed but not depressed enough to break my word to myself and start drinking and doing drugs again. Just the same I was depressed until one day I woke up to the realization that what was causing my depression was my ego. After all, this was a person that I couldn't even stand to be around most of the time and all we really ever had in common was sex. Once

I gained control of myself I wasted no time in getting a divorce from her. This ended marriage number four. This makes Sybil sound like a bad person, but she wasn't bad at all. Her problems stemmed from her upbringing and the fact she was constantly on some sort of drug. Speed, valium, marijuana and alcohol controlled her. If I had known then what I know now or if I had even remembered what I had learned before I let it all slip away I may have been able to help her find herself and perhaps our relationship could have worked. Although there was the 15 years difference between our ages some people will tell you that doesn't make any difference maybe it doesn't at 45 and 60 but at 21 and 36 it does make a difference. We couldn't relate to the same things so many of our conversations were limited. We had different sets of values. I wanted a home and she wanted no commitments. Our friends were usually her age when I felt the need to associate with friends my age. I felt trapped. I was addicted to a certain type of relationship that caused all of my relationships to end the same way. Not by accident and not on purpose. Poor relationships were what I knew best and what I was attracted to. Whenever a relationship began to feel healthy I would do something to destroy it because that's what our unconscious minds are programed to do. Keep us at our comfort level, whatever that is. It is what we have consciously programed it to maintain.

Secure Hell Hole

I discovered this in Stillwater by watching people come and go. I wondered what the reason was that causes so many to return shortly after their release. What I discovered is that no one really wanted to come back because they wanted to. It may have been a "hell hole," but it was a familiar, secure hell hole. The outside world had too many unfamiliar uncertainties. Life on the outside was too scary to face.

The subconscious mind says, "What I know best is always what makes me feel most secure. Whether it's good or bad, it doesn't matter. If it's what I know and it's what I find comfort in, then this must be what is best for me." So, with this plan as our guide, we continue our destructive journey back to our morbid comfort zone.

We follow the familiar path back until we find ourselves bound again in emotional, relational, spiritual, financial, and even physical prisons. Until we deal with the demons that are driving these misconceptions, we refuse to change destructive habits. There is true security, the kind Tyrone was looking for in a meaningful relationship. There's false security, the kind that leads to a dead end. It's a sort of addiction, a kind of deception. And it needs to be broken.

I began to remember the lessons I learned so long ago. Here was the turning point! My life was beginning to take shape. At this time, I was seeing a 23 year old bank teller and a 36 year old with a nine year old son both of whom I met at an Alcoholics Anonymous meeting. I felt very comfortable with the 23 year old but due to age knew it would never work. I discovered the 36 year old was demanding and needy. This I did not need in my life.

Then I met a forty-one year old Administrative Assistant. Amazing, someone my own age. She was mature and something about this made me uncomfortable, but it drew me in. She was my soul mate and I knew it. I had seen her in my dreams. I knew she was the one. In my dreams she didn't have a face but here she was, standing before me. We were total opposites; she was very much a lady and I was very crude. She was strong where I was weak and I was strong where she was weak. We decided, almost immediately, that our search was over and that together we could achieve anything. Years later, I can tell you that we weren't wrong. Her name is Carolyn.

Carolyn

Why You Are Holding This Book

That name has brought with it the single most positive influence in my life. She has stood beside me when I needed her most and against me when I would have destroyed myself. She has loved me unconditionally, and her belief in me has helped me believe in myself when I doubted I could hold on. Without her I can only shutter as to what I would be. With her, I have fulfilled all of the dreams of my childhood. We are secure in our relationship, and neither of us is dependent on any type of chemical. We love each other deeply and we are both at peace with who we are and the journey that brought us here. While we both live with regrets, and have constant reminders of how our former lives hurt others, we take responsibility for that, and leave it in the past. With that understood, we have risen above the dysfunction and are concentrating on helping others do the same. That is why you are holding this book.

Not one of us can change the past. But we can change the future. We only have today to work with, but that's enough to begin change for the better, both for ourselves and those we love. Each day, those we love can endeavor to do the same.

Just think, when Carolyn and I started out so many years ago, I was messing around with other young women. We both had dreams, but we were barely hanging on. There was pain and destruction all around. I was making $11 an hour as an employment counselor and she made $8.50 an hour as an Administrative Assistant. There was nothing exceptional about us except the lonely, broken path that brought both of us together. Today we are free of financial obligations. But I'm getting ahead of myself.

Let's go back to 1986 to just before Carolyn and I met. Like I said, I was seeing younger women. It was pretty much like my other relationships. We were trying to satisfy our own needs without truly being aware of what the other person might really need. If one of them wouldn't give what I wanted, or made demands of me which I didn't like, I became depressed. These were the kind of "bad" relationships I had become used to. I honestly believe that had I not been involved with them, I wouldn't have been able to recognize Carolyn for who she was. Believe it or not, it was the fact that the relationship with Carolyn didn't feel right that caused me to believe that it *was* right. It didn't "feel right" because it was the first good relationship I had ever experienced. She was different than all that had gone before. I wasn't very familiar with "good" relationships. Was it because she was older than the others? I was challenged by her, in a good way.

We surely have had our ups and downs and our share of hardships along the way. For whatever our differences were at the beginning, our love for each other grew stronger than the obstacle before us. We learned to be willing to communicate by sitting down to settle our differences rationally. I slowly began to realize that it doesn't matter so much who is right or who is wrong. What really matters is *what* is right and *what* is wrong. Carolyn and I discovered the answer to many "what is right and what is wrong" questions, because we made it a habit to talk things over.

After I first met Carolyn, I asked a coworker to go with me over to her office to check her out, to see what he thought. When we walked in, Carolyn was at the typewriter typing, sipping a cup of coffee, smoking a cigarette, and carrying on a conversation. She was sharp and talented. I didn't need my friend's advice, because I knew right then and there, this was the lady for me.

At eight fifty an hour, her talents were definitely being wasted. I knew it and told her so. Because of my position, I was able to get her working with me in the employment field. I began to learn more about her background.

She had been in sales before and was very successful. Her life had been in a tailspin, as she was medicating the loss of a ten-year marriage with alcohol. Her abuse of alcohol finally ended after she had a car accident. She took that opportunity to check herself into treatment.

The company I worked for came from the old school that did not believe that women should work in the industrial placement division, so they gave her a desk and a phone to make female, clerical placements.

I convinced the manager that he had nothing to lose by giving her a shot at industrial placements, in spite of the myth that woman didn't do that work. She was given the job and started working industrial accounts and soon out-produced me and everyone in the company, all within the first month. She moved up and became my boss for a short while, and then she stepped down, and I became her boss. She moved from the St Paul based industrial division, to the Minneapolis-based parent industrial division. Carolyn became the manager of that branch and I remained the manager of the St Paul branch. The owners became paranoid and feared that we might take over the company at which time the management position in Minneapolis was taken away and was given to someone with no management qualities, training, or skills. Carolyn held her tongue, took a sales desk and continued to work.

Then, one evening at home she declared, "Things are not going very well at work. I think I'm going to look for work somewhere else."

I responded with "No good decisions are made out of desperation". Why don't you hang in there, get back on top and then make your decision."

She agreed and soon she was out-producing everyone again. It was when our manager insulted her that she got the satisfaction to tell him to stick it and left.

From there she went back to work as a salesperson for the company that she had worked for in the transportation business. After a short time there, a new management group began to let people go left and right, especially the sales staff. Obviously Carolyn had some special value because she was the last salesperson to go. Just before she was laid off, I was let go from my management position in the St Paul based parent company where we had both worked. My position was given to the same person that Carolyn's management position was given to earlier. It was a bad economy in the mid '80s and companies were tightening their belts. I was more than just a little disappointed that I had dedicated ten loyal years of my life to the company and had taken them from a $16,000 per month business average to a solid $30,000 per month average with less payroll. I think they believed that those numbers just happened on their own.

The real kick in the teeth, was that their concept of one manager coordinating two separate offices in two different locations was my idea! I discovered that their bean counter, who knew absolutely nothing about the job placement business, had made the decision to cut me as a "high cost." True, I was making good money because I was producing revenue. A short time later, neither the Minneapolis nor the St Paul industrial division was in business.

So, I went job hunting and found a job at a transportation brokerage business. The pay was good and potential for growth was fantastic, but as much as I knew about sales, I knew nothing about transportation. The position I was hired into was a new division of an established business that was being monitored closely for profits and loss. I had very little time to learn the ins and outs of transportation. I was picking it up fast, but not fast enough. As it is with any sales job, once you have a firm grip on product knowledge, you need to find your personal niche within that market. It is rare that a seasoned transportation sales rep could come in to a new position and move freight, within the period of time that I was given. I was let go after only six weeks. I understand it now, but at the time, the old feelings of being a failure came back. Then I began to get paranoid thinking that maybe they found out about my prison record. The truth is, this was a high-security building that required card keys to get to the floor in which my company was located. I felt real uneasy about that and didn't really find myself fitting in with the people I was working with. In short, I was intimidated by the whole situation. I lost sight of my goals and jeopardized my chances at success. Regardless of my lack of product knowledge, I knew from much experience that when I lost sight of my personal goals, then everything started to go horribly wrong. Doubt and fear would begin to set in.

But not to worry. I had great experience placing talented people in the right jobs and I got a second chance with this company when I suggested Carolyn for the position I was let go from. Carolyn had the transportation experience. I knew it was a few steps down in pay from where she was currently, but I also knew that her current job would not last much longer.

The hiring authorities took Carolyn out for lunch and offered her the position. She decided to stick it out where she was, but a short time later, as predicted, she was let go, at which time she did accept the position.

The first year or so was very difficult working for less than half of what she was accustomed to. Plus, I was working for less than half of what I had been. I was now employed by a head-hunting firm. I could have done very well but I just couldn't seriously get into it. I rambled along and in the process made one very important placement into the company that Carolyn was now working for. I placed a guy named Pete, and between him and Carolyn, the two of them became the highest producers in the company and are largely responsible for what it is today. One of the most outstanding features of this company was that it was an employee-owned company where once fully vested, the highly compensated were awarded the highest number of shares in the company. Carolyn and Pete were two of the highest compensated employees in the company next to some of the managers, president and vice presidents of the company. When the company was acquired in 2007 all those highly compensated people became millionaires.

But I'm getting ahead of myself again. Let's go back to when we met.

How We Met

Before that day I walked into Carolyn's work place, we met on a mutual friend's 26-ft boat on Lake Minnetonka. By this time in my life, at age forty-one, I was completely alcohol and drug free. I had a squeaky clean record without so much as even a parking ticket. I was still smoking cigarettes, but I was in great physical shape from lifting weights at the local gym six days a week, doing two-hour workouts. Like I already told you, when I saw her sitting at that desk, I knew we would be together.

The first couple of months, we lived in St. Paul at Carolyn's place. She lived right next door to her landlord who seemed to enjoy verbally abusing her from time to time, which caused some feelings of inferiority. I saw this happen a few times, and I told her, "Hey, stand up for yourself."

Sure enough, one day I came home from work to hear the two of them arguing and Carolyn holding her ground nicely. The landlord didn't much like that and raised the rent on us in retaliation. We never had to pay the higher rate because we bought a home and moved. Shortly after we moved, we were married in the Woodbury Lutheran Church. It was 1987.

I knew Carolyn was something special, but like I've said before, we often don't see the whole picture right away. Carolyn is a strong, dedicated lady, and very determined. This made her an exceptional employee. I could see these qualities in her, and I was certain she had more talent in her than even she knew. I'm certainly not going to take credit for the hard work and dedication that she devoted to her work in transportation sales, although I will accept credit for influencing and encouraging her. I don't feel that I took unfair advantage of her as a means to fulfill my own selfish desires. I merely encouraged her to get maximum return for the energy that she was already spending. The requirement wasn't to work any harder than she already was. The requirement was to work smarter, by involving others to help her realize her goals.

One of her many outstanding abilities was her ability to take charge of a situation and get things accomplished. She took on messed up situations and turned them into successes. Every situation was a special challenge that she enjoyed.

In the transportation business, where people depend on various transportation modes to safely transport their valued goods to their customers, anything can go wrong. The transportation brokerage company such as the one Carolyn worked for, was responsible for hundreds of loads every day. Things often did go wrong.

The call no one wants to make is the one informing the customer that something has happened to their shipment. The response is never a good one. Carolyn's customers were no exception to the rule, but they loved the fact that Carolyn would make sure that the customer was the first to know when things went wrong and that she was already well on her way to solving the problem, which she always managed to accomplish. The dispatchers are the people in the middle. The sales staff depends on them to find transportation modes. They can make or break a sales person. Being the middle man, they are the ones that catch most of the crap when it hits the fan. They liked Carolyn and would work hard for her because she would lift the burden from their shoulders by handling customer complaints personally. Why would she choose to handle all the abuse of an angry customer? Two reasons. Control and compassion.

As with everyone's goals, obstacles will present themselves. Some are real, some are only imagined. Carolyn was always able to handle the real ones with great success. It was the obstacles she imagined that presented the most difficult hurdles to jump. My part was to help her stay focused on her goals and overcome the problems she only imagined.

As she was highly rewarded for her success at work, it became possible for me to retire. She had been doing well and her income was increasing.

Dreams Coming True

As her income grew, we were able to pay off all of our bills. We were instructed by our financial advisor to pay off our cars, which we did. Next we paid off the mortgage. It was a very fulfilling time.

As time went on and Carolyn became even more successful, she began to experience paranoia that caused her to often think that her superiors wanted to get rid of her. I assured her that was far from the truth, as they would be fools to get rid of their highest producer. I think she might have been resented, by her coworkers that were all men, for being the top producer in a position where men are generally the most successful. I think her supervisors were confused and even irritated about her methods and her failure to explain them. I think they would have liked to be a part of her success but were told by the CEO, "No one knows how she does what she does and I don't care. Just leave her alone and she will get it done." Actually, Carolyn did tell them how she did things on many occasions, but they didn't understand what she was telling them. Maybe some things just can't be communicated. Her best explanation was, "I can't tell you how I will reach my goal because I don't know how I will. All I really know is, that I will". And she did. She always exceeded her expectations and her goals.

"Sometimes, making careful plans and having it all figured out get in the way of achieving a goal." she said. "Just know in your mind that you're going to get there and pretty soon, there you are."

An onlooker, without emotional attachments, can often see and understand, as they look upon a situation, what others closer to the situation can't see. My role was to be that onlooker. We'd have little powwows in the morning to discuss our situation, offer advice, make changes and carry on. We kept each other on track.

Carolyn is results-oriented, whereas I am analytical. A results-oriented individual will rarely, if ever, be analytical enough to remove themselves from the circle where all the noise and confusion exist. In order to view the entire situation within the circle, you must pretend to be an onlooker without emotional attachment. This definitely provides the best possible understanding of what is really happening within the circle. This is something I often do in order to gain full understanding of the circumstances within any situation. It is, in fact, easier for me to turn off my own emotions and look at someone else's situation.

I watched Carolyn aggressively handle a certain difficult situation. She was given some accounts by her supervisors which were not expected to produce very well. I am sure that she was given these accounts because of her uncanny ability to turn junk into gold. This was probably unfair to give her the tough jobs, but they did. I suppose it was a compliment of sorts and a statement of confidence in her abilities. But she didn't see it that way. She took it as an act of discrimination and adopted an "I'll show you" attitude. That fierceness propelled her success. As you can plainly see, in every emotion, even a negative emotion like anger, there can be found some good applications that are beneficial, rather than debilitating. Hence "there is always some positive to be found in the negative," and vice versa.

This determination can be credited to her mother, who often discouraged her from doing things she wanted to do. After Carolyn left home, she fought hard against discouragement and consistently succeeded against all odds. In short, she became a strong willed, determined, take-charge individual, who views discouragement as a green light.

One of the accounts she received turned out to be the largest account in the company and another one turned out to be the second-largest account in the company. Clearly, Carolyn knew how to handle herself in rough waters.

I believe the people at Carolyn's work were not necessarily guilty of all of the things she may have imagined. What she took personally really wasn't meant to be personal. Some of the plotting and scheming she imagined was nothing more than misunderstanding. However, she was good at self-motivation and turned every situation into a success.

Within a year we were able to pay off an $80,000 debt to the credit union for recent home improvements. The next year, we paid off the mortgage on our home and purchased two new cars.

Carolyn's supervisors required everyone to set goals monthly, quarterly and yearly and everyone on staff was offered bonuses as an incentive to reach them. Carolyn consistently exceeded her goals.

And, again, when the supervisor asked how she would arrive at her goals, her answer was always the same. "I don't know, all I know is that I will." And she never failed to exceed her goals.

The other person most responsible for the success of the company was Pete. He was a salesman that I placed into the company when I was working as a headhunter sixteen years earlier. Isn't it funny how all things work together? I had worked for Carolyn's company for a short period of time and suggested just before I left, that they should consider hiring Carolyn in my place. I was told then that it was already a consideration. Shortly after that, Carolyn was hired, and the rest is history.

The truth is if you go back all those years to when Carolyn and I first met, when we didn't have anything, we agreed upon a vision to become successful, and we always have been. There certainly were hard times, but even then, we did all right.

If you really want to go farther back, look again at 1973, when I was introduced to Maxwell Maltz, and I became consciously aware of the power of visualization. That concept has been responsible for all of my success. Or, you can even go farther back, to when I was a child in school, daydreaming about who I would become, while my classmates studied.

Let's get back to how all of this came to fruition. In early 2007 Carolyn's company was acquired and all the people that were vested were well compensated. Carolyn was one of those people. None of us saw this coming; we had not even considered for a moment that this would be the way we would acquire the funds needed to become debt-free.

You see, how easy that was for me? All I did was help Carolyn maintain a vision through positive pep talks each morning as she got ready for work.

It doesn't really matter how you reach your goal or who you involve along the way, as long as you do it in a respectful way that is beneficial to those you involve. I can tell you this, you can choose to ignore this respectful way of life and reach your goals by lying, cheating, and stealing with no concern at all for your fellow man. You might reach some goals that way, but remember life's unfailing boomerang, "What goes around comes around."

We often had my youngest daughter, Jenna, on weekends, and both Carolyn and I really enjoyed her. She was attending a Spanish immersion class in St. Paul when her teacher told us that Jenna's mother, Loren, was about to take her away. I really couldn't believe that Loren would do such a thing without telling me. But sure enough, Loren took her off to Arizona, which explains why she was in Spanish immersion class. The idea was that Arizona has a lot of Spanish speaking people and Loren wanted Jenna to fit in. So that was the end of weekends with Jenna.

A few years later in 1989, when Jenna was nine, Loren agreed to send her back to me. Apparently, Jenna was causing problems that eventually required a counselor. The problem was that Jenna wanted to be near her father, so she was sent to me and I was told by her mother that Jenna had a learning disability. When she came back, I looked at her report card from the past year; it clearly indicated what her learning disability really was. Jenna would get an A in math on one report card and F's in everything else. Then on the next report card, she would get an F in math and an A in something else. Jenna's problem was self-discipline, which at the time I thought was laziness. That first year with us and a little encouragement, nourished by a few threats, Jenna got straight A's with hardly any effort at all.

By the next year, however, Jenna decided that she didn't like the responsibilities of maintaining high grades and began to fail again. We tried various methods of motivation. Mostly "punishment" by taking away something she really enjoyed. But it never did any good. She just continued to fail. Shortly after exhausting our methods, it was decided that it might be best for Jenna to go back to Arizona and live with her mother again in 1992.

Randy Jr.

During the time Jenna was with us, my youngest son, Randy Jr., got into trouble up north. He and a friend of his got into a bar fight and ended the life of another individual. I had not had any contact with him for many years. Once a few years earlier, I had contacted him and his sister and at that time, I promised him that I would pick him up over summer break. He was attending an Indian school and I didn't want to interfere with that. For reasons I don't even remember, I failed and never kept that promise to him. There have been many times that I have wished that I could go back and fulfill that promise because it destroyed any faith that he may have had in me at the time.

When I learned of his trouble from the bar fight, we immediately put a lien on our house to obtain the money to bail him out of jail. After posting bail, I brought him, with his two sons, home to live with us. I helped him find a good job at UPS and went with him to court. I spoke for him and helped him negotiate for workhouse time, rather than prison time. We had the promise, after three years of clean living, that the incident would be expunged from his record. It was a chance to start over, but he didn't see it that way. He seemed to be working hard at building a criminal record as bad as mine. It seemed that everything that he hated about me, he experienced for himself. He has children with several different women in different cities and states. He is not supporting any of them. At thirty-six years of age, he is already a grandfather. He has been gone from here for many years, but I still get bill collector calls looking for him.

A few years ago, we reunited with his three oldest kids, as they were the ones that had lived with us when we were helping Randy Jr. They were living here in Minneapolis with their mom when the youngest of the three called. Seeing them again after so many years was great! They had been through a lot since we had last seen them, so we decided that we would do something special for them. The second Christmas we took them to Disney World for ten days. After that, things started to come apart for their mother and before we knew it, they were out of our lives again. It has been several years since we have had any contact with them, as they went to live with Randy Jr., who thinks that he hates me for all I never did for him.

Then there was the episode when one of the mothers of two of his other children contacted me and wanted to arrange a visit. We had never met her or the grandkids. She claimed that Randy Jr. had not seen them or even been in contact with them in three years. I really wanted to see the kids, but I didn't want the disappointment of having them ripped from our life like the other three were. I was suspicious of their mother's motive for making the offer after so many years.

With that in mind, I ask her to let me think it over. I guess the real question was, "why is it important now that we be a part of their lives when we were right here and available in the beginning of their lives?" When Randy Jr. learned that I had declined contact with them (which I really never did get to choose one way or the other before their mother pulled the offer), he asked me why I didn't want to see his kids? I didn't defend myself. I just let him believe what he wanted to believe rather than tell him the truth. Maybe I just don't get the Indian ways, or maybe I just don't agree. Or maybe he just doesn't get me and my ways, or even agree with my ways. But the thing is, we really don't have to agree with each other in order to be at peace with each other. All we need do is respect each other for what we believe. There is no question about my love for him, as I love him dearly and though we have had very little time together, I miss him and think of him often and wish that we could be close.

A long time ago he asked me "What am I dad?" I knew he was referring to his nationality. His mother, Chick, was mostly, documented and registered Chippewa Indian, but he wasn't sure about my nationality. I have been mistaken for black, Mexican, and I passed for Indian, so my answer was "What do you want to be?" He seems to have made his choice and now he is a reservation Indian. I need to respect that and be proud of him for making a choice that gives his life meaning. Because certainly, there is no shame in being an Indian living on the reservation.

When I look back at those days with Randy and the kids living with us, they are certainly bitter sweet. Carolyn and I were going through some pretty hard times when my son and his kids lived with us. We had recently filed bankruptcy after losing our good paying jobs because of economical cutbacks. Our three bedroom town home was pretty full with Carolyn, Randy Jr., my youngest daughter Jenna, our three grandchildren, a 200 pound St. Bernard, a schnauzer and myself as occupants.

Randy Jr. received food stamps to help out with the grocery bills and that was much appreciated but always embarrassing to pay for groceries with welfare aides. I recall selling empty soda bottles for the deposit just to get enough money to rent a VCR movie for entertainment. We knew how to stretch a little food into a lot and make it taste good. We didn't have a lot but we had each other and that made everything worth the struggle.

Randy started to become restless after a while. He worked a late night shift at UPS and was home by midnight so that I would have the car for my commute to work in the morning. This worked out well until he started to stay out all night. He was failing to show up for work on occasion. I began to miss work because he wasn't getting home on time and some times, not at all. I really wanted to wring his neck, but every time he finally showed up, all was forgiven and I was just glad that he was alright.

Being in the job placement business and working as a headhunter for a local headhunting firm in St. Paul, I was able to secure full-time employment for Randy at a fairly good paying company that did electroplating. It was a nasty job, but in addition to good pay, provided good benefits. The owner wanted to groom Randy for supervision, which would have meant higher pay. But when it came time for him to turn himself in for workhouse confinement, he decided that he would rather do county jail time for a year and then be placed on probation for several years. It was pretty disappointing considering all that we had sacrificed to ensure his freedom. But then when it comes right down to it, what won't you do for your children? Even if they never do anything right, you still need to love them, always do your best to understand them, and never judge them.

After serving county jail time for a few months in a little town up north, Randy Jr. was allowed a furlough, so we drove the 300 miles or so where he was being held to pick him up. We brought him to a family reunion where he got to meet my oldest son, Tyrone, for the first time. It was the first and last time the three of us were ever together at one time. All too soon, a perfect day ended and it was time to take Randy Jr. back to jail. I didn't hear anything from him again until a while after he was released on probation. He went back to the reservation to live with his mother.

One of the calls I received from him was in a drunken state and he was asking for money. Two hundred dollars to be exact. I said no and then he gave me a little sermon on how I was to love him unconditionally. He just wanted the money. Anyway, to make a long story short, he said "You have more money than anyone I know and you won't do anything for anyone." After a final cuss word he hung up. That was it.

Randy Jr. and a couple of his reservation friends happened to be in the area sometime later, so he dropped in to say hi. He apologized to me for a few things and we teased with each other a little bit like we usually do. Then we hugged and said goodbye.

In about 1998 I heard from him again. He had violated probation and was serving time in the Stillwater State Penitentiary, the very same place where I had spent seven years of my life when I was about his age. We went to visit him as often as possible and when he was released Carolyn, Jenna, and I went to see him before he was transported back to the reservation by his parole officer.

He came out of the holding cell wearing an ankle bracelet. You know, one of those devices that sets off an alarm when you're more than so many feet away from your restricted area. I have been told that no one ever makes it on parole wearing one of those devices. They either cut the bracelet off or go beyond their restricted area.

During this period we got a call from a hospital after a suicide attempt by our granddaughter, Randy's girl. Shortly after that, my oldest son Tyrone died. Sadly, since then, we have not heard from Randy Jr. I would like to rebuild that relationship before either of us move on from this life. But, if this is all that we have, I am thankful he is my son. We have had some very special times together.

It's a very hard thing to review my life and come to the realization that if I had dealt with circumstances differently and made better choices, I might have been able to prevent some of the hardships my children and grandchildren are going through today. Sometimes I think I could have even prevented Tyrone's death, but then I, of all people, should realize that what's done is done and forever in the past. I have realized the lessons that I have learned came at the high price of my children's well-being. I cannot change the past, so the best I can do, is to be thankful that I have learned from these experiences, rather than deny my mistakes and keep repeating them. My sincere hope in writing this book, is that my own children and grandchildren can learn from my mistakes and not repeat them. I want to leave a legacy that helps repair all of the damage I was a contributor to. I cannot force anyone to listen to me. I am just telling you in every honest and open way I can, that, first, I am sorry for the trouble I've caused you. Secondly, you have a choice to break the kind of cycle of poor behavior that brings trouble into our lives and into the lives of others.

Backing up a few years, in January of 1996, the only father I ever knew, Wally, died of stomach cancer. About two years prior to his death, my mother and father were divorced after forty years of marriage. Dad was running around the country with a girl twenty years younger than he was. The girl was married too and happened to be the wife of one of my old schoolmates. Mom was pretty bitter about the way she was being pushed aside after all those years of devotion. I can't say that I blame her, but that didn't cause me or my brothers and sisters to love my dad any less. It was hard for our mom to understand what was going on at the time. She was ill and on many different medications that affected her thinking. We didn't take that into consideration when we learned Dad had only a short time to live. Since they were divorced, we catered to him because he was dying and pushed my mother aside at a time when she needed us most of all. None of us stopped to consider that the man she loved and cared about for the past forty years was leaving her forever. We felt that she had no right to have any say in the final preparations.

When we went to the funeral home to pick out the coffin and to go over the procedures of an American Veterans funeral, we were told that the youngest living child would receive a check for $2,000. My brothers, sisters and mother who were there at the time, agreed the money should go to Jason, who had been a foster child adopted by my mother and father just before they were divorced.

The flag that was draped over the coffin was to be given to the wife of the deceased. But since mom and dad were divorced, the flag would be given to be oldest living son. In my mind, I was that son. But my mother said the flag should go to Lee. She considered him to be Wally's first born son, although I am the oldest of all the children and was always told I was his oldest son. It was as though Mom had reached into my chest and ripped out my heart. The thing I feared most of all in my life was realized. I was never really considered as Wally's son, even though Jason, who had just recently been adopted, was considered his son. That day the truth finally came out. It was worse than pouring salt in an open wound. All of the pain and rejection came flooding back into my body and mind.

However, on the day of the funeral, when the flag was presented to my brother Lee, he walked over and handed it to me. Bless his heart. I hope he knows how much that meant to me. I built a case for the flag and give it a place of honor in my home.

To make matters worse, a short time later, Mom told me that Dad had never intended to leave me anything in his will, which really wasn't very much. Divided equally among the six of us, the amount only came to $1300.00 each. Mom told me it was "out of the kindness of my sister Joyce's heart" that she divided the money among us, as dads' intentions were to leave me a dollar. (Joyce was the executor of dad's will.) Well, that didn't feel so good. I had just lost the only man who had ever acted like a dad to me and now I was feeling wounded by my mother.

I began to realize the condition of my mother and the circumstances of her current health. I knew that she didn't mean to hurt me. Alcohol, pain and drugs had taken its toll. I knew what it was like to hurt someone when you are just trying to survive a situation yourself. My mother and I have since talked about those unpleasant times and I apologized for being so selfish and inconsiderate. It wasn't Mom who was wrong in all of that, it was us. Those were some very hard days.

Willie

The year was 2004. I had been working as an offset press technician for around 10 years machining, welding and repairing one-of-a-kind parts for obsolete machines. I was rebuilding and repainting offset presses as well as bindery related machines such as paper cutters and folding machines. I have always been fortunate in that mechanical things held no mystery to me. Therefore, I found it very easy to repair almost anything that involved moving parts. If someone had a broken machine that I was unfamiliar with or had never seen before, you could tell me what it was supposed to do, then I'd make it work again.

I believe I might have been displaying my mechanical talent when I parted out that toy in the backyard with a hammer. If you recall, that was the one that my grandfather whipped me for destroying? I was displaying the same talents several years later around age eight, when my mother whipped me for taking my Roy Rogers watch apart.

The company I worked for, PMC, was a small 4 man operation consisting of Pete our salesmen, Larry our field technician, Ken the owner and me. Last but not least, my dog, Willie. He was a silky terrier who had been coming to work with me for the past eight of those ten years.

Just like we never know when something hard is going to enter our lives, we also never know when something wonderful is going to happen. We never know when a little silky terrier is going to melt our hearts.

I just wish all of you had a "Willie" in your life. Let me tell you how great this little friend was to me.

Before Willie, Carolyn and I had a schnauzer and a St. Bernard. Their lives were a story in itself. A person never really stops to think when they acquire a pet, just how attached you'll become! All too soon we realize that pets don't live as long as we do and we also never imagined how hard it is to let them go when their quality of life becomes one of suffering. Caesar, our St. Bernard was ten, and Cassandra, our schnauzer, was twelve when we had to put both of them to sleep on the same day. The pain of that event was so great that I couldn't speak of it for two years.

I swore that I would never have another pet because I had no desire to ever experience that kind of pain again. But then along came Willie.

Carolyn and I were out and about doing a bit of window shopping when we passed a local pet store. We have always loved animals, dogs especially. We decided to go in and just look, because puppies are so amusing. Carolyn was at one end of the store and I was at the other when I discovered this little silky terrier that resembled a dust mop wearing a frown. He was more mature looking than the others and we found out later that he was four months old. I called Carolyn over to have a look and then I did a dumb thing. I asked the store owner, "Why can't we pet the dogs?"

He said "You can go ahead and pet them. Which one are you interested in?" I told him, but quickly added that I really wasn't interested in purchasing a dog. I was just asking the question. But, as you can guess, it was already too late. He had the dog out of the pen and in my arms before I could say another word. The dog began to lick me all over my face, while happily wagging his tail and wiggling around like he just couldn't get close enough to me. The pet store manager put us in this sectioned off area and put the dog on the floor. But someone opened the door and he made a break for it, then stopped and relieved himself on the floor. He ran all over the store causing all kinds of excitement with the other dogs. The whole place was a chorus of barks and howls before he was finally cornered and caught. We just barely pulled ourselves away and got out of the store without purchasing that cute little dog.

Throughout the day we couldn't help talking about that little dog. At one point I asked Carolyn what she would name the dog if it was ours. (I had read somewhere that if you name an animal then you become attached and the animal will be yours.) But, after every conversation, we always came to the same conclusion. Dogs tie you down and though it had been over two years since Caesar and Cassandra left us, we were just not ready for another dog.

At the end of the day, when we were heading home, Carolyn stopped, turned the car around and said "We can't leave that little dog there." We just couldn't believe that he was four months old and no one had taken him home yet. But we got control of ourselves, looked at each other again and repeated, "No. We're not ready." And we turned around and went on home.

That weekend, I went up north hunting deer. I use a compound bow and am a deadly shot but I had never really shot a deer and had no real desire to. It's just good getting out and meditating while sitting in a tree and getting together with family. When I returned home that Sunday evening, I was tired. I set down my bow, hung up my jacket and started up the stairs of our split entry. There at the top of the stairs was the little dog. We named him Willie. He never ever really grew up, as all of his life he played like a puppy.

Willie turned into a ball playing machine. He wouldn't just play with any ball. His preference was blue. Yeah, I know it has been said that dogs are colorblind and I say BS! Whoever made that statement had not met a dog like Willie. To every situation there is a skeptic and some people who weren't convinced Willie could see color, claimed that he could smell the difference in the balls. Others claimed that it was a hue that indicated a difference. But I would change their mind when I took two balls the same size; one purple and one dark blue. I would throw them at the same time. Willie would rarely even go after the purple ball and if he did get confused, sometimes while the ball was in flight, he would stop before he even picked up the purple ball, ignore it and begin looking for the blue ball. Like I said, Willie preferred blue balls.

I brought Willie to work with me for eight years and he was almost on salary by the end. Willie could sometimes be a real pain in the butt when we were flat on our backs under some machine performing repairs. He would often come over and stand on the part of you that was hanging out from under the machine and drop his ball on you expecting you to stop what you were doing and throw the ball. If you didn't cooperate with him, the next time you reached for one of the tools you had lined up within reach, chances are that tool would be missing and would require that you crawl out from under the machine that you were working on and look for Willie. Once Willie was located, the tool could be found nearby. It didn't matter what you were working with, Willie would take anything to get your attention. His rap sheet could go on and on, but it included razor blades, sandpaper, scuffed pads, wrenches of all sizes and anything else small enough for him to transport. What a brat! But everyone loved Willie and if I ever showed up to work without him, the first words out of anyone's mouth before "good morning" was, "Where's Willie?"

Ken the "boss" was a bit of a brat himself. He was always saying or doing something to make the work day more interesting. One of the things he liked to do, was sit at his desk and throw Willie's ball. He would throw it at a machine that was sitting on a pallet on the showroom floor about fifty feet away. Willie would continue to bring the ball back to Ken until he let the ball go under the pallet. Once Willie exhausted every option to retrieve the ball, he would begin to whine until I stopped whatever I was doing and got the ball out from under the pallet. Ken thought it was funny that he could get me to stop doing my job to come over and retrieve that ball for Willie. Being the bright dog he was, Willie learned that when he wanted attention, he'd stuff his ball under things and whine. Worked every time!

Willie is gone now, but I never grow tired of talking about him. I knew life without him would be tough, but I don't regret one moment with that dog. I find comfort knowing that we provided the best life we possibly could for him. As hard as it was to say goodbye, my heart is filled with gladness that will endure for as long as I live because of the unconditional love I experienced through Willie for so many years.

An Unusual Boss

I told you I would tell you about my job at the print shop. It was my favorite job of my life time. The guys I worked with were exceptional, and "Ken" was a very unusual boss. He had very good family values that extended into the workplace. I don't think Ken viewed any of us merely as employees, but more like an extension of his family. He never really seemed like a boss as much as he did a coworker or a working supervisor. He wouldn't ask you to do anything that he wouldn't do himself. He liked to play word games with us, upon which you had to be real specific about what you say, or he would have some wise ass answer.

For instance, if I said I needed a haircut, he would say "Don't you need all of them cut?"

Ken was also a prankster. Once, when I was rebuilding a big floor model folding machine, I had just replaced all of the rollers and calibrated them. Part of the job of rebuilding a folding machine requires reaming out the wooden bushings that the folding rollers turn-on. The trick was not to over ream the bushings making them sloppy and uncontrollable when adjusting them. The other trick was not to under ream them, making them too tight, for this would cause the bushings to overheat and smoke. I got really good at reaming bushings and never had to tear a machine down to make adjustments to them. Once the bushings had been reamed, the rollers were replaced into the folding machine and calibrated and the whole works needed to be tested. To test them, all of the gears, pulleys, and belts were replaced and the machine was powered up at full speed, while oil was being applied to the bushings. If none of them heated up or smoked, we were good to go. It would take between ten and fourteen hours to rebuild a twenty-six inch floor model folder with four folding plates that required six rollers.

I was about five minutes into the test run on one of these big machines, when this hellacious banging noise started somewhere to the rear of the folding machine. This was a noise I had never heard before and I immediately cut the speed down. When I did, the noise slowed down. When I speeded up, the noise picked up, and became louder. I shut the machine down and went to investigate. There was Ken laying on the floor with a ball pin hammer in hand. So that I wouldn't see him, he had crawled on his hands and knees across the floor with hammer in hand and was taping on the side frame. Why? Because he knew that I would do what I usually did when things went wrong with my work. I would cuss and swear, using almost every foul word known to mankind and even inventing a few unique ones of my own. Ken thought that was funny. Ken certainly was never one to let things get dull around the shop.

Aside from all the fun and games, Ken was also very intelligent in business, very knowledgeable about printing related machines and creative in the machine shop. Ken was what you would call "result oriented." He could find a problem with most any machine and fix it. He would make a big mess in the process, which he wouldn't bother to clean up. He would often invent things to make machines work better, but usually these inventions were very crude.

I, on the other hand, am a creative perfectionist. Needless to say, the two of us worked very well together. He would often create something crude that I would turn into a work of art. The offset presses that I rebuilt were a testimony to that. Before I came to PMC, the rebuilt presses looked like junk with new guts. Kind of like a demolition derby car with a new engine. With my auto body repair experience, I understood painting and welding. My farm experience trained me to repair various mechanical devices, such as wire and twine tying mechanisms, along with many other mechanical procedures required to maintain farm machinery and vehicles. With this knowledge, along with a lot of other jobs that I had over the years that required mechanical skills and machining abilities, I was able to turn a pile of junk into what appeared to be a brand-new machine. Often customers would mistake our repaired pieces for brand new. With what I already knew prior to PMC and what I learned from Ken over the years may be impressive. But all of us in that shop put together, didn't know as much as Ken about the printing business.

Ken was a clever manager and a good teacher. If he saw you assembling something wrong, he might ask if you wanted to continue and find out that you had done it wrong, or would you like him to tell you the right way now? He knew the value of letting you find some things out on your own and he often would let you choose. I have worked for a lot of people, but Ken was my favorite employer, and Pete and Larry were my favorite coworkers.

My Coworkers

Pete, our salesman and I went back many years to 1980 when we worked together as industrial placement specialists for the same company. Pete and I revolutionized that industry, by quickly becoming the top producers of placing personnel into industrially related jobs for a fee.

Pete and I worked very well together and always had more fee qualified applicants and place able job orders than everyone else put together in our company. We got together on weekends too, often to work on one of our broken down cars. Pete was a hunter and fisherman, so sometimes we would go fishing and sometimes we would go out to the gravel pits and just shoot at tin cans. I liked going fishing with him and his son John, who was a wise ass I soon dubbed, John "The Mouth."

One morning about 5:00 AM, Pete got me up for a fishing trip. The day would become the topic of conversation for years to come.

The deal was, he would pay for the gas and I would supply the vehicle. At the time I was driving a 1975 Cadillac Coupe Deville that was as big as a house and looked like it had been painted with a broom. My gas tank was empty as usual, when we stopped at the service station at the beginning of the trip. Even at the low gas prices of the time, it still cost $50 to fill the giant tank on that old piece of crap. After loading it down with gear, we then turned Pete's rowboat upside down and tied it to the top of the car. What a sight that was! Aside from having a 525 cubic-inch engine, the boat on top of the car caused a wind drag that helped us to get five to six miles to the gallon. We drove fifty or sixty miles to the fishing spot where our employer, Roger, had a cabin. We fished for hours and caught nothing.

I remember a time some years back, when Pete brought his company car to me for repairs. There was some front end damage that I repaired for him. Hours later his son, "The Mouth," smashed up the front end in his own driveway.

Pete and I did have a few differences throughout the years but always found a way to resolve those differences and remain friends. I recall a time when I was down that he was there for me and vice versa. Pete was one of the first people I called when my son died and he was the one I brought to meet my wife, Carolyn, before we were married because I valued his opinion and wanted to know what he thought of her. In a lot of respects, we were wired the same. We were good at the same things and helped each other be better at our jobs.

Back when we were placing people into jobs, many people took a dim view of how we did it. They didn't think it was fair to charge an individual a fee for placing them into a job. But we were successful at it. Strangely enough, some of the complainers were co-workers. The job paid almost straight commission, so needless to say, the counselors with animosities and complaints were not as successful as we were. They, themselves, were often soon out of work.

Pete and I, on the other hand, realized that finding a good paying job was no easy task. Especially in the early 80s when jobs were far and few between and a college degree didn't mean much of anything. At that time, high-level positions were being cut left and right and for every day you were out of work it represented a day of lost wages. I surmised that good people deserved good jobs and good employers deserved good employees. Our job was simply to bring these two together for the best possible outcome. For that service we charged a fee.

It was a very good service for the perspective employer in that they had no need to run costly ads and spend valuable time sifting through hundreds of applications looking for someone very difficult to discover. We would send one, two and sometimes three people to an employer for comparison purposes. The people we sent would often be exactly what they had asked for, which caused a dilemma about which one to hire. Often all three were hired even though only one was needed, because even in a time when jobs are scarce good, hard- working people are still difficult to find.

It was a good service for the applicant, in that it saved them thousands of dollars in potentially lost wages. We helped them find the right employer, offering the right job. We also instructed them prior to the interview, what to say and what to do, based on what the employer had told us they wanted in an employee. They were instructed to call us the minute they left the interview, so that we could call the employer and get the job offer and a starting date.

The way I see it, is that we literally changed people's lives for the better for a fee. Pete and I both became branch managers in charge of a sales staff. His office was in Minneapolis and mine was in

St. Paul. Unfortunately, when those jobs ended we fell out of touch for a while.

Pete was working for some firm in the placement industry and I was working for a headhunting company. But I was getting weary of the placement business. I enjoyed the employees and the employers and bringing the two together. I was beginning to dislike the people I worked for. They didn't seem to have anybody's best interest at heart other than their own. They were paring people that didn't fit together. I left the headhunting firm and returned to the industrial placement business that I had once managed, but it just wasn't the same.

It all ended for me one day when the manager called all of us in to his office and proceeded to scream at us about the quality of the job orders that were being written up. I might have been okay with his reasoning had it not been for the fact that he had just returned from lunch and was drunk. He was slurring his words.

I calmly called his attention to his drunkenness and suggested that he needed to sober up and look at the facts before opening his mouth. The next day I was fired.

Pete was back to work as a headhunter. He then accepted a position in sales with one of the companies he was trying to fill. The job was at PMC, a printing repair and sales company. Shortly after going to work for PMC, Pete approached me about going to work selling printing related equipment. I jumped at the chance. And so, that is how Pete and I came to work for Ken.

PMC resembled a junkyard when I got there. Remember, Ken was bright but not very organized. The place was a disaster. When I wasn't on the phone making sales calls or out on the road with Pete attending trade shows or knocking on doors, I was in the shop working on machines, welding, machining, cleaning and organizing the shop.

Ken finally noticed that I had skills that were more valuable to him than my sales skills. Besides, I was beginning to see that there was only room for one salesperson in the company. The commission structure was not working and I complained about it. They made changes that made things even worse. Then they tried to convince me that it was better until I showed them facts and figures to prove just how ridiculous it was. It was decided that I would dabble in sales, but be trained to repair folding machines and assemble offset presses.

I quickly became proficient at rebuilding folding machines of all kinds and sizes. From time to time, I would make sales, but mostly I repaired, rebuilt and serviced bindery and offset presses.

Things began to slow down in the printing business because of high speed copy machines. Almost everyone had one at home. Letterhead, business cards, literature of all kinds and many other things that the printing industry depended on, could now be done from a PC hooked up at home. Service calls became fewer and fewer and virtually no one was buying rebuilt small offset presses anymore. Things were beginning to look pretty bad in the printing industry for the small offset print shop.

We had another co-worker, Larry. Between us, we were our own version of the Three Stooges. I admired Ken for hiring both Larry and myself, as both of us had a history of back injury. Larry was an ex-Vietnam war veteran who had worked for a much higher wage before his back problems attached him to the crappy workman's compensation program. Workman's comp was about as demeaning as being committed to a nursing home before you really lost your ability to function independently.

Larry had been an honor guard in the service and had accompanied the bodies of many fallen soldiers on their final trip home. Larry talked about this from time to time, as if it was over with and in the past, but those experiences left their mark and took their toll on him.

It all began to torment him around the time his wife filed for divorce. He began to have mood swings much the same as an alcoholic does.

Our relationship was rather strange. I would be working at my bench and he would be working by his. At odd times I would be pelted by small screws, washers, and nuts. This was a declaration of war. I answered by air mailing some sizable bolts, which provoked him to send over chunks of hardwood. These wood grenades didn't feel good bouncing off my head. To this assault, I answered by launching larger objects in his direction. Not that I wanted to hit him with one, but I wanted to come as close as I could. Then we began to call each other names and trade insults. He was an adopted child, so I told him, "Your own mama didn't even want anything to do with your worthless rear end." The things we said were terrible, but for some sick reason we enjoyed the verbal abuse we took and dished out. I had his name on speed dial as "Larry the Prick." He simply called me "Asshole."

Larry gained a lot of weight, because all he ever ate at work was popcorn washed down with Coca-Cola and followed by one cigarette after another. Whenever there was a sale going on for Coca-Cola, he would buy out the store. We shared a big office and the wall on his side of the office was often filled from top to bottom with cases of Coke. The same went for Winston cigarettes. He would search the net for deals and buy hundreds of dollars' worth of them. Judging by his habits, Larry had no desire to quit smoking, even though Pete and I had quit.

One day, he and I had to go out on a service call to pick up a machine. He had his cigarettes and a bottle of Coke. We were driving down the road with his stash in the front seat between us, when he began to smart off to me. I grabbed his cigarettes and Coke and threatened to chuck them out the window if he didn't retract the statement that he had just made referring to my sexual preference. I gave him a chance by counting to three. The grin on his face was one of assurance that I wouldn't really throw his goods out the window. But on the count of three, his grin turned to shock as his cigarettes and Coke left the cabin of the truck by way of the window.

It may sound like Larry and I were more enemies than friends. The truth is, we got along very well. These games we played served to liven up what could have been a dull day. There was never a dull moment with Ken, Pete, Larry, Willie, and me.

Larry was online one night visiting in one of those chat rooms with a lady from New York by the name of Mary Beth. She was in the copier business and worked for a company that had a large account in the Twin Cities. Copiers were supposedly being reconditioned in another state and were being stored until needed, then transferred to the Twin Cities.

Since our business was slow and they were both in the printing business and PMC had available warehouse space, Mary Beth thought she could do business with us by storing the machines closer to their destination.

Mary Beth asked Larry if we would be interested in storing some machines and cleaning them before they were picked up by a company who would in turn, deliver them to one of their business locations around the five state area. The proposition wasn't all that great, but it was business that we didn't have at the time, so we agreed to store and clean copiers.

Within a few days, we received 13 copiers from the company that was supposed to be servicing, rebuilding and repairing the copiers we received.

Since Larry spent more time out in the field repairing offset presses, I was left mostly in the shop machining parts, painting, and rebuilding machines along with repairing walk-ins. I got the dubious honor of cleaning the machines. I had absolutely no idea what I was doing in the beginning. The machines we received looked like they had been through a war. They were discolored from being exposed to sunlight. PMC was only supposed to be storing and cleaning them. I discovered that they didn't work at all because of broken and /or worn parts. I also discovered that the "fix it" company was charging hundreds of dollars to repair them, yet was not repairing them at all. After a lot of hassle, I was able to get a hold of some books and within weeks, I could repair any part of the copiers that failed. In addition to this, I began to repaint the copiers so that they not only worked like new, they looked like new as well. It wasn't long before our 13 machines grew to be several hundred machines and I had more work than I could handle. Most of the repairs were pretty simple and only required changing paper feed, rubber tires, belts, and charger wires. I was making about $1600 a week for the two hours of work involved in painting the machines, plus my regular hourly rate for repairing and cleaning the machines.

A lot of the machines needed to be repaired because of the damage that was done in transportation. Larry liked to drive truck much better than his job as an offset press technician. He made service calls in his own personal car, which was a hopped up Ford

Mustang Cobra. Larry opted out of the Cobra and into a delivery truck, as he began to make deliveries, in the five state area, of the copiers that I was repairing.

This "small" storage job, was turning into a huge money maker and we couldn't keep up to the demands. I hired and trained two young men, James and Cory, from a local technical school. I hired James first but needed more help. James was in a band with Cory whom James also attended school with. James kept telling me how smart Cory was and I finally told him to bring him around for an interview. I hired Cory on the spot.

I took a personal interest in James, because in some ways, he reminded me of myself when I was his age. I also admired him, because he was actually doing something with his life in spite of his battle with alcohol and the fact that he was miles away from the place he called home in Alaska. James was the bass player in a band and a very good one at that. James was more results-oriented and worked fast in order to get things done. Unfortunately, the type of detailed work that we were doing, required a lot of attention to those details. Consequently, James made lots of mistakes that he didn't like to be made aware of. It was my responsibility to often inform him of his mistakes by way of retraining.

Cory was the lead guitar player in their band and one of the best I had heard in a long time. Cory was one of those people that picked up a guitar and started playing it as if they had been playing for years. It was just a natural talent that he had. Cory, unlike James, was detail oriented and didn't really require any training. In fact, if I tried to tell him how to do something, he would become confused. If I just handed him a copier part and told him to install it in a machine, he would do it in record time with no confusion or mistakes.

The boys liked loud, heavy metal music as they worked. I would tolerate it even though it made the hair on the back of my neck stand up. When I had enough, I would tell them to turn it down or play something different. Being the rebellious little shits that they were, they would usually turn up the volume. But I had the antidote. I had a sixty gallon 5 horsepower compressor that made the most annoying noise that you can imagine. It resembled a constant scream. For the first couple of times, I simply walked over to the compressor, opened the condensation valve at the bottom of the tank and drained enough air to kick the motor in. I let it scream for about ten minutes before it built up enough air pressure to automatically shut itself off. After that, the third time I asked them to turn the noise, they called music, down or play something different all I had to do was threaten to turn on the compressor. Problem solved!

Yes, I was their boss and I could fire them as quickly as I hired them, but I couldn't easily replace them and never once considered it, because they always got the job done and we all had a lot of fun in the process. Both of them loved Willie though he got on their nerves by dropping his ball in their department wanting to play. Cory would throw the ball as hard as he could across the parking lot and into the woods hoping that Willie would never find it or at least it would take him a long time to find it. But Willie always found it and brought it back.

I still hear from them from time to time. I gave both of them very good references when they left. Last contact I had with Cory, he was a field technician at one of the copier companies around the Twin Cities. I'm surprised that he isn't famous for his music, but then, there are a lot of people out there with a lot of talent working regular jobs because they don't have the courage to let themselves be known.

James went to work for a very well-known industrial company in the Twin Cities. He was planning to get married. Carolyn and I took him and his bride to be, out for dinner one night. They looked like they would make a very nice couple.

Within about 10 months of starting the copier business our parent company lost their contract with our five-state region. The copier business began to die. But during those ten months we had done almost half a million in copiers.

Trying Something New

We hobbled along for about a year living on the revenue from those ten months, until there was no more work and no more money. Larry announced that he was leaving PMC to go to work for another company driving semi. He called me a couple times while on the road and I could hear him grinding gears. I told him that the Kennedy transmission company was looking for him; they wanted to put him on the payroll for sending so much transmission work their way. It felt like old times as we insulted each other over the phone. As soon as he figured out how to shift gears and handle a semi, he bought his own rig and went into business with his girlfriend, Mary Beth.

In October of '04, on a long ride home from work, I decided to call my oldest son Tyrone. We hadn't spoken to each other for a long time because of some silly misunderstanding the last time he, his wife and kids visited. He said that he'd gained so much weight that it was beginning to consume his life and that he needed to do something about it. We will visit the results of that conversation later.

PMC was pretty close to going down in flames, when Ken and Pete came up with an idea. They had discovered eBay. One particular company on the east coast attracted their interest. The concept was simple and seemed to have unlimited possibilities that would provide prosperity for everyone concerned. But in reality, it turned out to be a lot of work where we invested a lot of time, effort, and several thousand dollars, for the opportunity to learn another one of life's hard lessons.

The business idea was an online auction of unwanted stuff that local people had lying around the house collecting dust. They brought it in to be sold to the highest bidder on eBay where the possibilities were much better than a local garage sale. It was thought that we would be so successful that our business, which we named Easy List, USA, was kept hush-hush until the opening day. We had hopes and fears of more business than a three-man show could possibly handle.

It was days before we received our first customer. We tried advertising in newspaper and television. We still didn't have any business to speak of. At one time, we had several hundred items listed. But I looked at everything we had listed and realized that if we sold everything at top dollar, not one of the three of us would take home a paycheck. I looked at the numbers and realized that the product we needed to auction had to be worth $50 or more per transaction. Even then, the work involved to receive, list, and ship enough product at $50 per auction was not possible to be done by three people.

Setting Bigger Goals

I personally began to do research online in order to find out why some people became millionaires on the Internet, while others did nothing more than waste time and money. What I discovered, was that the most profitable Internet businesses were not bricks and mortar type businesses that stock and shipped product. Some did okay, working with companies who would drop-ship product, meaning that the product was advertised and sold through their website but was shipped from another location. They made it to appear as though it was shipped from the website owner's location. Another thing I checked into was affiliate programs where Internet gurus would sell you the opportunity to own your own business through them. For as little as $98, they would give you a website and the rights to sell all of their product, including their business opportunities, for which they would give you 50% and sometimes even more, of the profit of each sale. All you had to do was find a way to bring traffic to your website; they would even give you the tools and tell you the tricks of the trade in order to attract traffic to your website. I thought this was a good idea but rather than be an affiliate myself, I would rather be the one collecting 50% of every transaction that all of my own affiliates were doing.

Since I couldn't really get Ken and Pete to seriously consider what I had discovered as a possibility, I took the concept to one of my brothers and his son. The reason I didn't keep it to myself is that my brother has a good head for business and organizational skills and his son is a computer nerd. I really don't have any of these skills, or at least that is what I told myself. My skills lie in ideas that require me to find the people with the skills to do the things that need to be done in order to prosper. I've been most successful when I employed people to do the things that I already knew how to do better than the people I hired.

Unfortunately, or maybe not, my brother was committed to his current job in the theater business and his son needed to work at his current job so that he could pay his bills and neither could see a way to find the time needed for a new startup business. We succeeded in building a website, but it was unusable and hasn't gone anywhere. I had a business goal of reaching $500,000 within a year and a personal goal of owning a new car. I had been online with an internet teacher and he thought my business goal was unrealistic, but he recommended that I set the car goal in front of myself and pay for it in cash. I was driving a 2000 Cadillac SLS that I still owed over twelve grand on. My dream car was a black SLS 4 with every option available. It listed for $67,000. With that said, I got a brochure about that car and found a picture online and ran a copy of it. I had my goal identified and just needed to work and wait.

In the meanwhile, I wanted more understanding about the internet, how some folks could start with nothing and end up financially loaded. I watched how a guy started his business. He started out, a few years ago, by making affirmation tapes to help himself out of his predicament of losing job after job, while living out of his van wondering where his next meal would come from. His idea was to record messages to himself in triplicate. These messages would be positive and would remind him of the things he needed to realize in order to accomplish his goals. After making the recordings, he then listened to them while he slept. His idea worked and he went on to become a renowned salesman for Reader's Digest.

A few years ago, he started his own business by studying some of the most successful people in the world and some of the most unsuccessful. He set out to find out what thoughts successful people have that make them successful. He then took all of the thought patterns and recorded them in triplicate, using a person with a very entrancing voice accompanied by background music designed to put you in the alpha state of mind. He sells several different CDs that help to develop self-esteem, motivation, goal setting, becoming organized, ridding yourself of anxieties and a whole host of other things that you can accomplish by listening to the thought patterns of the extremely successful. He sells these CD's on the internet for as a little as $29 for each life-altering change. Do they really work? I can testify that they do. Last year, his little website made $200 million. Not too shabby an income for helping people to realize their potential, wouldn't you say?

How did my internet business pan out? Well, OK, I'll confess, it hasn't yet. Did I acquire my dream car? The answer is parked in my driveway. It is the exact $67,000 black Cadillac STS 4 that I imagined and I did pay cash for it. Did I reach the $500,000 goal? It was exceeded. How did that happen? Easier than you might think, but I'm getting ahead of myself, even though the windfall that pushed me past the original $500,000 actually began to materialize the moment I conceived it 30 years ago. It wouldn't be fully developed for another two years from the time I set out that $500,000 goal, but the important fact is that I was looking and aware that how I acted, thought, and planned could bring me the very things I wanted. My goals could be born into reality. This may have been a very important lesson in patience for me and the apparent need for better self-discipline in order to reach my goals on time. To this day, I don't think I have ever reached a goal by a specific time, but I always do eventually succeed in reaching my goals. Sometimes, I reach them ahead of time and sometimes not. Upon reflection, most of my goals have not been reached the way I thought I would reach them, yet the end results have always been what I imagined.

This then sheds light on the truth, "If you know every step you need to make in order to reach your goal, your goal isn't big enough."

Creative Habits

My obvious lack of control that would enable me to reach goals on time, is most likely due to a lack of self-discipline that stems from former conditioning, causing doubt, even though I know the truth. In the end, it's just another habit that needs to be broken. Since I possess the knowledge that all habits, good and bad, are realized the same way, (which is by repeating them over and over, until they become habit) my doubt that once caused hopeless despair, was overcome by the knowledge that I can overcome what holds me down by replacing old debilitating habits with creative habits. All of the debilitating habits I have ever overcome have been accomplished exactly the same way. You start by suppressing the urge, one second at a time in the beginning, until the distance between these begin to get further and further apart. Seconds become minutes, minutes become hours, then hours become days and days become years. There is great danger in thinking that just because you have mastered a bad habit, you are free of it. What once was, will always be and so it is that every bad habit I have ever overcome still exists at some level of consciousness, just waiting to consume me. For this reason, I am always recovering from those habits I have overcome. The urges are far apart now, but every now and then a strong urge will come over me and challenge my self-discipline and then quickly fade away when I stand my ground.

Habits always seem to leave a space that needs to be filled. So rather than fill that space with another bad habit equally as debilitating, I choose to take this as an opportunity to continue developing self-discipline. I begin by filling that empty space with something beneficial to my personal endeavor.

Choosing Truth

If everything I'm saying is beginning to sound real familiar and appearing to be nothing more than the common sense things you've heard repeated over and over again throughout your life, in some ways, you're right! My point is, that we have always been in possession of the knowledge. Still, even though it's common knowledge, I have still been guilty of taking it all for granted, ignoring what would set me free, while clinging to false beliefs and ways of thinking that hold me down. No amount of truth is ever going to make you choose it. The difference between truth and choice is clear. Truth stands regardless of whether you are aware of it or not. It is truth and always will be truth. Choice is a personal matter and we all have choices to make in our own lives. If we look for truth and choose it, that brings us to positive places. But let me be very clear, just knowing the truth does not mean good things will flood into your life. You must choose truth, which requires discipline and good habits.

A Blood Clot

Getting back to my life's story, it was right around this time that my daughter-in-law called me. Tyrone had been battling his weight, and had decided to have a gastric bypass operation done in Fargo. When she called, she was in tears and said Tyrone was in the hospital and that she was very concerned for his life. The word was that she was a bit of a drama queen. Although I had no definite proof that this was true other than hearsay, I took her concern lightly, until the second call, when she told me that he had been diagnosed with a blood clot and was hospitalized. I'm not a doctor, so I had no idea of how serious a blood clot could possibly be. But, she was worried and I decided to pack up and go to Fargo to see for myself.

When I got there, a lot of the family was gathered in the waiting room. I was standing in the hallway when the elevator doors opened and a young lady stepped out and said, "Hi grandpa! Do you remember me?" Of course I remembered her, but it had been so long that I couldn't remember her name. This was Leah, Tyrone's oldest daughter. His oldest son, Chris was in detention for drug possession, but besides Leah, his other three kids, Kaleigh, Aubrey and Dennis, were there with Tyrone's sisters, Charmane and Crystal.

The room was full as I looked around to Tyrone's Aunt Shirley, a few cousins, and Tyrone's mother, my first ex-wife, Gloria. I hadn't seen Gloria in quite a while. She had always been slim and shapely, but she was on some kind of emphysema medication that caused her to appear overweight. Despite our past, Gloria was good to me. She always treated me with respect and kindness and this evening was no exception. Crystal must've taken after her mother, because you couldn't ask for a more polite girl. She wasn't my daughter, but I sure would have been proud if she was. I hadn't seen my daughter Charmane for quite a while either. She hadn't changed very much. She was still as pretty as always. Tyrone's wife told me that she had a boyfriend who was a lot older than Charmane and that he was a biker with long shaggy hair and a scraggly beard. That night when I met him, I knew who he was because of the hair and beard. He had a Harley Davidson motorcycle and he certainly was older than Charmane, but he was also one of the nicest guys I've ever met. The respectful way that he and my daughter communicated with each other, made me very pleased that he was a part of my daughter's life. He certainly seemed to be a different person than the filthy biker with bugs on his teeth that I had imagined from the first description.

Tyrone was pretty much out of it when I arrived. He hadn't been out of surgery long and wasn't very responsive. They had just completed removing a large part of his intestines, as a large portion had "died" because of a blood clot. I couldn't really be a comfort to him, as he really wasn't coherent enough to even know that I, or anyone else, was there.

So, I decided to make the night about Charmane.

A Priceless Evening

I went outside, with her for a smoke, although I quit the habit and really didn't care to be around smokers. It was a good chance to do some father-daughter bonding. We weren't ever very close. She always had issues with me and I never really knew why. She told me that night that she was always left out, while Tyrone and I had a relationship because we had things we related to such as cars, stereos and other electronic equipment. But the truth is, the relationship between Tyrone and myself was pretty superficial compared to the depth to which Charmane and I communicated that evening. Being the inconsiderate, self-absorbed idiots that we were, neither one of us had ever realized how neglected Charmane felt when Tyrone seemed to get all the attention. She desperately needed and wanted a dad too and I just never realized it. Charmane and I talked openly and honesty about our relationship that particular night. We shared a lot, yet I could still tell there was a lot of resentment and anger in her that needed release. That was a priceless evening, standing there and talking with my daughter.

Once I was assured that Tyrone was going to be okay, I headed home.

Pain, Regret and Truth

Throughout this book, I have told you that the pain I caused my children and the ripple effect on my grandchildren, is the biggest regret of my lifetime. As I have told you, my son eventually died and I didn't take some of the chances I had to connect with him. Now when I think about him, I have regrets. Such pains are etched in the deepest parts of my own, father's heart. There is no amount of talking, writing, fancy words or deep thinking that can ever change the way things were for Tyrone. The challenge for me is to carry on with my life without letting these painful memories ruin what is left of my own life and the people who are dear to me today. I caused so much hurt. Yet, I must carry on. There is no purpose in living the rest of my life poorly just because of the past.

So, why am I telling you all of this? Why is it important to conjure up the events of the past, especially my checkered past? Because there is a true way for all of us. I want to be sure we all find it, despite mistakes made in our past.

Just Tell Me

I will continue to tell you because for anyone who is searching or willing to learn, I want to share what I've learned in order to help you avoid making the mistakes I made. You can do better than I did. Just tell me, sometime, that something in this book has changed your life for the good. I long for there to be something redemptive in all of this. The opportunity to make a difference in someone else's life is something I would treasure! It would be as important to me as it would be to you. But perhaps this book is my chance and your chance to see truth win out in the end.

Author's Postscript

Since Tyrone's death, Charmane and I have become good friends. Besides being friends, we have a father daughter relationship that I will cherish for the rest of my life. She calls me often, keeping me up to speed on what's going on in her life. We have been known to talk for hours and we have never covered the same ground twice. I love that girl. She is mine.

I never hear from my son Randy Jr. He has decided to walk a different path. Even though we do not have a relationship, I still love him. He is my son.

My daughter, Jodie, calls from time to time but we just never seem to connect. She is mine and I do love her very much.

My youngest daughter, Jenna, has always been in touch with me. She certainly has a pile of issues that I continually work with her on. She has always been under the influence of someone or something not so good and she often fails to accept the responsibility for herself and her actions. I point out her involvement in her situations, and even then, it seems like her attitude is "Oh, crap! I'm busted". I never get the feeling that she fully accepts her shortcomings because she makes the same mistakes over and over. On the other hand, she is very intelligent, she has a vibrant personality most of the time, and is very easy to like. I sometimes want to pull my hair out when I see the potential that she is throwing away, never realizing that time is running out for her, just like it does for everyone else. No matter what is going on in Jenna's life, whether she takes my advice or not, I have always believed in her and I always will. It is my heartfelt wish that she would believe in herself as I do. I don't think I ever get angry at her. She has a little boy, and he is a delight to his grandpa. They presently live in Arizona close to her mother. It wouldn't matter where she lived. She is my daughter. I love her.

You see, things are pretty screwed up aren't they? It is definitely an ongoing process to straighten the things out that I messed up so many years ago. I take full responsibility for so much of my children's pain. I was not there for them like I should have been. I am sorry for hurting them. Despite the dysfunction that I contributed to, I'm good with myself. I note that I can't change what is done and that I can only learn from all my mistakes and pass that knowledge on.

I don't feel that I owe anyone anything, but rather, I feel like I need to give all that I can of myself to those less fortunate. There is no time like the present to turn it all around and make yourself proud. I believe that each of us has had glimpses of what our potential is. We have moments of choice. These choices shape our lives and lead us down one path or the other. How many times did I come around to the same circumstances? You have read my story. Sometimes it reads more like a merry-go-round, doesn't it?

I am deeply touched to have all of these pages full of my story and to somehow be making an impact in your life. I know that I have used many words to say the same thing. I will end this book recapping the moments that impacted my life most.

I had a lot of hard things happen in my youth that lead to predictable problems. Despite the wounds from my childhood, I was loved. I needed to look at the entire picture. You need to pick yourself up every time you fall down. Seek help from others. You will need it. The difference is in the way you seek help. If the only reason you are in your current situation is because you were "forced" or "got caught", chances are, you are not ready for change yourself. Others are intolerant of your behavior, but you haven't reached the point of admitting your life needs radical change. When it comes right down to it, there really isn't any personal achievement that we can take full credit for. There is always someone who has had input. Take movie credits, for instance. Or the dedication in the front of a book. Or listen to all of the actors and actresses when they accept an award at the Oscars. Don't they list all the people who should be credited for making their success possible? Clearly, if we are to do great things, there should be a host of others that we feel deserve to share the spotlight with us. With that thought, be certain that you are actively involved with people who can help you achieve your goals.

We need to briefly revisit how to handle the hurt and pain you have caused someone else. You cannot go through your life self-destructing because you made some mistake that really hurt someone. How is it going to make anything better if you stay drunk, high, or continue to punish yourself? The answer is simple: It won't. What you have already done cannot be erased. You have to honestly face the pain you have caused others, and move on. When is this the most difficult to do? When those that you have hurt refuse to forgive you and continually remind you of the very faults you yourself dislike. Just let it go.

Now we get to one of the most important concepts that I can share with you. You will never get from where you are, to where you want to be, without a very clear vision of the goal you have. You don't have to know how to get where you are going, you just need to keep a clear vision of what it is you want! Through the years, there have been many goals that I have personally set and achieved in various ways. When I imagine a goal, I only see the end results and I have no idea of how or even when I will get there. I only know that I will get there! In my mind, I have already reached my goal, even though the path at the time is not known. That path is just a formality that will eventually be revealed to me when I am called upon to take action in one way or the other. I have heard a lot of visionaries' claim that you only get to where you want to go through hard work. I have not found this to be necessarily so. I am certainly not saying that hard work doesn't have its place, because I enjoy hard work. (Although it rarely ever pays very well!) The benefits of working hard are the hands on experience, the chance to be creative and the exercise that keeps us healthy. These are all positive things, but if you think that something good can't come easy, then you won't be looking for it when it does. You will inadvertently make everything in your life a struggle. Why? Because if that is how you think it has to be, then that is all you will be ready to see and accept. If you or I imagine that good things acquired don't have to be realized through hardship and struggles, then it certainly won't be a struggle to realize. Remember when I said that some of the concepts that I most wanted to show you are truly simple? This is a very simple concept that trips most people up. If you get this concept and master it, you will have the vision that will lead you to take action at the right moment. That, in turn, will bring you to happiness, contentment, and the reality of your dreams coming true.

I have had many inspirations to write this book. My wife Carolyn. There is no one I would rather share these glory years with than her. She is my soul mate, and I love her more deeply than anyone I have ever known. My life is so full because of her and I can only smile and say, "We did it, babe! What a ride"! We have dreams of a retirement home. I am sure that we will be smiling at each other over a cup of coffee some morning and chuckling when we hear the cold temps from "home" in dear old Minnesota. Do I know when we will get to our dream destination? Nope. But I am not worried. We will get there when the time is right. And we will know when it comes.

To all of my children, I love each of you. My son Tyrone, I will miss you always. Charmane Rae, Randy Junior, Jodie Lynn, and Jenna Rae, you all inspire me to tell my story and have my life make a difference. I am sorry I hurt you. I know I did, but I surely didn't do it on purpose. I want you to know me now and I would count it a great honor to stay involved in your lives. I want to know my grandchildren and great grandchildren. I hope they do not have to follow the same paths I did, but rather, that they can learn from my mistakes.

To all of the people that I have harmed along the way, this is my apology to you. Maybe you will understand, as you read my life's story, that while I was selfish, I wasn't out to hurt you. Please forgive me and go from this place peaceful towards me. That would mean a lot to me.

To the people I served time with, as well as the ones who are serving time right now, this book is my hope for you. To the families of those behind bars who don't understand, maybe you will see glimpses of how you can help them now.

All those "without hope" let this give you hope. I do not believe you are worthless and there isn't anything you could have done to convince me of that. Beginning today, set out to quiet your critics and make a plan to fulfill the desires buried deep in your heart. Those visions are unique to you. Make them your reality.

Special Thanks

Thanks to Leah Greuel for her editing and a very special thank you to her for her creation of the cracker box analogy and the house with no electricity.

Thank you to Landis Lundquist for his help with writing, editing, cover design, title and getting this project into print. He gave me a sense of urgency to complete this ten-year endeavor. No words can express my thanks for his encouragement and expertise.

I wish to thank the people that I have never met who have been inspirational to me. Also, my very good friend Rob Adams, another writer, and many other inspirational authors whose thoughts I have had the honor of reading over the years. They have encouraged me along the way.

But most of all, I feel deeply thankful to Maxwell Maltz, author of Psycho Cybernetics, the man who turned my life around when I had finally reached the bottom.

What Have I Learned?

I have learned that things don't just "happen" and that people make things happen for a reason. What is your reason? I feel that I was reborn that day so long ago in 1973. I read the book that began to change my life and enabled me to write this book, even though I only had an 8th grade education and a broken, confusing life filled with mistakes, depression and wants.

It is often the worst that we can imagine that inspires us to do the best that we can. All of my worst mistakes are my inspiration for the things I have shared with you on my personal journey.

I hope that this book might be a new beginning for you in the direction of your desires. If so, "Happy Birthday!" Today is the beginning of a new life for you!

Acknowledgments

The following sources have been an inspiration to me.

Edgar Casey, Hue Lyn Casey. Einstein, Maxwell Maltz, author of *Psycho Cybernetics* Matt Furey, internet guru, Leslie Householder author of *The Jack Rabbit Factor*, Dr. Robert Anthony, Mike Brescia creator of *Think Right Now*, The book *Message of a Master* presented by Tenzin and Christy Whitman on the 7 laws of the universe.

Made in the USA
Las Vegas, NV
29 December 2020